AUSTRO—HUNGARIAN EMPIRE 1914

SHTETL MEMOIRS

Jewish Life in Galicia under the Austro-Hungarian Empire and in the Reborn Poland 1898–1939

by

JOACHIM SCHOENFELD

Foreword by
Michael Marrus,
Professor of History,
University of Toronto

KTAV PUBLISHING HOUSE, INC.
HOBOKEN, NEW JERSEY

Library of Congress Cataloging in Publication Data

Schoenfeld, Joachim, 1895-
  Shtetl memoirs.

  1. Schoenfeld, Joachim, 1895-   2. Jews—
Ukraine—Sniatyn—Biography. 3. Sniatyn (Ukraine)—
Biography. I. Title.
DS135.R95S367   1985   947'.718   85-5553
ISBN 0-88125-075-9

MANUFACTURED IN THE UNITED STATES OF AMERICA

In loving memory
of my
father Asher, mother Chayye Sara,
and
wife Ola and sons Zygmunt and Stefan,
who perished in the Holocaust.
Zichronam livrachah
May their memory be for a blessing.

Contents

Foreword

"Although I never returned to the *shtetl* after the First World War," writes the author of these memoirs, "all my love and most fervent feelings go back to that era." In the work that follows, Joachim Schoenfeld explores the world of his youth, a world of small-town Jewish life in Eastern Europe, finally destroyed by the Nazis in the course of the Holocaust. The author's deep affection for his birthplace and its inhabitants infuses practically every page. So too does the sadness of one who watched this world die its violent death. In addition, however, Schoenfeld's account is enriched by the skilled stroyteller's or the anthropologist's eye for detail—the keen description that enlivens his world for us, giving substance to nostalgia and explaining why his affection, and that of many other Jews, is so durable.

Schoenfeld's account centers upon Habsburg Galicia, a province that was integrated into the ramshackle Austro-Hungarian Empire after the partitions of Poland in the latter part of the eighteenth century. Around 1900, over 800,000 Jews lived in Galicia, mainly in its eastern portion, where they constituted 12 percent of the total population. Throughout the region, as the author implies in his chapter on occupations, the Jews were part of a lively, largely preindustrial market economy, traders and merchants in an overwhelmingly rural environment. The *shtetl* examined here is Sniatyn, a sizable market town of about 18,000 souls in the foothills of the Carpathian Mountains, only a few miles from neighboring Bukovina, which was also under Austrian rule. Close at hand was the administrative capital of Bukovina, Czernowitz, where Schoenfeld and his friends used to bicycle after the Sabbath to attend the Yiddish theater. On the outskirts of the town ran the railway line from Vienna, the nerve center of the Habsburg domain. And in the nearby countryside,

Jews lived scattered in numerous smaller *shtetls*, scaled-down models of the Jewish core of Sniatyn, which was plainly a town of some importance.

Culturally, these Jews lived in a universe of their own. And as these memoirs suggest, the cohesive force was far less hostility from the outside than an inner commitment to Jewish tradition and religious practice. Austrian rule was relatively benign, particularly after the Jewish emancipation of 1867, and the Jews had a warm affection for the Habsburg Kaiser, Franz Josef, affectionately known as "Froyim Yossel." Some anti-Semitism persisted, exacerbated by the three-way struggles of Poles, Ukrainians, and Habsburg officials. But Galician Jews lived in a political paradise compared to their brethren in tsarist Russia, some of whom showed up as refugees in Sniatyn following pogroms in the early twentieth century. The real enemy of Galician Jews was poverty, a crushing burden which, according to Schoenfeld, afflicted about half of the Jewish population of his *shtetl*. Galicia was among the poorest Jewish settlements in Eastern Europe, and its rich cultural and religious inheritance contrasted markedly with the material deprivations that were so widespread.

Schoenfeld was born in Sniatyn in 1895, when important changes were beginning to affect the life of Galician Jewry. In the decade after 1891, according to the historian Raphael Mahler, 67,000 Jews left the province for America, 80 percent of the total Jewish emigration from the entire Austro-Hungarian Empire. Relations between the Poles on the one hand, and the Ukrainians and Jews on the other, worsened notably about this time, as Polish leaders pressed for autonomy within the empire—often against the interests of minority groups. Jewish nationalism established a foothold in the 1880s, and the earliest Zionist periodical in Galicia appeared in Lwow in 1890. In 1898 Galician Jews established their first colony in Palestine, known as Mahnayim. Given the relative backwardness of Galician industry there was nothing comparable to the powerful Jewish labor movement that was emerging about the same time in the cities of Poland and Lithuania. Nevertheless, a Galician offshoot did appear in the 1890s, but it was limited to a few larger cities and does not enter the author's description. The overall picture is of a tradition-bound society, stirred occasionally by new forces from the outside.

The greatest upheaval before the Nazis came with the First World War, which rocked the foundations of Jewish life in Eastern Europe. Much of Galicia became a battleground. Schoenfeld, who began postsecondary studies in business in 1913, was soon fighting *für Kaiser und Vaterland,* as were many of his fellow Jews. Tens of thousands became refugees, uprooted in the face of Russian advances. Then, after the tsarist regime collapsed in 1917, pogroms rumbled across the country, involving hideous massacres that lasted until 1920. Galicia was now transferred to Poland, whose postwar rulers proved far less protective of Jews than Habsburg officials had ever been. Like many others, the author left his *shtetl* at this point, never to return. Immediately after the war he completed his studies in Vienna, later practiced accountancy in Cracow, and eventually became Director of Finances for the Cartel of Wire and Nails, with headquarters in Warsaw.

Joachim Schoenfeld's *Shtetl Memoirs* examine the workings of a gentle society, portrayed with remarkable clarity. Encompassing the whole panorama of life in what was a kind of Jewish homeland, they offer a good-humored, knowledgeable, and spirited guide to a world that disappeared long ago. Through these pages, across the wreckage of time, we glimpse a vibrant civilization, in the last moments before its tragic demise.

Michael R. Marrus

Acknowledgments

.ברוך אתה ה' אלוקינו מלך העולם שהחינו וקימנו והגיענו לזמן_הזה

Blessed art Thou, Lord our God, King of the Universe, who has granted us life and sustenance and permitted me to reach the age of ninety, and who has enabled me to survive and to write this Yizkor Book in memory of the martyrs who are no longer and of the way of life, the culture, and the folklore of a bygone era in the history of Polish Jewry.

I am grateful to the Memorial Foundation for Jewish Culture for the support provided me.

I wish also to express my gratitude to Rabbi Bernard Baskin, Professor Emil Fackenheim, Mr. B. G. Kayfetz, Rabbi Irving Lehrman, Rabbi Gunther Plaut, Mr. Isaac Bashevis Singer and Professor Elie Wiesel for having taken of their precious time to read the manuscript of this book and for encouraging me to have it published.

I am particularly indebted to Dr. Michael Marrus, Professor of History at the University of Toronto, for reading the manuscript and for contributing a foreword to this book.

I also acknowledge my thanks to Mr. Bernard Scharfstein of KTAV Publishing House and to Mr. Robert J. Milch for their advice and guidance in polishing up my work and preparing it for publication.

Finally, I would like to thank Mrs. Sherry Skibo and Mrs. Michel Strok for their untiring typing, retyping, and retyping again of the manuscript.

Introduction

NOWADAYS THE SEARCH for family roots is very much in style, and the younger generation is interested in gaining knowledge about the life of its ancestors. My nieces, the instigators of these writings, have told me that they, as well as their children, are very much interested in knowing about the roots of our family and the way in which our ancestors lived in the past. Therefore, complying with their request, I shall first introduce a concise account of the origins of our family, known to me from what I was told by my grandfather, *alav hashalom* ("may he rest in peace"), and then I shall describe some details of Jewish life in the lands of Eastern Europe in times preceding the Holocaust.

Our ancestors came to Poland from Germany in the fourteenth century, when King Casimir the Great invited German Jews in order to build up and develop the Polish economy, which at that time was in a deplorable state. As the legend goes, King Casimir was in love with a Jewish girl, Esther by name. As long as he was on the throne the Jews in Poland enjoyed special privileges. However, after his death these privileges were intermittently revoked by some of his successors and granted again by others. When, at the end of the eighteenth century, Poland was partitioned by her neighbors, Lenczyce, the town in which my grandfather was born and lived with his parents and two brothers, and where before them many generations of their ancestors had lived and died, came under Russian sovereignty.

The fate of the Jews, bad enough under the Polish regime, became still worse under the Russians. In 1827 Tsar Nicholas issued a decree ordering that Jews from the age of twelve to twenty-five, and even sometimes as young as eight, should be conscripted for twenty-five years of service in the Russian army. Once in the army, the Jews were placed in special camps, called cantons, with the implicit intent to convert them to Christianity. In the camps, which were located mostly in Siberia, the cantonists, as the Jewish recruits were called, were treated with the utmost cruelty. They were forced to eat pork and to cross themselves, and many were forcibly converted to Christianity.

On each of the Jewish communities was put the obligation to provide a certain quota of conscripts. Since, however, the Jews made every effort to avoid conscription, the elders of the communities, who were responsible for the filling of the quota, used *khappers*, as they were called, for kidnapping recruits.

For some time my great-grandfather, *alav hashalom*, was able to buy out his three sons by paying ransom money to the *kahal* elders. But when he was later blackmailed with requests for more money he decided that the only way his sons could be rescued from becoming cantonists was by fleeing the country.

With an adequate bribe the three brothers were able to escape to Germany. From there one of them went to England, another to Hungary, and my grandfather went to Austria and settled in Sniatyn, a shtetl in Galicia, where he got married, set up a family, established a business, and lived until he passed away there in 1905 at the age of 95.

For a better understanding of the life of the Jews in Poland prior to their destruction during the Holocaust, I shall draw a picture of my *shtetl* in Galicia, which was similar to hundreds of other *shtetlekh* there, and describe it as it was at the end of the nineteenth and the beginning of the twentieth centuries, as I see it when my memory takes me back to that place where I was born ninety years ago, from the time when, as a three-year-old boy, I started *cheder,* where I graduated from high school, and where I spent the first eighteen years of my life. I shall follow it up with a description of the events during the First World War, when I first was under Russian occupation, and then, from 1915 till the end of the war, when I served in the Austrian army on the Russian and Italian fronts.

I shall also describe, as I remember it from my own experience and observations, the life of the Jews in the Polish state that was reborn after the war, where I lived with my wife and our two sons, first in Cracow and then, till the outbreak of World War Two, in Warsaw.

Galicia once belonged to a Roman colony. It was a province of the Kingdom of Red Russia (red only by name, not to be confused with communist Red Russia). Its capital city was Halicz. The Ukrainians, also called Ruthens or Rusyns, called their country Haliczyna, hence Galicia.

Poland captured Galicia in the fourteenth century. Jews had lived in Poland and Galicia since the ninth century. They played a significant role in the economic life in Poland, but were always treated by the Gentile population, especially by the clergy, with enmity. Throughout the centuries Jews had to suffer from persecution by the noblemen and the church, which often arranged debates and disputations between rabbis and priests, most of whom were converted Jews. Following such disputes student riots often occurred. Expulsions from large cities, preceded by robbery, plunder, and pillage by unruly mobs, often took place.

Pogroms and ritual-murder charges were recurrent, and economic restrictions were placed on the Jews. However, the most vicious blow suffered by the Polish and Ukrainian Jews took place in 1648 when a Ukrainian hetman named Chmielnicki, who bore a grudge against a Polish nobleman, fled to the eastern Ukraine, which at that time was ruled with ruthless terror by the Poles. There, in Zaporozhe, Chmielnicki organized an uprising of the Cossacks. As their leader he marched against Poland, heading 50,000 Cossacks in alliance with 100,000 Tatars. On the way his bands killed hundreds of thousands of Jews and wiped out approximately 750 Jewish communities in the Ukraine and Poland.

If we take into consideration the primitive means and tools of destruction available to the Chmielnicki bandits, and their field of operation, minuscule in comparison to that over which the Nazis laid their brutal hand, it can be said that they were, relatively speaking, not far behind Hitler in their métier of killing Jews.

Yet a larger-than-life-size monument, cast in bronze, of Chmielnicki on a horse dominates one of the main squares in Kiev, the capital of the Ukrainian Republic of the Soviet Union. To them, Chmielnicki is a hero; but we Jews will always remember him as no less a murderer than Hitler. Chmielnicki preceded Hitler by 300 years. One may well ask how long will it take until, in a capital city of another country in Europe, a monument glorifying Hitler is erected. Certainly not 300 years, I am afraid.

Whenever a liberal king was on the Polish throne, conditions improved and Jews even occupied key positions in the Polish economy. There were Jewish revenue collectors, bankers, physicians, and so forth. Jewish learning blossomed, and Poland was a renowned center of rabbinic study and great talmudic scholars.

At the end of the eighteenth century, when Poland was partitioned between Russia, Prussia, and Austria, the latter acquired Galicia. Galicia was composed of two parts, namely western Galicia, including Cracow, the ancient Polish capital, with a prevalent Polish majority, and eastern Galicia, including Lwów, the capital city of both parts of Galicia. In the eastern part of Galicia the Ukrainians were in the majority, except in the cities, where the Poles and Jews made up the majority.

The new rulers of the annexed Galicia, the Austrian Empress Maria Theresa and later the Emperor Josef II, were both convinced anti-Semites and in no way sympathetic toward their newly acquired Jewish subjects. They got them in the bargain and willy-nilly had to take them, but they could not go as far as to recognize them as citizens with full rights. They only tolerated them. Emperor Josef II proclaimed the so-called *Toleranzakt*. attempting (unsuccessfully) to abolish *chederim* and to force Jews to send their children to German schools. He tried also to forcibly settle Jews on farmland, and introduced other innovations, such as asking Jews to change from their traditional garments to the European style of dress. Moreover, Jews were ordered to acquire family names given to them by the Austrian officials. The officials usually assigned names according to one's profession, such as Lehrer, Schuster, Schneider, Goldschmied, Kantor, Shoichet, Dayan, Kaufman, Shames, Melamed, Belfer, and so on. But some officials gave names with the aim of making fun of the individual involved. Some of them were Ochs, Loch, Laufer, Langsam, Schnell, Graf, Mehlsack, and some unprintable ones.

For all these reforms a special tax, the so-called *Toleranzsteuer*, was introduced, in addition to other taxes. However, Jews were resourceful and managed to cope with all the restrictions imposed upon them. As the saying goes, *M'gewaynt zikh mit tsores, laybt man in frayden*, which means, "Accustomed to grief and want, one will live with them in joy."

And, as a matter of fact, the lot of the Jewish population in Galicia eventually did take a turn for the better. In the aftermath of the revolution of 1848, the Austrian Emperor abdicated. His nephew, the eighteen-year-old Prince Franz Josef, ascended the throne of the Austro-Hungarian dual monarchy as Emperor of Austria and King of Hungary. After his ascension to the throne, Jews in Austria were granted full rights. We may say that from then on, Jews in Galicia enjoyed, at least formally, equal rights with other nationalities, even though some restrictions still remained on the books.

In contrast, under the Tsars, Jews in the Ukraine and Russia were crammed together in a vast ghetto, the so-called Pale of Settlement. They had no rights to settle beyond it and lived there under a tyranny organized by the government. For Jews in Russia, a *numerus clausus* applied. Since the universities were usually located in the big cities, where Jews, with the exception of the very few wealthy industrialists, rich bankers, and merchants of the first guild, were not permitted to live, the student quota couldn't be filled.

There was, however, a way to break through this barrier. But it was for girls only. Since prostitutes were given permission to live in the big cities regardless of their nationality, Jewish girls who wanted to gain *pravo zhitielstwa* (a resident's license) in a city where they could enroll in a university could obtain this privilege through the acquisition of the so-called Yellow Ticket. Jewish girls who were eager to get a higher education formally applied for the "Yellow Ticket." Having received permission to live, for example, in St. Petersburg or Moscow, they did not become involved in the profession for which they had been licensed. Ironically, this license opened an opportunity for them to enter a university where they studied for the profession they craved.

But for Jews to enter a university in Austria, however, was no problem. Comparing the conditions under which the Jews had to live in the neighboring Russian Empire with the relative freedom they enjoyed in Austria, and remembering also their fate under the Polish regime, Jews were thankful for the change of the overlord.

The Austro-Hungarian monarchy was a conglomerate of nationalities—Czechs, Poles, Italians, Serbs, Ukrainians (Ruthenes), Rumanians—all kept together by the dominance of the German minority. (Jews, who lived throughout the monarchy, were not considered a nationality.) The master race in Hungary were the Magyars, who ruled over Italians, Rumanians, Croats, and Slovaks.

Emperor Franz Josef ushered in a constitutional era. He granted universal suffrage to all nations of his empire. Emperor Franz Josef was a benevolent ruler. Everyone who came to the palace with a plea or a complaint would be brought before the monarch. If the petitioner was right, justice was rendered. Among the petitioners one could often see a bearded Jew from Galicia in his black kaftan and with the *yarmulke* on his head.

In 1908, which was the emperor's jubilee year, he passed through our city on the way to Czernowitz, on the occasion of the so-called *Kaiser Manoever*, or "Emperor's Maneuver," which was conducted close to the Russian border. The streets of the city and especially of the shtetl were lined on both sides with people, old and young, waving black-yellow flags. When the Emperor reached the shtetl and saw the representatives of the Jewish community holding Torahs and waiting to greet him he got out of his carriage, approached the group, and shook hands with the rabbi, who said the appropriate blessing when meeting an Emperor. The Kaiser asked the rabbi to repeat in German what he had just said in Hebrew. The rabbi did so, much to the great pleasure of the Emperor. The Kaiser then exchanged a few words with some other members of the Jewish delegation. This event was later discussed with great satisfaction and pride among the Jews in the shtetl. They pointed out that *"our* Kaiser" didn't stop to talk to the priest but did stop when he saw the *hadras ponim* (the "majestic face") of the rabbi with the Torah.

Austrian Jews were patriots. They loved their Kaiser, whom they nicknamed *"Froyim Yossel."* Each year on his birthday, August 18, the Jews celebrated with great joy. Streets, houses, and synagogues were decorated and illuminated. Services with prayers for the well-being of the Kaiser were conducted in all *shtiblekh.* In the great synagogue a special service was held, attended by officials and Jewish reserve officers, who afterwards paraded in their gala uniforms on the streets of the shtetl. On each Saturday and on holidays a special prayer for the well-being of the Emperor was said in the synagogue and in all *shtiblekh.*

When the Emperor's son, Crown Prince Rudolf, was found dead at his Mayerling hunting lodge beside the body of Baroness Vetsera, after he had shot her first and then himself, the Emperor's nephew, Franz Ferdinand, became the successor to the throne of the Austro-Hungarian monarchy. The next in line was his brother Otto, who, however, died shortly after Franz Ferdinand became Crown Prince. Otto's son Karl became successor to the throne after his uncle, Crown Prince Franz Ferdinand, was shot in Sarajevo in 1914. He became Emperor after the death of Franz Josef in 1916.

Crown Prince Franz Ferdinand and the Emperor differed vastly on questions of external, as well as internal, politics. The Emperor was in favor of introducing electoral reforms; his successor was against this move. The Emperor appointed members of non-German nationalities to high ministerial posts in the government, but the Crown Prince saw in them a threat to the monarchy.

Another stumbling block between the Emperor and his successor was their different approaches to the problem with the radical parties in Vienna. There was the All-German Party, headed by Dr. Schoenerer, who dreamed of uniting Austria and Germany in a true *German Reich*. Austria, he felt, should break with Hungary and get rid of all non-German parts of the monarchy. He made his party *Judenrein* ("free of Jews"), and to join the party one had to supply proof of four non-Jewish grandparents. It was a prototype of the policy of the Nazis, and we may say that Hitler followed in the footsteps of Dr. Schoenerer, whose ideas he adapted and developed.

Another preacher of anti-Semitism was Dr. Lueger, who headed the Christian Socialist Party, which was associated with the anti-Semitic Catholic Education Society. The Emperor refused three times to confirm the avid anti-Semite Dr. Lueger as mayor of Vienna and succumbed only after Dr. Lueger was elected a fourth time.

Notwithstanding the anti-Semitic tendency of Dr. Lueger's parties, the successor to the throne of the monarchy agreed to serve as patron of the Catholic Education Society. This was bad news for the Jews, who could imagine how well they would fare under the reign of an Emperor who was a patron of the Christian Education Society, should he follow the fatherly Emperor Franz Josef on the throne.

1

The Shtetl

I WAS BORN and raised in the shtetl of Śniatyn. Since the life of the Jews in all the shtetls of Galicia, and indeed throughout Eastern Europe, was, with slight deviations, more or less the same, my picture of life in Śniatyn reflects that in hundreds of other shtetls as well and can be taken as an approximate description of all of them.

Although I never returned to my shtetl after the First World War, all my love and my most fervent feelings go back to that era. Even today, although thousands of miles away from it, after having fought in many trenches on different battlefields during the First World War, after having survived Hitler's concentration camps, and after having traveled through many countries, happiness overcomes me when I think back to those days and manage to recapture some of the tableaus of former years.

This happiness, however, is soon overshadowed by sadness and sorrow that this, our past, doesn't exist anymore. With affliction and grief I mourn the desolation of the Yiddish shtetl: *Aychou yoshwou bodod ha-shtetl.* Actually, it may be wrong to call the place a shtetl, and not a city as it really was. However, having in mind the core of the city, where the Jews lived on a kind of isle, surrounded by a sea of Gentiles, I call it the shtetl.

The shtetl is located in the foothills of the Carpathian Mountains in the so-called Pokucie region of Galicia, on the tip of an angle, one arm formed by the mountains being the border between Galicia and Hungary, and the other arm, along the Dniester River and her tributaries, being the border with Russia. Two kilometers south from the center of the city was the border with Bukovina, which was also part of the Austro-Hungarian Empire. Through the city there ran a south-north highway which for centuries had been a convenient trading route connecting the Balkans and Southern Europe with the North.

A railroad connecting Bucharest with Vienna, running at a distance of approximately four kilometers from the city, was built in the late nineteenth century. In the middle of the city was a large rectangular area paved with cobblestones, the marketplace. Early every morning, with the exception of Saturday and Sunday, stall-keepers put up their stalls. Jews displayed a variety of merchandise for sale to the peasants, and the peasants piled up all kinds of produce—vegetables, fruits, eggs, fowl, etc.—which were bought by the Jews. In the afternoon the stalls were stored in the yard of a nearby building, to be used again the next morning.

On the outskirts of the city was a large meadow which was used as the yearly fair grounds. Still farther away from the inner city was the Christian cemetery, and bordering it was the Jewish cemetery, the *git ort*, the *haylig ort*, the *bays hachaim*, which was separated from the other and fenced in by a high stone wall. According to the dates, some of the tombstones were 500 to 600 years old. There were also a few mausoleums, *ohelim*, where rabbis were buried. Behind the entrance gate to the cemetery there was a small chapel where the *chevra kadisha* (burial society) stored the *tahre brayt* and the *mitah*, the board used for cleaning the corpses and the stretcher.

As everywhere, the living conditions differed from family to family, depending on their means. Accordingly, the location, size, and type of construction of the buildings varied.

On all sides of the marketplace were rows of two- to three-story brick and stucco houses under sheet-metal roofs. On the ground floor of these houses stores were located. The upper floors were occupied by their owners or were rented out as living quarters. The houses and the stores all belonged to Jews, and the tenants also were Jews.

Three- to four-story office buildings, such as the district's government administration building, the public school for girls, three churches belonging to different Christian denominations, the district council, the hospital, the district courthouse, the Baron Hirsch school, the high school, the Polish exclusive club, called *Sokól*, and the telephone, telegraph, and postal offices were conveniently located not far from the center of the city. Also, close to the center was the new city hall, a four-story building with a forty-meter-high watchtower. From this tower firemen kept watch for fires.

In the city hall was located the city police headquarters, the city jail, the fire department with the stables for its horses and the coachhouses for its equipment. The equipment of the fire department consisted of three or four wooden tanks mounted on wheeled platforms, a few pumps, some lengths of hoses, and a few ladders. The horses were also used for garbage collection. In the event of a fire alarm, the coachmen, who were actually the firemen, left their garbage wagons and hurried on horseback to the fire department, where they gathered their equipment and then proceeded to the fire. The upper three floors of the city hall building accommodated a public school for boys.

Farther away from the center of the city, to the north and west, the streets became wider, had good sidewalks, and were lined with trees. Some houses were connected to the waterline and the sewer system and were equipped with inside plumbing. This was the domain of the Polish residents and a sprinkling of wealthy Jews—doctors, lawyers, teachers, and clerks who owned or rented homes in that area. The houses in this section of the city were large, mostly brick covered with stucco, and decorated with gypsum ornaments and carvings under tiled or sheet-metal roofs. The houses were usually set back from the street and had gardens in the front yards with orchards in the back. This district had a fair amount of greenery and a park which was usually frequented on Saturday afternoons by Jewish teenagers who were not Chassidic. Most of the houses in this district had, in the backyard, a one-room building with a hearth and an oven for cooking and baking during the hot summer days.

In the center of the city, in the shtetl, one would find no greenery at all, and rarely anything growing except in the flowerpots on the windowsills. The houses in this area consisted of many rooms. There usually was a living room, called the salon, a few bedrooms, depending on the size of the family, with separate bedrooms for the father, the mother, the children, and, if necessary, for a widowed parent. There were also one or two bedrooms for guests. If a son-in-law was taken into the family with the promise of *kest* (room and board for a certain period of time), the couple, and eventually their children, if there were any before the period of *kest* was terminated, were also quartered in the house.

Also, depending on one's means, the furnishings differed from family to family. As a rule, however, there was a glassed-in cabinet, or at least shelves along the walls, for *sfarim* (books), a buffet containing silverware, such as cutlery, candlesticks for Sabbath and *Yom tov*, a box for spices for *havdalah* (the Sabbath evening blessing), a *menorah*, and a box for an *etrog*. The latter was seldom missing in a well-to-do home. From the ceiling hung a candelabra. Those who didn't have all the silverware at least had the candelabra, the candlesticks, and the menorah of brass, which were usually received as a *drushegeshank* (wedding gift). Some houses had parquet floors, while others had either painted or unpainted hardwood floors. Maids, as a rule, had their own rooms. Where there was no room available they would sleep in the kitchen. In the bedrooms there were many featherbeds (eiderdown) and numerous pillows stacked up high on the beds. On the walls of the kitchen hung many shiny copper pots and pans. The way they shone provided a means of judging how good a housewife, the *balebuste*, was. Of course there were two sets of kitchen utensils, *milchig* and *flayshig*, which were easily recognizable by their different colors.

Since not every house was connected to the waterline, a barrel for water, a jug, and a basin and a towel were kept in the hall or the kitchen. The houses were heated by burning wood in ceramic tile or brick ovens with dampers for exhausting the fumes, which if closed too soon caused carbon monoxide poisoning. This happened quite often.

The nicest and largest house in this district belonged to a Jewish landowner whose estate was located only six kilometers from the city. This man had built on his premises a special *shtibl* in order to pray twice daily with a *minyan*, so there was no need for him to go to the synagogue for this purpose. He used to drive to his properties in a huge open coach which was drawn four-in-hand by fiery horses, all the same color. The coachman, high on the coachbox, proudly and skillfully driving his horses, looked funny in his cap and uniform, which didn't suit his red beard and his long *payes* (earlocks) very well. The valet always accompanied his master on a seat mounted to the rear of the coach. The boss, with his nicely combed, snow-white, long beard, and with a long-stemmed pipe in his mouth, sat comfortably in his seat, looking majestic in his black silken caftan. Whenever his wife rode with him she sat on the opposite side, never beside him.

There was another man who had a *shtibl* on his property. He was the banker, and he always had a *minyan* because his patrons always came to his *shtibl*. They wanted to be friends with him in case they needed to apply for a loan one day.

In contrast to the district mentioned above, the farther away one went from the center of the city, to the east and to the south, the streets became narrower and dirtier. Here the poorer people lived. The houses were smaller and shabbier and were made mostly of wooden frames with walls of clay and straw under thatched or shingled roofs. There were no sidewalks, only boards laid out in a few places where the mud was ankle-deep. This district had no sewer connections, and the water, pure or dirty, was drained out onto the streets.

Behind the houses, chicken, geese, ducks, and turkeys were kept in fowl houses which were nailed together from wooden orange or tea boxes, or they ran freely around the house. Here and there was a shack for a goat. It cost very little to feed a goat, and one could have milk for his children. For the same reason, other people kept a cow in a shack. Some even kept a few cows for business purposes.

In this area lived the water carriers. Also, the *balagulas* and the *fiakers*, the former being a coachman who transported goods and the latter a cabman. Behind their houses were the stables for the horses which they used in their trade. Tailors, shoemakers, and porters also lived in this area.

The houses in this district were small and consisted of one or two rooms with a hall in the middle. Seldom was there a house of three or four rooms. The houses were crowded with large families. Many children, and often an elderly parent, lived in these cramped quarters. The cooking and laundry were also done in this area if the weather didn't permit them to be done outside. Cooking was done on a trivet, a metal stand over an open fire over which an opening was made as a smoke vent to the flue.

In such a room might also have been the shop of a tailor or a shoemaker; even a *melamed* might have had a small *cheder* in his one-room quarters. In these houses, beds were taken out for the day. Children slept alternately with the heads of some at the headboard and the heads of others at the opposite end of the bed. They were all covered with one comforter. Some slept on the floor on straw-filled mattresses. If there was a cradle it was usually close to the mother's bed.

Seldom would one find wooden floors in this district. The floors were made of packed earth, and usually on Fridays, when preparing for the Sabbath, they were plastered smooth with a mixture of cow manure and clay and sprinkled over with fine sand.

In nearly every house, rich and poor, there were boxes for charity, for *yeshivahs*, for *kizwah* (for Jews studying and living in Tiberias and Jerusalem). Without exception, there was always a *pushke* (box) for Reb Meir Bal Haness. Whenever a *Yiddene* had a *shwayr hartz* (was depressed due to a sickness in the family), or was begging God for a *zivik* (a match for a daughter) or a better *parnusse* (livelihood), she always put a few cents into one or another *pushke* before *lechtbentshen* on Fridays.

In most of the houses throughout the city one could always find hanging a picture of Sir Moses Montefiore. This English philanthropist was honored in appreciation of his missions on behalf of Jews in faraway countries such as Morocco, Palestine, Syria, Russia, Romania, Italy, and so on, wherever Jews were in distress.

The city had no electricity. Only in 1912 was the building of a hydroelectric station started, but it was not completed before the outbreak of World War I. The streets and houses were lit by kerosene lamps. Only one house had electricity, and it belonged to the Jewish owner of the flour mill. He used the electricity generated by a diesel unit for the mill to also supply his house, which was located directly in front of the mill.

The city, originally built for strategic purposes on a hill, had no water wells inside her limits. It obtained its water supply by means of a pipeline from a distant place with good water sources. On various corners of the streets were posts with taps installed for use by the population.

Not too many houses were connected to the waterline. But the buildings with public offices and some of the private houses in the Polish section were. This was also the case with the connection to the sewer system. Most of the houses had outhouses located behind them. There was a scavenger who, when the outhouse pits were full, would drive by at night with a wooden tank on a wheeled platform and pump out the contents. He would then carry them to the ravine or sell them to peasants for fertilizer.

Since the city had no natural sources of water inside her limits, and because a *mikveh* (ritual bath) must be above a natural spring, the *shwitz* (steambath) and the *mikveh* had to be built and located in a valley a far distance from the center of the city.

Nevertheless, this distance didn't prevent the pious residents of the shtetl from using the *shwitz* and the *mikveh* every Friday, the latter by men on Saturdays also. Some evenings were also set aside for the use of the *shwitz* by women. But this distance was no hindrance to the women for the use of the *mikveh*.

The city had, at that time, a total population of 18,000, of whom 70 percent were Jews. The remainder consisted of an overwhelming majority of Poles and a small number of Ukrainians.

It was a city with a rural hinterland of forty-nine mostly one-street villages, which were inhabited by Ukrainians. Only the estates belonged to the Poles. Among the Ukrainian villages were a few which belonged to Germans who had settled there after the annexation by Austria of this part of Poland when it was partitioned. This farsightedness by Austria in bringing in German colonists paid good dividends during World War II, when the German armies were met by the colonists with great joy and sympathy, helping them in every way they could.

In some villages, among the Ukrainian peasants were also sprinkled a few Jews who made a meager living out of farming and as innkeepers. However, they were constantly exposed to many kinds of vexation and annoyances. The Poles lived exclusively in the city and in the nearby suburbs.

Most Poles belonged to the Roman Catholic Church, but a minority of them were Armenian Catholics. The Ukrainians belonged to the Greek Catholic Church. All three Christian denominations adhered to the Pope in Rome. The Roman and the Armenian priests lived in celibacy, each of them having a housekeeper. The Greek Catholic priests were married and had families. The Greek Catholics didn't recognize the Gregorian calendar, and their holidays usually fell on the thirteenth day after the corresponding Roman and Armenian Catholic holidays. Schools were closed on the Roman as well as on the Greek Catholic holidays, and the students had an abundance of school days off. Of course, Jews were free from school on Jewish holidays as well.

The Poles were mostly civil servants, from the officials on the highest level down to the caretakers, messengers, and janitors. All the offices were occupied by them. The Ukrainians were engaged in farming, breeding of cattle and sheep, raising poultry, working in the forests, cutting, hauling, and floating timber, domestic handicrafts, wood carving, rug weaving, pottery making, and the weaving of linen from which they made their own clothing.

The relations of the Jewish population to the Gentiles were limited to business matters, or when dealing with officialdom. The knowledge of the Ukrainian language by the Jews was limited to the minimum of words which were absolutely necessary in order to transact business.

When dealing with officialdom, which was exclusively Polish, the Jews usually used Yiddish, which the clerks normally understood because of its similarity to the German language, or they sent someone who knew Polish to speak for them. Most of the Jews, with the exception of the younger generation and, of course, the intelligensia, spoke only Yiddish. Many Jews whose businesses brought them in touch with the world outside of the shtetl and who traveled extensively knew many languages very well, especially Polish and German. And, because the shtetl was only a few kilometers from Czernowitz, the capital of Bukovina, German was the second language used in the shtetl.

The Bogdan Chmielnicki monument in Kiev

Emperor Franz Josef

Jews in a village in the Carpathian Mountains

Reprinted by permission of Schocken Books, Inc., from Image before my eyes by Lucjan Dobroszycki and Barbara Kirschenblatt-Gimblett. Copyright © 1977 by Schocken Books, Inc.

Sir Moses Montefiore

Galician Jews, from a postcard

Reprinted by permission of Schocken Books, Inc., from Image before my eyes by Lucjan Dobroszycki and Barbara Kirschenblatt-Gimblett. Copyright © 1977 by Schocken Books, Inc.

2

Anti-Semitism

IN OUR SHTETL, as everywhere else in Galicia, the Jews were an entity unto themselves. So were the Ukrainians and Poles. Most of the time Jews lived in harmony with the Gentile population, but a wall of anti-Semitism always separated the Jews from the Poles and Ukrainians.

A peasant who came to the market might sell a horse, and as was the custom, would invite a few friends for a vodka at an inn (in the city all the inns were kept by Jews). After having a few vodkas himself, he would begin "treating" everyone present at the inn, so that in no time all his money would be spent. When the innkeeper refused to serve any more vodka without being paid, the peasant would start to yell, "Where is my money that I got for the horse I just sold? The dirty Jew robbed me! He stole all my money!" Grabbing the Jew by the collar he would begin beating him while the others helped themselves to everything that was in the inn, at the same time breaking the fixtures and furniture.

They would then spill out into the street, yelling, "Brothers in Christ, help us! The Jews are robbing and murdering Christians!" Thereupon the war cry "Kill the Jews!" was raised at the marketplace. Stalls were overturned, merchandise looted, and a march through the Jewish streets was started. Windows were broken, and wherever a Jew was found, he was mercilessly beaten. By the time the gendarmes arrived everything was over.

The next day all was quiet. Yesterday's *pogromoczyk* was once more a customer in the Jewish inns, stores, and at the marketplace. As for the Jews. Well, some were at home in bed nursing their wounds, some were in the hospital with broken ribs or

11

arms, others were once again tending their businesses and re-pairing the broken doors and broken windowpanes, some with glass and others with cardboard.

When a Ukrainian wedding was celebrated, and the wedding guests, who were already drunk, rode on wagons into the city from their villages to have the wedding performed at the church in the city, Jewish innkeepers locked up their premises, not wanting to pour oil on the flames by selling vodka to a drunken bunch of peasants. The wedding guests, already high in spirit, embarked from the wagons and first fell upon the Jewish musicians they had hired for the wedding. They had already entertained them at their village and had come with them to the city. The Ukrainians beat up the musicians, breaking some of their instruments, and blaming them for allegedly having notified the Jews in the city, in advance, that they were coming. Having finished with the musicians they tried to take further revenge on other Jews.

When a priest was on his way to administer extreme unction to a dying Christian soul, the Jews, as soon as they heard the ringing of the bell by the deacon accompanying the priest, left the streets quickly and locked the doors of their homes and stores lest the Christians, who knelt on the streets in front of the passing priest, would accuse them of not having behaved with dignity at such a moment by remaining standing when everybody else was kneeling. This would have been enough to set anti-Jewish disturbances in motion.

The same thing happened when a procession was marching through the streets bearing holy images and banners, for example, on the Corpus Christi holiday. No Jew would dare remain on the streets because he might be accused of host desecration.

Even at times when everything was quiet, heroic Christian boys didn't fail to harass Jews. It often occurred in school that two or more Polish or Ukrainian boys would grab a Jewish classmate and rub his mouth with pork fat. The teacher usually didn't see or hear the commotion. But when called to the scene by other Jewish students he had no other alternative but to act. What he did was to gently reprimand the Christian students and explain to the Jewish student that it was only a joke and that there was really no reason to make such a fuss. After all, they hadn't hurt him, had they?

A Jewish boy would never venture into the streets inhabited by Christians, even when accompanied by an adult. Christian boys would make fun of them, call them names, throw stones at them, and set their dogs upon them. Also, for simple fun, Christian boys would drive pigs into the Jewish streets and throw manure through the open windows of Jewish homes. Twice a year, in the spring and in the fall, nineteen-year-old boys from the surrounding villages came to town. In the spring they appeared before a military draft commission which had to decide whether they were fit to serve in the army, and again in the fall after the harvest to be transported to their units. As a rule all were drunk and they were always spoiling for a bloody fight. Jews would, on such occasions, lock themselves in their houses and keep quiet, because to respond to violence with violence was "not Jewish." But around 1910 the Jewish youth said, "Enough is enough!" Students organized a self-defense unit and, with the help of porters, coachmen, and butchers, armed themselves with clubs. As soon as trouble started, the Gentile "heroes," not expecting to encounter any resistance, but fully prepared to have a good time harassing Jews, learned that the Jews would no longer rely on the gendarmes, who in most cases arrived at the scene too late. Met with strong resistance, the "heroes" learned that the Jews were capable of hitting back very hard, and many fled with bloody noses.

Anti-Semitism is not a monopoly of the Ukrainians or Poles. There is not a single state in Europe which, at one time or another throughout the ages, did not persecute Jews. This hatred is characterized by the fact that for any wrongdoing, actual or alleged, perpetrated by a Jew or Jews at any given time or place, the Jews as a whole have been made responsible.

The reasons for anti-Semitism are manifold and can be understood only when viewed in terms of centuries-old social, economic, and religious differences. Although unable to analyze all the reasons for anti-Semitism, let us try to analyze at least some of them: apartheid, competition, envy, the need for a scapegoat, hostility of the debtor toward the creditor, and Jewish ability and zeal for reforms. And finally, the common denominator of all of them—the teachings of the Church, which contain the oldest and strongest roots of anti-Semitism.

Wherever we lived we didn't melt into the majority which surrounded us. We were regarded as strangers who looked, dressed, and spoke differently, and who had strange customs and beliefs. We preserved our Jewish way of life, clinging to our faith and traditions, no matter how much we suffered. In order to make a living, Jews were forced to compete with Gentiles. This was, for the Gentiles, reason enough to combat Jews. What they couldn't obtain by means of fair competition was achieved by violent attacks on their Jewish competitors. It was an easy way to do away with the Jewish businesses. Whenever Jews were allowed to breathe a little freer they prospered. If a Jew became successful he engendered envy and was regarded with jealousy and hostility. The means by which the Jews achieved success—their diligence, their hard work, and the sacrifices they endured—were overlooked. The Jews were always judged in the negative.

A scapegoat is needed by rulers to divert subjects from real problems. Wherever we lived we were weak and therefore easy prey for scapegoating. We were accused of any calamity suffered by the majority, such as spreading the black death, poisoning the wells, and so on.

Hostility of the consumer toward the shopkeeper, of the debtor against the creditor, also played an important part in stirring up anti-Semitic feelings. As long as the Jewish shopkeeper could be milked by buying on credit, everything went well, but when it came to paying the debt, the Jew became a bloodsucker.

Our abilities, our resourcefulness, our thoughts, our open-mindedness and knack for reform, brought Jews to the forefront among the leaders in science, economics, and political change. The result: again, for the deeds of individual Jews, all of us were branded Bolsheviks, capitalists, and counterrevolutionists.

Anti-Semitism spread in sermons was the heart and soul of Jew-hatred. The teachings of the New Testament paved the way for pogroms, autos-da-fé, ghettos, massacres, and so forth. Religious indoctrination, full of hatred against Jews, was force-fed into the brains of Christians from childhood and throughout their lives. The desire to obliterate the Jews is characteristic of the Christian educational system. Two thousand years of catechism presented the Jews as the source of all evil. They preached that the Jewish mob had cried out, "Kill him, kill him!" (Jesus), for which we were branded "Christ-killers." But Jesus was born a Jew and died as a Jew. He spent his energy trying to get the Jews of his own time to obey the law and the spirit of the Jewish religion. The New Testament describes how the Jewish masses loved him and that huge crowds pressed into the synagogues to hear him, and how they followed him. How, then, could the "mob," the masses, predominantly his Jewish followers who loved him, have cried, "Crucify him"? It was the Romans who crucified him.

The Christians proclaim Jesus to be the savior of mankind. One would therefore expect them to be thankful to the Jews who gave them the savior. In the minds of Christians remains the assumption that as long as we don't "see the light," and do not accept Jesus, no salvation can come. Thus we are in the way of their salvation. In the Soviet Union, where equality is supposed to be the substance and the pillar of communism, the curse of anti-Semitism is nevertheless burning red hot. The Soviets do not blame Jews for the death of Jesus, but find enough other excuses for Jew baiting. Jews are branded counterrevolutionists and spies serving the Western countries. In addition, Jews have had to suffer from Soviet anti-Zionism. As soon as it is known that a Jew has the desire to return to the land of his forefathers it's enough to exclude him from places of higher learning, and to the dismissal from his job. Jews are accepted at the universities in limited numbers only, and are dismissed from higher posts if they are ever promoted.

Another kind of anti-Semitism and anti-Judaism, where the question of the guilt for killing Christ is not utilized, is the one practiced by the Arabs in their aim to destroy Israel. Their weapons are the fragrance of their oil and their mighty coffers filled with petrodollars, which enable the sheiks to manipulate the policy and economy of many countries, among them the mightiest. Some of these countries, blinded by egotism and selfishness and in order to adulate the Arabs, are ready to sacrifice Israel and the citizens of their own countries who, as well as Israel, are subject to an economic boycott. Nobody wants to take the risk of losing Arab oil deliveries. Not wanting to lower the standard of living in their own countries, they feel it is better to sacrifice Israel in order to get enough oil to keep the wheels of their economies rolling.

3

The Jewish Community

WHEN GALICIA AT the end of the eighteenth century came under Austrian rule, a new order was prescribed for the organization of the Jewish community.

The government wanted to deal with only one organization representing the entire Jewish community—a council composed usually of five *parnassim* (councillors), the so-called *Juedische Kultusgemeinde*, the Board of Jewish Worship and Education. The *parnassim* were elected only by taxpaying members of the community. The councillors chose one from among themselves as president, the *rosh hakahal*. The catch, however, was that the *parnassim* had to be confirmed by the government. The board represented the Jewish community before the government and was responsible for the slaughterhouses for poultry and cattle, the ritual bath, the registration of births, marriages, divorces, and deaths, the main synagogue, the *hekdesh* (asylum), the Talmud Torah, and so on.

The community's main income came from taxes imposed on its members by its own assessments. Government tax collectors acted for the community. Other income came from leasing the slaughterhouses and the ritual bath, and from the fees for burial plots at the cemetery. Depending on the wealth of the deceased person, a higher or lesser fee was asked, and hard bargaining with the surviving family took place. When a rich but stingy man died, who in his lifetime hadn't contributed enough to charity, this was the time to balance the account. Accordingly, a larger sum was asked for the burial. If the family didn't come up with the money, burial was refused until the family gave in. If they stubbornly refused to pay the amount asked for, then a plot close to the fence, where suicides were buried, was given to the deceased.

The rav and the dayanim were appointed for life. Usually different groups of community members supported their own candidate. As a result they would be at war with each other. There were always various opinions among the groups in the shtetl, in keeping with the saying that three Jews discussing a matter have four different opinions.

Purely religious matters were in the hands of the rabbinical authority. These included *kashruth*, officiating at weddings, making out a *get*, attending at *chalitza*, and so on. The *rav* presided over *din toyras* (rabbinical court) in conciliation with a *dayan*. Their verdict was always binding. It seldom happened that a Jew called before the rabbi to a *din toyra* would refuse to appear or wouldn't accept the rabbinical verdict. It was considered a sacrilege to use the secular courts. Even a judge would sometimes ask two quarreling Jews, "Why don't you go to the rabbi?" Often a Gentile would suggest to a Jew with whom he had a dispute that they submit the dispute to the rabbi for a decision.

There were many classes of Jews in the shtetl, depending, first of all, on wealth. Who, for example, took the seat on the *mizrach* (eastern wall) of the *shtibl, klouze, beth hamidrash*, or synagogue? Not the learned man, but the rich one who had contributed the most for it at the time the building fund was being collected. Who got *shishi*, the more *bekuvete aliyah* to the Torah? The honorable one who paid the most when the *aliyas* were auctioned off. Even among the tradesmen and the laborers there were differences in *yiches*. The tailors were on a higher level than the cobblers. Behind them other trades followed, *balagulas, fiaker* owners, porters, and so on.

Nevertheless, one characteristic quality common to all Jews must be mentioned. It is the *yiddishe neshume*. Deep in the Jewish soul a sentiment of solidarity is ingrained. *Kol Yisroel achim*—All Jews are brethren. This feeling of solidarity comes to the forefront because the Jews as a whole are held responsible for any transgression perpetrated by an individual Jew. If the need arises and help is required for a Jew in distress, nothing would stand in the way of helping the individual or group by another

Jew. Many organizations were instituted for this purpose, based principally on charity of a local character. But to a Jewish helping hand, borders were no hindrance.

Before listing the many charitable organizations which acted in our shtetl, philanthropists such as Baron Hirsch and Moses Montefiore must be mentioned. Institutions such as the JCA (Jewish Colonial Association) and the Israelitische Allianz in Vienna shouldn't be forgotten. The Baron Hirsch Institution organized a school in our shtetl, and the JCA organized a farm not far from our shtetl in Slobódka Leśna, where Jewish youth were taught agriculture. Speaking about this farm, I would like to mention that after World War I, Polish soldiers murdered three students at the school.

Baron de Hirsch

When a fire destroyed more than one-half of the shtetl in 1911, help was available the very next day, not only from neighboring Jewish communities, but from places as far away as Lwów, Cracow, Prague, and Vienna. The Israelitische Allianz provided ample funds and building materials. The shtetl was rebuilt very quickly.

There were many voluntary religious and secular organizations. The *Chevrah Kadisha* (Holy Burial Society) arranged that a Jew who died would be brought to *kever Yisroel* (have a ritual funeral) without delay, that the corpse would be washed and cleansed, receive *tachrichim* and men a *talles*, and would be buried in a Jewish cemetery. For all this work no remuneration was received. The funds, donated to them, were used to cover the expenses for the burial of the poor. They did this as a *mitzvah*. If an unknown Jew was found dead, the *Chevrah Kadisha* acted immediately. This was done in order to prevent an autopsy from being performed. There was also a *Chevrah Nosay Hamitah* (pallbearers). If the dead person had no relatives to serve as pallbearers, then these men were always ready to do so. Also, there was the *Chevrah Ner Tamid*, which made sure that there was always a light burning in the synagogue or shul on behalf of the deceased.

The *Chevrah Shass* was made up of people whose only aim was to study. Whoever was not able to study by himself, for example, as a result of lack of education, could stay in the *shtibl* after *maariv* and there was always a member of the *Chevrah Shass* who would study with him until late into the evening. The same applied to another group, the *Chevrah Mishnayes* (studying the Mishnah). The *Tillim Sooggers* were on hand whenever a calamity occurred in order to recite Psalms, which, it was hoped, would speed up the recovery.

The *Chevrah Talmud Torah* was concerned that no Jewish boy should be left without an education. Although the Talmud Torah *cheder* was financed by the community, this organization collected money to bolster its funds in order to pay poor parents who couldn't afford to let their boy go to school because they needed his assistance.

A very important institution was the *Gmilas Chassudim*—the loaning of money to people for various purposes, such as the establishment of a business, in the case of an illness, and for any other emergency. No interest was charged. In many instances funds were even given as a subsidy.

Tomchei Yesoymim ("help the orphans") was an organization which cared for the well-being of orphans. Since no orphanage existed in the shtetl, the organization arranged for foster homes and paid the costs.

Matan b'sesser was a charitable organization which helped needy people who were ashamed to admit that they might require assistance from charity.

Malbish Arumim ("clothing the naked") collected used clothing from the rich and distributed it to the poor who couldn't afford to buy clothes. This organization was very much in demand just before winter.

Bikur Cholim was an organization which visited and comforted the sick people in the hospitals and at home. They were supplied with kosher food, especially chicken soup and preserves, and where it was required, assistance was given with the housework.

Matir Assurim cared for the imprisoned Jews. Kosher food was supplied and ransoms were paid if a Jew was jailed on false charges.

Hachnassas Kalah did what was possible in order to help a Jewish girl get married by collecting money for a modest dowry, providing dresses, and obtaining linen for a trousseau, as well as arranging the wedding.

Hachnassas Orchim cared for every Jew who was a stranger in the city. They made certain that he obtained a place to sleep and that he would be invited by a family for the Sabbath meal. This organization cared for the *hekdesh* (asylum) as well. Beggers wandered from shtetl to shtetl, some of them in groups having in partnership a wagon and a horse. They were given alms by the community and were supposed to stop begging. However, this they usually continued and would beg aggressively and curse if they did not receive what they considered to be sufficient.

Moes Chittin was an organization which arranged that no Jewish family would be without matzah, wine, and other necessities for Pesach. Collecting the funds for this purpose was started before Purim so that everything could be ready in time.

In the shtetl were many people known as *tzduke gebers* (spenders for charity). If there was an emergency the charitable organizations knew exactly where to go for funds. The best-known among the spenders was the Jewish landowner. Each year, after Sukkot, his wagons unloaded sacks of potatoes, cabbage, beets, carrots, and firewood from his estate and forest, and left them in front of the community building. His administrator distributed them to the needy people. For those who were ashamed to pick up the things which they so dearly needed, a committee of young men picked up their share and delivered it secretly. Everybody in the shtetl knew that whenever there was a need for help, the landowner, Reb Hershel by name, would do whatever was possible in order to help a fellow Jew.

In the *hekdesh* of the shtetl lived a harmless *meshuggene* (crazy man). He walked the streets the whole day and collected every scrap of paper and pebble he could find. He would put these into a sack which, when full, he would deposit at the garbage dump.

One day, the *meshuggene* went to the office of the *rosh haka-hal* and said, "I have had enough of this shtetl and can't take it any longer. The boys run after me calling me *meshuggene*. I am therefore moving to another shtetl. However, since a shtetl like ours can't be without a *meshuggene*, I appoint you as the shtetl's *meshuggene* from today on."

In the new shtetl the *meshuggene* enjoyed being left alone and not being teased. He said to a few boys in the shul, "You know, I like your shtetl very much. When I was in Śniatyn, everybody called me *meshuggene*, but here nobody provokes me." Yes, you guessed it. From then on he had his old *tsores* and preferred to return to Śniatyn, relieving the *rosh hakahal* from his duties as his deputy.

4

Occupations

BEFORE DESCRIBING THE Jewish *parnusses*, let us have a look at the occupations of non-Jews.

All the jobs in the government offices and enterprises from the top to the lowest post were held by Poles, or to a more limited degree, by Ukrainians. Jews might also have been found working in a government office.

The Ukrainians were devoted to farming, with vegetables and fruit growing predominant.

In the city there was a Polish butcher shop which sold pork, ham, sausages, and the like. Wildlife was shot by the hunters, and the butcher sold it as well. This usually consisted of hares, venison, brawn, rabbit, and all types of wild fowl. The beef he sold was the hindquarter of the cattle which had been slaughtered by the Jews but which they did not use.

A Polish restaurant, a cake and pastry shop, an ice cream shop which was open during the summer months, and a bakery functioned in the city. Of course, a kiosk which sold Catholic devotionalia was open on Sundays and on Catholic holidays. The city also had a few non-Jewish craftsmen. There were Ukrainian shoemakers, a Polish blacksmith, a locksmith, a saddler, barbers, midwives, and so forth. The notary public, the veterinarian, the pharmacist, and three doctors were Polish. The Poles looked upon the merchants and tradesmen with scorn. They considered waiting on customers beneath the dignity of a Pole and therefore left these fields open to the Jews.

As for the economic situation of the Jews in the shtetl, it may be assumed that 20 percent of them were rich and lived comfortably. Thirty percent would be considered as doing well, somewhere in the middle of the ladder. Another 30 percent had difficulties making ends meet, although they somehow managed to do so. The remaining 20 percent eked out an extremely meager existence. Many of them depended on charity.

Jews were engaged in two types of work. One group worked for and serviced the Jewish population. A second group followed occupations of a general character in the professions, carrying on businesses, plying trades, and performing many types of hard and backbreaking work.

There were also Jews who did nothing but study the Torah all day and late into the night. The *parnusse gebers*, the ones who worried about *parnusse* and cared for the upkeep of the household and the children were their wives. The men lived an ascetic life. Some fasted every Monday and Thursday and didn't bother about money. The wives were proud of their husbands and happily convinced that the mode of life their husbands pursued would bring them straight into heaven. When their time came, they too would be rewarded and would be allowed to accompany their husbands into paradise. It did not matter what kind of life you had to endure on earth, as long as you were able to earn the "other world." Meanwhile, these poor, overworked women worried about *parnusse*, the household, and the bearing of children.

The Rav. To fulfill the obligations of the *rav* was no easy task. In his fervent piety he wanted to spend his time primarily on his studies. But being an employee of the community, which paid his meager salary, he had other obligations. He had to preside over *din toyras* (rabbinical court), perform marriages, attend some funerals, arrange for divorces, be present at *chalitza*, and so on. Of course he had to resolve questions of *kashruth*, such as when a housewife opened a chicken and had some doubt concerning spots she noticed on the liver. The *rav* then had to decide whether the chicken was kosher or not. Usually when the *rav* was pondering a hard problem he encountered in the Talmud, a maid brought a chicken to be examined and he had to interrupt his thinking to consult many books before making his decision.

The Soifer. There were three *sofrim* in the shtetl. A *soifer* (scribe) must be a very pious Jew. In commissioning a *soifer* to write a *Sefer Torah*, as a donation to a congregation, the most pious *soifer* was chosen. The Torah was written with goose quills and ink made by the *soifer*. He also tanned the parchment. His work lasted for hundreds of years. Before starting his day's work, the *soifer* went to the *mikveh* and said a blessing. Before writing a *Shaym* (the name of God), he again went to the *mikveh*. During the writing he had his *talles* on and was very careful not to make any mistakes and to have each letter and word perfectly written. In case a mistake was made, the entire page had to be cut out and kept in a special place in the synagogue, the so-called *pulish*. Besides Torahs, the *soifer* wrote *tfillin, mezuzaas, kol korays* (proclamations), *megillas, ktubas* (marriage contracts), and so on.

The Shoichet (Slaughterer). In the shtetl there were six *shochtim*. Before being accepted as a *shoichet* one had to study all the rules concerning *shchita* and had to pass an exam. A *shoichet* had to be a *boidek* as well. This was an inspector who had to decide whether the slaughtered animal was fit to be declared kosher. He slaughtered with an extremely sharp knife so that the animal would not suffer, and he had to have a steady hand. He was also usually a *mohel* who performed circumcisions. The *shoichet* was paid by the community.

The slaughterhouses were leased to the highest bidder, who in turn charged for the slaughtering of fowl and/or cattle at the fees prescribed by the community.

Melamdim. The *melamdim* (teachers) conducted *chederim* ("rooms," i.e., classrooms). The shtetl had ten *chederim*, each conducted by a *melamed*, who would or would not have a *belfer* (helper).

Restaurants. There were two kosher restaurants in the shtetl and a kosher delicatessen with a large room behind the store where the young boys used to drop in to discuss politics.

Printing and Books. There was a printer who made letterheads, business cards, invitations, and so on. He also had a bookstore in which he sold textbooks for all the schools, and Jewish books such as *sidurim, chumashim, machzorim,* complete sets of *Tenach, Gemaras,* and any other kind of holy books. Also, *tallesim, tfillin, tzitzis, mezuzos,* and books in Yiddish, such as the *Tsenah Ureehnah* ("Let's Go and See"), written around 1600, full of folk tales, legends, and rabbinical commentaries combined and intertwined with the Torah portion of the week. He also had story books in Yiddish to bolster *Yiddishkeit.*

Butchers. There were many butchers in the shtetl. They bought cattle at the marketplace or direct from the peasants in the village and had them slaughtered. The kosher part of the animal, the front part, was sold in their stores, and the hindquarter was sold at a cheaper rate to the non-Jewish butchers. Butchers who knew how to perform the so-called *traybern* (extracting some veins from the hindquarter of the animal) were allowed to sell this meat to Jews after it had been inspected by a *shoichet* and found to be kosher.

Chazanim. There were no full-time jobs available for the *chazanim*, so they had to be content with finding jobs for the High Holidays. They supplemented their income with perquisites which they received when they were asked to sing at a family *simchah* or a funeral.

Shamossim. Every *shtibl* and synagogue had a *shames* (beadle) who received a small weekly wage from his congregation. It was certainly not enough to live on. He depended upon tips, but they were not enough to enable him to solve all his *tsores*.

Bath Attendants. Although the bath attendants, both men and women, received tips for their labor on top of the small price for bath tickets, they hardly made enough money to pay the community for the lease on their facilities.

Musicians. There was a band of Jewish musicians with string instruments and flutes, but with no drums or horns. This band was considered to be the best. They were asked to play on many occasions, including Polish or Ukrainian festivities. It was the only one available, and since there was no other band in the shtetl, how could anyone say that they were not the best?

Badchen. A special profession was the so-called *badchen* (jester), who officiated at Jewish weddings and family festivities. A *badchen* used to make fun of everyone present. It was considered in bad taste to show that one felt offended by the jokes.

Shadchen. The *shadchen* (matchmaker) was an important profession. In this occupation there was no discrimination against sex: there were male and female matchmakers, who sometimes worked together. The woman would deal with the mothers of the boys or girls who were to be matched, and the man would discuss the matter with the fathers.

Sarvers. The *sarvers* (caterers) were women, good cooks, who were hired for cooking and baking by a family who was preparing for a *simche.*

Batlunim. The *batlunim* (idlers) were pious Jews who, although not very well learned, knew enough to recite psalms or read *Mishnahyes* when hired by a family which was suffering a sickness, or when called to a home for the *layl shmirah*, the watch night before a *brith milah* (circumcision) was to take place, or when remaining overnight at the home with a corpse. They were also hired to say *kaddish* for a person who passed away without a son.

The gravediggers at the cemetery, the *bays oylam*, were also Jews.

Matrikelführer. The *matrikelführer* was the registrar for births, marriages, divorces, and deaths. He was appointed by the government on the suggestion of the Board of Jewish Councillors and was paid by the community. He had the right, however, to charge an extra fee for issuing any certificates.

Luftmensh. The *luftmensh*, the one who "made money from the air," was an agent, a broker, a middleman without a store or an office, and also without money. He always knew who was selling what and who was buying what. A *luftmensh* bragged that there was no trick in selling somebody what he was looking for. The art of selling is to sell not what someone else wants to buy but that which you want to sell.

Winkelschrayber. The *winkelshrayber*, an unlicensed councillor, masterfully fluent in Polish and German, wrote petitions, suits, appeals, and had extensive experience in judicial matters and court proceedings. His advice was as much sought after as that of the lawyer.

Barbers. The barbers' main job was haircutting and shaving, but some patrons had a subscription to be shaved every second day, or twice a week, either at the barber's shop or in their home. Anyhow, there were not many people in the shtetl who shaved their beards. Even a *dajtsh* did not shave, but used instead some depilatory chemical. At that time shaving was not a simple matter. There were no safety razors, and a straight razor was used for this purpose. Not everybody had the courage to do it himself.

A barber called the *royfe* (the healer) supplemented his income by performing paramedical jobs, such as giving enemas, regular and cut-cupping (*gehakty bankes*). When the skin was sucked very high into the cup, the cup was removed and the barber made an incision with a straight razor in the skin, letting a fair amount of blood flow. Another form of bloodletting was done by simply cutting into a vein in the arm. For this kind of operation peasants used to come on market days from far-off villages. The belief was that all sicknesses were caused by poison in one's blood, so that the more blood you lost, the less poison remained in the body.

Applying leeches to the body was also very much in use and was even recommended by some doctors. The leeches were put onto the skin near a vein. They would suck the blood until they were blown up full and would fall off. As a matter of fact, even today one may find that some pharmacies in Vienna or in many German cities display in their windows jars with leeches for sale.

Another specialty of the barber was the extracting of teeth, which was done without any anesthetic, except that the patient prepared himself for the operation by taking a good swig of vodka. In case of any sickness in a family, the barber was called first.

Midwives, usually wives of barbers, assisted at childbirth. A doctor was called by the midwife only in case of an emergency.

All other Jewish occupations were spread over a very wide range: professions, wholesale and retail businesses, trading in many commodities, light industry, importers and exporters, craftsmen, and artisans. The businesses were based on and adjusted to the needs of the peasantry and the landowners of the estates.

Professionals. There were Jewish doctors, lawyers, a judge, a few clerks in the civil services, a banker, high school teachers (called professors), public school teachers, and a special teacher for Jewish religion for all the schools, the public as well as the high school. There were private teachers, *layrers,* who didn't like to be called a *melamed;* they tutored Hebrew, German, and the most important subject at that time, caligraphy.

No Jewish pharmacy was in the shtetl, although according to the population there should have been at least three. There was only one which was owned by the burgomaster, a Pole with good connections at the top, and as a result no other pharmacy in the shtetl was permitted to be licensed.

Wholesale and retail businesses and import-export firms dealing in any commodity needed locally and available for export functioned in the town as well. So did forwarding and shipping undertakings, mostly branches of internationally known companies in Vienna or Hamburg with connections with firms located all over the Austro-Hungarian Empire, Germany, England and other European countries.

Every Tuesday was market day in the shtetl. The surrounding shtetls also had their market days once a week. They were set up on different days so as not to coincide with the markets held in the other shtetls. *Costermongers* were out through the week, every day attending a market in a different shtetl, except on Fridays, when they didn't leave home because they wouldn't be able to return home for Shabbos on time. The *costermongers* had their own, or hired, horse-drawn wagons on which they loaded their merchandise for sale, with stalls ready to be put up. Others left for the market with empty containers and boxes to be filled up with merchandise bought at the market from the peasants, such as eggs, chickens, geese, ducks, turkeys, goose feathers, hides, wool, bristle, beans, wax, grain, corn, honey, and so on.

In the afternoon the merchandise bought during the day was packed and brought home to the shtetl, where it was sold to the wholesalers or exporters who specialized in the relevant commodity. On the other hand, the ones who were not buying but were selling merchandise at the markets replenished their stock at the wholesalers and loaded their wagons for the next trip. After a few hours sleep, and upon rising in the early morning, they left for another shtetl where on that day the market was held.

All the wagons traveled at the same time, following closely one after the other for security reasons. Often, when a single wagon passed a village it was harassed, if not attacked, and the Jew was beaten or even robbed by the teenagers of the village. However, when many wagons appeared, driven by strong *balagulas* (coachmen), the teenagers would not dare to attack. Instead, they would satisfy themselves by throwing stones at the wagons.

The exporters sorted the merchandise bought from the *costermongers* and readied it for export. Hides were dried, beans cleaned of dirt, bristle sorted, and feathers plucked. Chickens were loaded into coops and were shipped immediately in carloads to destinations such as Vienna and Prague. Such a carload was usually escorted by a man who was responsible for looking after the birds on the way to their destination, replenishing the water and grain in order to deliver them alive to the importer. Horses which were no longer fit for work and were being shipped to butchers in Prague, where they would be slaughtered and sold to special butcher shops for horse meat, were also given escorts.

Another source of *parnusse* was the cleaning and drying of the intestines from slaughtered animals and their export for making sausages.

Horse and cattle trading was also one of the larger businesses. Horses were bought and sold locally as workhorses for the estate owners, peasants, forwarders, coachmen, and so on, with the army being the largest buyer of horses. After tenders were invited the traders went to Hungary and Russia, returning to the shtetl with the best available horses, which were never rejected by the army. Cattle were purchased locally and at the marketplaces of the neighboring shtetls, and sold to the landowners, peasants, butchers, and the army. Cows were also sold to the Jewish dairymen.

Once a year there was a big fair in Olmuetz in Moravia. It was the biggest fair in Europe, where cattle were exclusively traded. The shtetl's cattle traders attended this fair and bought large quantities of cattle, which they in turn sold mostly to people whose business was cattle fattening.

Almost all the landowners of the estates surrounding the shtetl manufactured alcohol in distilleries on the estates. Vodka, which was distilled at the distilleries, was made from potatoes. The Jews rented large stables from the landowners, bought a couple of hundred head of cattle, put them into the stables, and contracted the waste left over after the process of fermentation, which mixed with chaff was used as fodder for the cattle. After a few months, normally in springtime, the cattle became fat and the business-man reaped a nice profit, if it was not wiped out, as so often happened, by an outbreak of hoof-and-mouth disease.

A fruit merchant imported from Hungary and Rumania melons and grapes, and pineapples from overseas. He also imported dates, figs, tea, coffee, oranges, and spices. He exported apples, pears, and plums, which were plentiful in the orchards of the surrounding villages. He also had his own coffee roaster. Traders in grain exported all types of grain and corn.

There was an exporter of eggs. On receiving the eggs from the peddler, the eggs were candled, sorted according to size, packed three-score (60) to a case in straw or wood shavings, and then shipped in carloads to Germany or England. There, a broker was ordered to sell the eggs. However, as so often occurred, instead of the bank draft which the exporter was waiting for, a wire arrived notifying him that the eggs were not fit for sale, and, since it was a perishable item, the carload had to be auctioned off at a very low price. After having suffered a few losses, the exporter dispatched his brother to the Saar district in Germany. There he opened a few retail stores, selling eggs at a competitive price, and from that time on no shipment was rejected. Because eggs are usually cheaper in the springtime, the exporter had pits on his premises, made of concrete, in which he preserved the fresh eggs in a solution of lime and other chemicals. When December arrived and the prices were high because of the demand before Christmas, the eggs were removed from the pits and exported.

There were a lot of *pigs for export,* and this business was also carried on by a Jew. For this reason he was held in contempt by his fellow Jews.

The abundance of excellent fruit in the district of the shtetl gave some Jews another kind of *parnusse.* In the springtime they would contract to buy that year's yield from the peasants' and/or landowners' orchards. This was a gamble because nobody could know in advance how big the crop would be. It was not until the fruit was picked in the fall that they would know what kind of a deal they had made. Fortunately, the crops were good most of the time. The fruit was picked and sorted. There was some fruit which was not ripe but which would be ready closer to Passover. These fruits were stored in special cellars, and from the remainder of the crop the better-quality fruit was selected and shipped out in carloads. The fruit of lesser quality, or that which was damaged, was sold to the local preserve factory. This factory produced marmalade, jam, and syrup from the different types of fruit and berries, which were collected from the neighboring hillsides by the children, who brought them to the shtetl.

Another *parnusse* was *pickling cucumbers.* The cucumbers were sorted according to size and pickled in wooden barrels, which were then stored for the winter in a nearby creek to be sold in the spring. Making sauerkraut and pickling apples and tomatoes also belonged to this line of business.

Different types of herring were imported from Holland in truckloads, primarily for sale to the public. But the importer opened a small factory as well, where he marinated the herring and sold them in small wooden barrels. The very small herring were sold in jars. This herring, called *rollmopses* and *moskaliki,* was sold all over Galicia.

Other importers brought in all kinds of manufactured goods, such as steel, pipes, sheet metal, wires, cast-iron ovens, nails, building materials, textiles, seeds, foodstuffs, and so on. The shtetl had many light industrial enterprises. There was a brick-yard, a flour mill, weaving shops of *kilims* and rugs, and clothing material made of raw wool for the peasants. There was also a soda-water factory which bottled the soda water in syphons and made lemonade or soda water with raspberry syrup.

There were representatives of breweries in Plzen, Okocim, and Lwów who had beer-bottling installations. In the winter ice was cut from the river, stored in special ice storages, and covered with straw for insulation. Throughout the summer, when beer was delivered to the inn a certain amount of ice was provided. Ice was also sold to private households.

Another *parnusse* was a bargain store which opened only occasionally. The owner of this store had a son who lived in Vienna. His only occupation was to find out about bankruptcies or liquidations of businesses there. He would then buy the entire stock for next to nothing, and without even looking at the list of merchandise, would ship it home to his father. When the merchandise arrived it was not even sorted. The customers came into the store, grabbed what they liked, and paid the modest price being asked by the merchant. Everyone got a bargain. This was the only store in the shtetl where haggling never took place. In all the other stores haggling was the manner in which business was conducted.

There were traders who attended the yearly fur fairs, the largest in Europe, which were held in Leipzig. They bought huge quantities of pelts and sold them to furriers in the shtetl and in the surrounding towns. There was also a furrier who manufactured, on a broad scale, sheepskin coats and parkas for the peasants. He imported dry, raw sheep hides, tanned them in vats filled with bran and lime in his small factory, and then blanched and dried them outside. The stench from the factory poisoned the surrounding air.

There were a few dairy businesses, each with a few cows. The dairy women milked the cows in the wee hours of the morning and then, carrying two heavy cans filled with milk, would go from house to house, delivering fresh milk to their customers for breakfast. The unsold milk was made into butter and cheese.

Although the woman and her husband were pious people not everyone would buy the milk. The really pious people didn't trust anyone when it came to *kashruth*. They preferred to go to the stable with their own bucket and be present when the milking was done.

A lumber dealer, apart from trading in all kinds of lumber, manufactured prefabricated log cabins in his yard. For this purpose rafts of raw timber from the Carpathian Mountains were floated on the Czeremosz and Prut rivers which ran behind the lumberyard.

Jewish enterprises in which Jewish labor was used, as a rule, interrupted their work in the evening for the *mincha-maariv* service.

The city had two hotels. One belonged to a pious Jew and was patronized exclusively by pious Jews. The food was *glatt kosher*. In the big dining room of this hotel one could listen to the evening discussions and arguments when a problem from the Gemara was brought up and analyzed, point by point. If one stayed during the Sabbath, he had to order his meals on Thursday, as no money changed hands on the Sabbath.

The other hotel was a larger one with a big backyard and stables for horses. Here the *commivoyageurs* (the traveling salesmen) would stay. The Gentile travelers patronized this hotel as well. This hotel had a hall with a seating capacity of over 250 people. This room was rented for Jewish banquets, festivities, lectures, and weddings, and for visiting Yiddish theater companies.

There was a larger and nicer room with a stage in the city which belonged to the Polish club, *Sokól*, but they wouldn't rent it to the Jews under any circumstances.

There were a few inns located on the streets around and close to the marketplace which sold beer, vodka, cheese, herring, pickles, and hard boiled eggs to the peasants. During market days they were usually filled up. There was also an inn where no alcoholic beverages were sold. A specialty of this inn was the so-called *kwas*, an ale made by the owner from a variety of fermented dry fruits. It had a tasty acidity. During a market day the entire family, consisting of the husband, wife, and three daughters, was busy serving the customers this beverage. They would drink it while biting into their own black bread. A condition for being served was that no pork would be eaten.

The government had a monopoly on the manufacture and sale of alcoholic beverages and salt. Wine was free, and so was beer, but tobacco for smoking and sniffing, as well as cigarettes, were under the government monopoly, as were the lotteries. To open an inn for the sale of alcohol a special license was required, and this was also the case with opening a tobacco store or lottery agency. Of course, there were conditions under which one could obtain a license, and the officials used the issuing of licenses as a means of pressure, for example, at election times.

In the surrounding villages Jews kept inns, *kraytshmes*, in premises rented from the landowners. There was no reason to envy such Jews, who lived as a single Jewish family among Ukrainian peasants. But the saying was, *"Woos teit man nisht far parnusse,"* which translated means, "One must do anything possible in order to make a living."

There was a store where one could buy the best kosher wine, which was imported from Hungary or Rumania. During week-days there was no traffic, but on Thursdays and Fridays one had to elbow his way to the counter to buy a liter or half-liter of wine for the Sabbath. The poor people made their own wine by fermenting raisins a few days before the Sabbath.

The majority of stores were located around the marketplace called the *Ringplatz.* There you could find the largest wholesaler with a big warehouse behind the building, down to the smallest store selling a few herrings, pickles, slices of bread. Or a store selling glasses of sour milk, cheese, a few buns and butter, the whole stock of which was worth no more than 20 crowns.

Till 1912 no shoe stores or stores selling ready-made clothing were in the shtetl, for the simple reason that nobody would buy ready-made shoes or clothing. Shoes were ordered from the shoemaker, who took measurements with a piece of paper folded lengthwise into the form of a tape. He would make a mark on the paper by tearing the edge of it where necessary. For men's and women's clothing, material was bought at one of the many textile stores, and the clothing was made-to-measure by a seamstress or a tailor.

There were hardware and dry goods stores in the shtetl, along with a leather store, which usually sold leather to the shoemakers and saddlers.

The stalls in the marketplace were set up in rows upon rows, and each huckstress using a stall had to pay a few pennies for it. Peasant women offered various types of fruits and vegetables, as well as flowers, from their gardens and orchards. Others displayed eggs, butter, milk, and cheese. Still others sold berries of different varieties and mushrooms from the forests in the mountains. Chicken, geese, ducks, and pigeons were also offered for sale in another corner of the marketplace. Pigeons were brought in by boys mainly, who raised them at their houses for either fun or business. No Jewish boy had time for such nonsense.

The Jewish market women displayed different kinds of merchandise in their stalls which peasants could use in their households, such as pots and pans made by their tinsmith husbands, leather for boots, especially for soles, and paints in powder form which were used for whitewashing the walls. There was no ready-made paint in cans available except for painting ironwork. Dyes for cloth, nails, screws, wires, locks, padlocks, and any other kind of hardware needed in a peasant's household were displayed. Also, candies, rolls, and buns were available which the peasants bought as a gift for their children. Bottles of lemonade, herring cut into small rings, pickles, pretzels, different kinds of home-made baking, bagels, corn on the cob, and even hot *vareniki* were sold at the market.

On Friday mornings the fisherwomen waited at the wholesaler's store for the arrival of the water-filled vats with live carp which were shipped from Galatz, Rumania.

It was no easy task to be a huckstress. From the early morning until late into the afternoon, the women had to be at the stalls, rain or snow. It was especially hard when they had to leave small children at home, sometimes under the care of a five- or six-year-old daughter. It was even worse if the huckstress had a baby at home which had to be breast-fed. The mother had to cover her stall with a sheet and run home to breast-feed the baby if a wetnurse couldn't be hired to feed the baby three times during the day. Winter was especially hard on such a woman, with cold and frosty days and the wind blowing snow into her face simply to spite her. On such days the women put on innumerable skirts, blouses, coats, and shawls. Sitting on a small stool they kept under their skirts a pot filled with glowing embers which were checked from time to time to be sure that they did not go out.

The competition between the huckstresses was very keen, and

they often quarreled and wrangled with each other. When one huckstress undersold her neighbor the controversy ended in cursing. Listening to their yelling one could become deaf or get a headache from the profane abuse, the reviling, and the invectives they shouted at each other.

There were two kinds of peddlers wandering from village to village. They left home on a Sunday afternoon and returned on Friday before noon. One type sold cotton, thread, needles, soap, candles, kerchiefs, and so on. The other were wandering tailors who made all kinds of alterations and patched old clothing. Each carried a bundle on his back. The tailors needed a sewing machine with a hand crank, threads of different colors, scissors, and some pieces of material which they would use for patches. Both had with them *talles* and *tfillin*. If there were no Jews in the village from whom they could buy kosher food, they lived on bread, eggs, and cheese which they washed down with hot water boiled in the pot they carried with them.

Another place of business in the shtetl was where fodder for the horses and cows, grain for the fowl, and straw and hay in bundles or hacked to pieces with a chaff cutter was sold. Firewood, cut and split, ready for the oven, was also sold there.

Another occupation should be mentioned: maids, cooks, waiters, and sales personnel in the stores. These were usually young boys or girls from poor families who worked for their bosses for little pay, receiving food and board and some clothing. If they behaved well the boss or woman of the house tried to arrange suitable matches for them and even helped them to get married. They also, at times, assisted them in establishing their own businesses.

The many Jewish craftsmen and artisans included carpenters, cabinet makers, tinsmiths, blacksmiths, ornamental ironworkers, coopers, tanners, bricklayers, butchers, upholsterers, saddlers, weavers, bookbinders, shoemakers, seamstresses, modistes, wig makers, tailors, goldsmiths, watchmakers, painters, jewelers, bakers, umbrella makers, corset makers, rope makers, photographers (who didn't have very much work, since the pious Jew wouldn't allow a picture of himself to be taken), and also a denture maker, who although not licensed was quite good. (He was forced to do his work in secret.) Some of the craftsmen made a very good living, owning nice homes and shops, while others had to fight very hard to make a living. And . . . *oy vay*, was it a living?

Artisans were organized in guilds, and to become a master one had to go through a period of apprenticeship lasting anywhere from three to five years. A boy who was sent by his parents to a master in order to learn a trade was, in the beginning, actually nothing more than a servant to the master's wife. He swept floors and cradled the baby, and all this without pay. Only after a year or two would he be introduced to the secrets of the trade. After another year, during which period he would receive some remuneration for his work, he became a junior master. After an additional two-year period, followed by an exam, he was entitled to work and to open his own shop as a master.

To a special group belonged the *balagulas* and the coachmen. They transported huckstresses and peddlers with their merchandise from the market in one shtetl to the market in a neighboring shtetl, returning them home for the night. They were also hired for delivery of merchandise locally or to another shtetl. Coachmen with carriages on springs would take passengers to the railway station to meet every arriving train, and then transport the arriving passengers to the shtetl. The competition between the cabmen was sharp, and two or three of them might pull at an arriving passenger at the same time in order to get him into their own coach.

In a corner of the marketplace there was always a group of men standing and waiting for a job. These men were the porters who did the loading and unloading of any kind of merchandise which was brought in by the forwarders. They carried on their backs sacks of 100 kilograms or more in weight. They also transported goods from the wholesalers to the retailers, and some had carts on two wheels to which they harnessed themselves for this purpose.

The water carriers had large wooden barrels mounted on a two-wheel horse-drawn cart. The barrels were filled up at an outlet of the waterline and the water was then delivered to the customer's homes. The horses knew which house to stop at without being directed, having stopped there so many times previously. The water carrier took as many buckets as were needed to fill the water barrel at a given house. He was paid every Thursday. After buying fodder for his horse he would often be unable to give his wife sufficient money to buy the necessities for the Sabbath.

The list of occupations in the shtetl wouldn't be complete without mentioning the thieves and beggars, as well as the running of the bawdy house—although it was not located in the shtetl itself, but on the outskirts of the city.

Weekly markets were held in the shtetl, and two or three times each year, a larger fair, called a *yarid,* was held at a huge place farther away from the center of the city. It was usually held on a Ukrainian saint's day.

A few days before the *yarid* buyers and sellers from near and far began to arrive with their wares loaded on horsedrawn wagons. Peasants from faraway places brought their horses, cows, calves, pigs, sheep, goats, grain, produce, fruit, chickens, geese, ducks, turkeys, pigeons, eggs, butter, cheese, and so forth for sale or barter.

Mountains of earthenware were displayed by potters. Coopers displayed all sizes of barrels with wooden hoops, wooden bathtubs, pails, buckets, troughs, and so on. The cartwrights displayed wheelbarrows, sets of wooden parts with which the buyer could assemble a wagon, spinning wheels, churns, wooden shovels, flails, grain threshers, and neckpieces for ox yokes. Wood carvers brought wooden spoons, beaters, dishes, plates, cups, spindles for thread spinning from hemp, flax, or wool, and also liquid tar for greasing wooden cart axles. In the spring the *hutzuls* (mountaineers) bought many sheep which they drove to the pastures in the mountains. When the fall fair arrived they would sell the sheep, wool and the salted cheese called *bryndza,* which they had made during the summer.

Jewish craftsmen displayed their merchandise, such as saddles, harnesses, and leather made from cowhide treated with a mixture of lime and ashes, and then put into oaken bark, which the peasants preferred to the industrially tanned leather. There were sheepskin coats treated with bran and chaff, cords, ropes, boots, leather for soles, and different types of hardware.

Every craftsman had a stall at the fair, and the items bought and sold were too many to detail. Around the stalls, boys sold bagels, pretzels, buns, cookies, candies, lemonade, hot corn on the cob, and hot *vareniki.*

Horse and cattle traders haggled in a special way. The buyer and the seller clasped hands with each change of the bidding until a final price was agreed upon.

In every corner of the marketplace beggars sat on the bare

ground, exposing their wounds, begging in a singsong. Some played the *liras*, which is a national Ukrainian instrument. Pickpockets had a heyday, and more than one peasant who had realized a large amount for selling a horse or a cow ended up discovering that he no longer had horse or money. Often a Jew who had a good day was left crying that his purse with all his money had been stolen.

Finally, it should be noted that the Jews of the shtetl were not in the business of murder. No murders occurred, not could any drunkards be found. *Doos past nisht far a yid* ("It is not Jewish").

5

Superstitions

SUPERSTITIONS PLAYED AN important role in shtetl life. Superstition involved believing in good angels and bad ones who were out to get you. Painful and unpleasant events were attributed to irrational forces. There was a belief that some people had the power to curse, and that their curses always came true. Being cursed was the worst thing that could happen to a person. It was also believed that the blessings of a saintly rebbe brought good luck.

Mazal Tov—Good luck! This wish is based on mystery and astrology. Luck depends on the position and the movements of the stars. *Mazal* meant "constellation," and *bar-mazal* meant "a lucky man who was born under the right constellation."

Some rites were based on superstition. Psalms were recited to chase away the evil spirits who might do harm to a woman lying in childbirth. A newborn baby had a red woolen thread knotted around its wrist immediately after it was delivered. The night before a circumcision was especially dangerous. In order to prevent any harm from being done to the baby, precautions were taken. This was called the *wach nacht* (watch night), the *layl shmourim*. A *minyan yidden* recited *tillim* (psalms), and amulets made by a *tzaddik*, a rebbe, a righteous man, were placed on the bed of the mother. The walls of the room where the mother and the baby rested were plastered with printed psalms. A *krishmah laynen* was held. For this purpose a *melamed*, usually the one to whom the baby would be sent at the age of three, brought his pupils into the room of the mother and child. The children said

39

the bedtime prayer in order to chase away the evil spirit. For more protection for the newborn who would be brought into the covenant, the help of Eliyahu Hanavi (Elijah the Prophet) was sought. A special chair was set aside for him at the ceremony of the circumcision, and he would protect the baby against the trials of the bad angels.

During *Sefirah*, the seven weeks between Pesach and Shavuoth, marriages were not allowed and haircuts were forbidden, except on Lag b'Omer.

On the first day of Rosh Hashanah at *Tashlich* one emptied his pockets, throwing the crumbs into the stream, and with them, his sins.

On Hoshanah Rabbah, by beating willow sprigs against the ground, one cast off his sins, as the leaves fell off.

People whose parents were still alive had to leave the synagogue during the *Yizkor* prayer.

On the eve of Yom Kippur, *kapoures shlougen* was performed. A chicken was raised above and circled around the head. At the same time a prayer was pronounced that the chicken should be the *kapoureh*, the scapegoat, and should die instead of the person involved.

At *Havdalah*, a little alcohol was spilled on the table and ignited. Then, with a gesture of catching the flames and putting them into his pockets, one might expect good returns for the coming week.

Cutting one's nails was also done in connection with a superstition. The cutting began with the thumb and the clippings had to be burned, together with a small piece of wood.

Magic was the reason for the custom of the bride circling around the bridegroom under the *chupah*, as well as for the bridegroom's breaking a glass under the *chupah*. The noise would chase away the demons. Also, as a precaution against the demons hurting the bride, the bridegroom lowered the veil over her face. If the bride stepped on the foot of her bridegroom when under the *chupah*, she would surely be the domineering one in the family.

Those guiding the bride and groom in the procession under the canopy should never be divorced or widowed lest the same happen to the young newlyweds.

The three neighboring houses to the left and the right of the home where a person died had to empty their water containers. The Angel of Death might have washed his sword in that water after having killed his sacrifice.

Upon leaving the cemetery after a funeral one was supposed to use a route other than the one used for the funeral procession.

Inside a mourner's home the mirrors had to be covered with black cloth. If one's reflection appeared in the mirror the parting soul might take the person with it.

Pieces of small branches were placed in the hands of the dead. This enabled him to tunnel his way to Jerusalem at the time of the arrival of the Messiah. The eyes were covered with shards.

When visiting a grave at the cemetery one had to leave a pebble beside the tombstone. This was to notify the person buried that he might rest in peace wherever he was.

All unpleasant, painful, and troublesome events in everyday life were generally attributed to a *git ojg* (evil eye), an *ayn-hora*. The belief was that some persons by merely looking at others could make them ill. Looking at somebody with jealousy could bring misfortune to the person. Some women had an evil eye, and they were to be avoided. Some had supernatural powers and were able to cause or cure sicknesses. Children, especially, were susceptible to an evil eye, and when a child fell ill the first diagnosis was the "evil eye."

Instead of calling in a doctor who readily made home visits, usually an old woman was called who was famous and renowned in the shtetl for being able to do away with the evil eye by using her special remedies. Looking at the child, she decided, "No doubt in my mind, the poor child was struck by an evil eye. First of all, let him urinate to let the evil poison come out. Now, tell me where the child was, who looked at him, and who talked to him. There are people who always give an evil eye, and I know them all. If I know whom to suspect my task will be a lot easier."

And so, after a lengthy discussion with the mother, having decided who the culprit might be, the woman began to apply her remedies. First came the *upshprechen*, the murmuring of some secret sentences—her own "abracadabra." If that didn't help, *koylen upleshen* was applied, the extinguishing of glowing wooden embers, accompanied again by lengthy murmurs. Not having achieved any visible result this time either, the hocus-pocus was carried on with a much stronger remedy, the melting of wax, i.e., pouring melted wax into a bowl with cold water. From the shape formed by the cooled wax the woman was able to determine the cause of the high fever. The child as it usually happened, felt better in a day or two, and the fame of the woman as a healer would increase.

There were, however, occasions when a child with a very serious illness was left for some time without proper medical care. By the time a doctor was called it was often too late. If it was a contagious disease, it was kept a secret in fear that the house and also the store (if one was owned by the parents) would be placed under quarantine. The family therefore preferred to have home remedies applied.

An evil eye (mostly caused by jealousy) could be the cause of any misfortune which befell a person or a family. A prosperous businessman could suddenly lose his patrons, a young man's engagement to a rich and beautiful girl could be broken, a woman with the nicest dress at a wedding could have it ruined by the waiter accidently spilling sauce on it, and so on.

To avert an evil eye, one should spit three times and say each time, *"Tfu, tfu, kaayn ayne-hora."* To avert an evil eye, a *fig* was recommended. This is done by inserting one's thumb between two fingers and pointing the so-called *fig* in the direction of the person who might give an evil eye, but keeping the *fig* hidden in a pocket or under the blouse. Another remedy was to place a small piece of bread and some salt in a child's pocket.

Salt and bread were also a remedy against bad luck, so before moving into a new house or apartment, bread and salt were brought into the premises. This would not only prevent bad luck but might bring good luck.

Breaking a glass or a plate inadvertently was a sign of good luck. A cricket chirping somewhere in the oven brought good luck. Finding a horseshoe was considered good luck, and the horseshoe might be nailed to the threshold of the house or the business. An itching palm meant that you would be counting a lot of money. Meeting a chimneysweep was a sign of good luck, and if one then quickly touched a button on his clothing his wish would come true. If cutlery dropped to the floor when your table was being prepared for a meal, it meant that you would have visitors. Bread falling to the floor butter-side down meant that failure awaited you. When you sneezed, everyone who was present would utter some good wishes for you and would say, "*Zu gesund, zu lange yourn*" ("Good health and many years").

A lost button should never be sewn back on with the garment on your body, because this way your wisdom would be sewn in. It was better to take off the shirt, or whatever the piece of clothing might be, and sew it on. Putting on two garments at the same time might cause loss of memory. Children playing with fire during the day would wet the bed the following night. A bad dream was always a forecast of bad happenings, and the belief in dreams was a guide to life. Different books explaining the meanings of dreams were best-sellers. To have a piece of rope on which a person was hanged meant good luck.

If somebody was in a bad mood it was because he stepped out of bed with his left foot. If a pregnant woman saw a mouse, was frightened and touched her face, her child would be born with a birthmark on its face where the mother touched her own. Also, looking at a cripple might result in the birth of a crippled child.

Once one had left his house he should never return to pick up a forgotten article. If he did, he would fail to achieve the purpose for which he left the house.

Counting people was not advisable. However, when one had to know how many people there were in a room, as in the case of a *minyan*, he would count in a negative manner: not one, not two, not three, not four, and so on.

Walking beneath a ladder brought bad luck. Stepping over a child who was lying on the floor or on the grass might cause the child to stop growing. It was best to go around him or her. Stepping into a circle of dust or sand which was blown into the air by the wind might cause instant death. Piercing your finger when making a garment meant that your work would please everyone.

The first coin received by a merchant after opening his store in the morning should be spat on. The merchant would sell a lot of merchandise that day. It was a good *potshontek* (beginning). Conversely, if the first customer who entered the store bought nothing, or bargained very hard, the whole day would bring only bad business.

Putting on underwear inside-out was a sure sign that the wearer would be quarreling with everyone he dealt with on this day. The loss of a wedding ring was a bad omen and meant that the marriage would break up. Shaking hands over a threshold was to be avoided. It might spoil the good relations between the two people. Bad luck was in store if a cat, especially a black one, crossed your path. The same applied if you met somebody going to the well with empty buckets. Only misfortune awaited you. It was best to go back home.

A candle over which a blessing had been said on Friday evening which was blown out, or suddenly ceased to burn, was a bad omen. It meant that somebody close to you might have died at that very same moment, even in a faraway place. When a person was dangerously ill, candles equal in the total of their length to the size of the patient were offered to the synagogue.

To end a plague in the shtetl, two orphans were married at the nearby cemetery, at the expense of the community.

It was better not to spell out that one was seriously ill as it might conjure up the evil spirit.

Figures played an important role in planning and making decisions. Some figures were lucky and some might bring misfortune. The letters in the Jewish alphabet, having their counterparts in figures, were calculated in various ways to forecast future happenings by using *gematria*. Eighteen was a lucky number: eight corresponds with the letter *chet*, and ten with the letter *youd;* therefore *chetyoud chai*—"life." Seventeen, the *gematria* of *tov* ("good") was also a lucky number. *Tov* was spelled *tet-vav-bays: tet* equals 9, *vav* equals 6, and *bays* equals 2 . . . 9 + 6 + 2 equals 17. For some reason odd figures were considered lucky. The number seven meant a falsehood.

Monday was a bad day to start any kind of affair, business trip, move into a new house, or to have a wedding. Tuesday was a lucky day. Common, also, was the belief in fate. *S' is bashairt:* What is prescribed for you cannot be averted; regardless of what you might do, it will happen anyway.

It was nevertheless possible to prevent misfortunes by wearing a *shmirah*, a talisman or amulet given by a *tzaddik*, a rebbe. An amulet was worn as a bracelet or hung around the neck, or carried in the pocket. The amulets were mostly coins which were blessed by a rebbe. Amulets could not only prevent mischief and disease but were capable of attracting good fortune and luck.

Nobody should enter the synagogue at midnight. This was the time when the ghosts of the deceased were there praying for their salvation. Many people would assure you that they had witnessed a procession of ghosts in white shrouds and *tallesim*. The ghosts would leave the synagogue a few minutes after midnight and would vanish in the direction of the cemetery.

Spirits could also be cheated. A second name was given to a sick child. The Angel of Death, arriving with a summons for, let's say, Moishele, would become confused if he did not find Moishele at this home but instead found Avroomele.

A mother who had lost a number of her children in infancy might sell her child, in order to save it, to a lucky mother who had many healthy children and who had never lost a child. This was done for a token sum of money. The child was moved over into the new family home, remained there for a certain period of time, and had to call the new parent "Mommy." Afterwards, without canceling the deal, the child moved back to its own mother's home. It still formally remained the child of the foster mother and lived in the home of its natural mother as a visitor only. And so, the Angel of Death, wanting to take away another child from this poor woman, would find that she had no more children of her own.

It was a widespread belief that there were good spirits as well as bad ones. The spirits of some people entered into the soul and body of a living person, tormenting him or her as a *dybbuk*.

If a person, especially a young girl, was depressed and showed signs of schizophrenia, everybody was convinced that she was possessed by a *dybbuk*. The only thing to do was to chase out the *dybbuk*, to exorcise the devil. It started with prayers and charms. If this didn't help to conjure the devil a method of carrot and stick was used, involving cruel and violent beatings. The poor girl usually ended up with bad injuries to her body, if not worse.

The fear of the unknown was ingrained in the minds of the people. So, one should never refuse to give alms to a beggar even if he was aggressive and cursed you when he was not satisfied with what he had received. The beggar should be invited into the house and treated well, for he might be Eliyahu Hanavi in disguise, or one of the *lamedvavniks*, the thirty-six just men on whom the existence of the world depends.

6

Education

JEWS ARE KNOWN as *Am Hasefer*, the "People of the Book." The purpose of Jewish education was, by constantly studying Torah and Talmud with their many commentaries, to achieve the highest possible knowledge of religion and tradition.

As soon as a child began to talk, the mother taught him to say *modeh ani* (the morning prayer), *krieshma laynen* (the bedtime prayer), and some *brookhes* (blessings).

Jewish education concerned the menfolk only, and no great importance was attached to the education of girls. A girl was sent to *cheder* for two or three years where she learned the *aleph bayis* and how to read the *siddur* (prayer book). Later she was taught to write and read Yiddish. That was about all that was asked of a girl.

A boy's lifetime was marked by several milestones until he reached the age of eighteen, at which time he was ready for marriage, *ben shmona esray l'chupah*. At three he began with the *cheder*. After the *upshayrenish* ceremony, when his hair was cut for the first time, leaving the *payes* (earlocks) only, he was carried, wrapped in his father's *talles*, to the *cheder*. *Cheder* means "room," which is certainly the correct name for this kind of school, as it consisted of only one room. The shtetl had ten functioning *chederim*. In most cases the *cheder* was also the *melamed*'s (teacher's) living room, dining room, and kitchen. It was converted in the evening into a bedroom by bringing in some mattresses.

The *melamed* usually employed a *belfer* (helper), whose main task was to carry the small children on his back to and from the *cheder*.

No sacrifice was too great for Jewish parents when it came to the question of letting their son attend a *cheder*, and there wasn't one Jewish boy in the shtetl who didn't go to a *cheder*. A boy whose parents couldn't afford to pay the *melamed* was sent to a Talmud Torah *cheder*, the upkeep of which was paid for from public funds, such as subsidies alloted by the community and those alloted by the *Chevra Talmud Torah*. Another source of funds for the Talmud Torah stemmed from donations which were pledged when a man was called to the reading of the Torah on a Sabbath or *yom tov*. Boys attending Talmud Torah were also fed and clothed by the community. Orphans were placed with families, as there were not enough orphans in the shtetl to justify the opening of an orphanage. It should be mentioned that there was not one illiterate Jew. At the very least, every Jew could *daven*.

During the first two years in the *cheder*, called *dardeke* (beginner's *cheder*), a boy learned the *aleph bayis* and the prayers from the *siddur* (prayer book). At the age of five the boy was sent to another *melamed* who had a *cheder* with a more advanced curriculum. Here he learned to translate the *chumash* (Pentateuch) into Yiddish, and was taught the appropriate *sedra*, *parsha* (chapter) of the week. Later he studied the commentaries, especially those of Rashi, and learned to write and read Yiddish as well. The boy spent his entire day in *cheder*, with a short break for lunch and for *davenen minche maariv* (the evening prayers), until late in the evening. The streets of the shtetl were only dimly lit, and the boys used lanterns lighted by candles to find their way home.

In the *chederim* the children, usually sitting along a table, studied with the rebbe, chanting the words and their translations into Yiddish, which they repeated after him in unison.

Following King Solomon's proverb that "he who spares the rod spoils the child," the rebbe often used a belt, stick, or *kantshik* (whip) to inject, through the bottom part of the child, the knowledge which might not go straight into the child's head. The poor child was expected to absorb the rebbe's teachings by mechanically echoing him word for word.

The school year had two *zmanim* (semesters); one began on *chol hamoed* Pesach, and the other on *chol hamoed* Sukkot.

Five-and-a-half days a week the boys sweated under these conditions in the small *chederim*, with the exception of holidays and, of course, one day every year, Lag b'Omer, the thirty-third day of *Sfirah*, when the *melamed* went with them from the shtetl into the fields. The children took their lunches with them, and they played games with bows and arrows and wooden swords. They were able to breathe fresh air which they had lacked during the entire year. However, on many occasions these excursions ended abruptly when the Gentile boys noticed that the Jewish boys had dared to go for fresh air outside the shtetl into their domain.

In time, according to his abilities, a boy advanced to another *cheder* with a higher grade. At the age of eight he began Mishnah and later Talmud (Jewish law)—its doctrines with all the *payrushim* and *toysefots* (commentaries).

Then, at thirteen years of age, the age of fulfillment of the commandments, the *Shulchan Aruch* was studied. A gifted boy who wanted to be a rabbi continued his studies at a yeshivah. The shtetl had no yeshivah, but a few bright boys studied in a *klouze* (house of prayer), under the guidance of an old man, a *talmid chacham* (wise man), and some also with the *rav*. They studied by the dim light of a candle until late into the night, and then they slept on the benches in the *klouze*. They were provided with board every week by different families as a mitzvah. Some families did so, perhaps, in order to catch a *khosen* (bridegroom) for a daughter.

The study of spoken Hebrew was neglected in the *chederim*. For this purpose there were special *layrers* (teachers). After the pogroms in Kishinev in 1903 and 1905, the shtetl received a large influx of young Jewish refugees from neighboring Russia. These young men were all well educated, and most of them made a living by tutoring Hebrew.

The law of the land compelled every parent to send his children to a public school. Of course, there were no exemptions for Jewish children. However, since secular schools did not allow a head covering and required students to stand while the Lord's Prayer was recited at the beginning and ending of the school day, Jews considered sending their children to such *trefe poosol* (idolatrous) schools a *chilul hashem* (blasphemy). Everything was done to evade and disobey this law. Children were not registered at birth, or were sent away to a relative in another city. They were also kept away from school on the grounds of alleged physical incapability, or the parents simply bribed the officials or paid a fine in order to keep their children from attending these schools.

On the other hand, the authorities opposed the *chederim* on the grounds that the facilities were unhygienic and unsuitable for a school. Building inspectors often made unannounced inspections. But as soon as the inspector was seen coming, the children would run out of the *cheder,* and with a *shnaps* for the inspector the matter was settled.

However, with time the need grew to give the children some secular education. Those who began to send their children to the public schools prevailed. The Jewish children would attend the public schools in the forenoon, have a quick lunch, and then run to the *cheder* for the rest of the day, leaving for home late in the evening.

Apart from the *cheder* and the public schools, the shtetl had many private tutors who taught the children, first of all, the German language and caligraphy. Good handwriting was of the utmost importance. There were no typewriters in use. Therefore, no carbon copies could be made, and in order to have a copy in the file a special pencil, or special ink, would be used. A thick book with thin, cigarette-paper-like sheets was used for copy-making. A slightly wet piece of linen was put under one sheet in this book and the written letter or document was placed on top of it. The entire book was then put into a press and after a moment the contents of the letter would appear as a copy in the book.

Merchants, as a rule, used German in their correspondence, as their suppliers and/or customers were in all parts of Austria and Germany. The business correspondence among Jews was also conducted in German, but was written in the Hebrew alphabet, and not in the Gothic or Latin style. Private letters between Jews were written the same way.

A learned Jew did not, however, use German or even Hebrew. Instead he wrote his letters in a mixture of both Hebrew and Yiddish. Such a letter would begin with "*Baruch Hashem* [Praised be the Lord], *Po kehila Kedosha* so and so [Here the Holy Community of (the name of the shtetl)]," followed by the date according to the Jewish calendar only and the *parsha* (the chapter of the reading of the Torah for the week). He began with endless citations from Holy Books, mixed with praise for the addressee,

calling him "My beloved teacher, friend, *chacham* [wise man],"
and so on. All this could take up to four or five pages, none of it
relevant. The purpose of the letter was finally mentioned in short
form at its end.

Two public schools, one for boys and one for girls, functioned in
the shtetl. Jewish students were not forced to attend public
school on the Sabbath. There was a special teacher for Jewish
religion. The classes were held at the same time that the priests
taught religion to the Christian children. Because there was only
one teacher for both the boys' and girls' schools, Jewish religion
was also taught on Sundays to some of the students.

In the shtetl a Baron Hirsch school functioned extremely well
and received full recognition from the authorities. The school was
funded by the multimillionaire Baron Maurice de Hirsch with the
purpose of furthering education among the Jews in Galicia. The
school, which was for boys only, was housed in a fine building
erected by the fund. Competent teachers were hired and, in
addition to the public school curriculum, trades were also taught.
Students at the Baron Hirsch School received free lunches, and
before Pesach and Sukkot those who were poor received suits,
shirts, shoes, and coats.

Around the year 1890 there was a high school in the shtetl for
about a year. The Jews boycotted the school, as they did not want
their children to stray from the study of Torah. Also, it was
compulsory for the students to attend the school on the Sabbath.
Eventually, due to the lack of students, the school was closed.

However, since it was in the interest of the Polish population to
have a high school for their children in the city, so as not to have
to send them to schools in other cities, the authorities attempted
time and time again to organize a minimum of Jewish parents
who would agree to send their children to high school. The need
to prepare their sons for a better life made some Jews change
their minds, and in 1905 the *Oberrealschule* (high school) was
reopened. Many families enrolled their sons in the high school
(girls were not admitted) and awaited the day when they would
see their son achieve the profession of engineer, architect, doctor,
or lawyer. In 1906 the Jewish students were in the majority.

A few Jews were among the teachers, called professors, at the
high school. Each of them had a Ph.D. degree. They were unable
to obtain positions at schools in the larger cities and were forced

to accept the positions available in this small city. On the other hand, Gentile teachers consisted of those transferred to this school from other cities for disciplinary reasons. With minor exceptions they were anti-Semites, and a Jewish student had to work twice as hard in order to pass an exam.

Jewish students in the high school were not exempted from attending classes on the Sabbath even if their parents wanted them to go to shul. Moreover, they had to listen to the Lord's Prayer twice daily, had to keep their heads uncovered and cut their *payes*, and were faced with anti-Semitic needling from both their Gentile colleagues and some of the professors. Parents who were unwilling to subject their sons to such inconveniences but nevertheless wanted them to have a secular education, engaged tutors, mostly professors or graduate students, to teach them at home. At the end of the school year the boys were allowed to take exams for the appropriate grade. The girls, who were not admitted as students, were also allowed to take yearly exams, as externs.

Jewish boys were seldom active in sports, on the skating rink, the ski slopes, or on the football fields.

Among the Jewish youth were also a few autodidacts. They sharpened their brains on the study of Gemara and self-study. They told nobody about the *trayfe* studies, and when they were ready they left the shtetl for Prague, Vienna, Zurich, or Rome, where they passed their entrance exams at a university with flying colors. To reach this point they taught themselves languages from dictionaries and perfected their knowledge of the German language with the aid of Mendelssohn's translation of the Pentateuch into German.

One such *bocher*, Joske the Illuy, who came from one of the poorest families, disappeared one day. No one knew what had happened to him or what had become of him. After a few years he returned to the shtetl as Dr. Rabbiner Josef Selinger. After he had vanished from the shtetl he went to Geneva, passed the required entrance exam at the university, received his Ph.D. and went to Berlin, where he received his *smikha* (diploma as a rabbi). Later he went to Palestine and opened a chain of Hebrew schools in Jaffa and Jerusalem around 1907. Unfortunately, he failed in his endeavor.

Professor Arie Jakob Sternfeld, the co-inventor of the Russian *sputnik*, was also a *bocher* from a neighboring shtetl who began his studies in *cheder*. The Nobel Prize winner S. Y. Agnon was another *cheder bocher* from a shtetl in Galicia, not far from our own. To this trio should be added Naftali Herz Imber, the author of our national anthem, the "Hatikvah."

The older generation of the Jews in our shtetl stubbornly condemned secular education and knowledge. For them, a discussion about the Darwinian theory, or the question of whether it was the earth or the sun that moved, was anathema and considered sinful.

Girls received very little education in *cheder*, but were not hampered if they desired to further their education.

7

Family Life

IT IS A mitzvah to establish a family. No matter how learned one might be, he would not be accepted as a *rav* if he was not a married man.

Marriage. The Hebrew word for "marriage," *kidushin,* comes from the word *kodesh,* meaning "holy." At a Jewish wedding ceremony there are no vows, such as "till death do us part," and even the presence of a rabbi is not necessary. The reciting of a simple formula, *haray at mekadseshet li* ("thou art consecrated unto me"), and the groom's placing of a ring on the bride's finger in the presence of witnesses formed a bond which could only be dissolved by a *get* (divorce) or by death.

Faithfulness, *zniuth* (modesty), and conjugal love are the characteristics of a Jewish family. Once married, family ties are strong and closely knit. *Sholom baayis* (harmony of the home) and great respect for parents prevailed. For example, no matter how long the father might be away from home, even if he was on a trip, no one dared to sit in his chair.

Only a *beth-din* (rabbinical court) had the right to grant a divorce. To obtain a divorce the husband and the wife had to both agree. If one did not agree, the rabbi would try to reconcile the couple, and only after failing to bring back *sholom baayis,* would he agree to perform the *get.*

Divorce was rare among the Jews in the shtetl. Nevertheless, I can remember three cases of divorce which were performed in the ten-year period between 1904 and 1914. One was at the insistence of the husband because the marriage was childless. The wife later married another man and bore him many children. The second divorce was performed because the husband was a gambler, did not support his wife, deserted her, and lived with another woman. The third divorce was a special one, performed by proxy. The man left his wife and children and emigrated to the United States, promising that as soon as he had saved enough money he would send the family passage to join him. Years went by and nothing was heard from him. The woman, left alone with no knowledge as to what had happened to her husband, was considered an *aguna*. In order to marry another man she would have to prove her husband dead or she would have to receive a *get*. The *rav* of the shtetl began a search for the deserter. He wrote to rabbis in many different cities in the United States. It was finally established that the man was living in Philadelphia and under false pretenses had married another woman. The rabbi in Philadelphia, using all possible pressure, forced the man to sign a divorce for his wife in the shtetl. The document was sent to the *rav* in the shtetl and was delivered to the wife. She was now legally divorced.

I remember another performance of a religious ceremony in connection with Jewish family life. A widow was left childless after the death of her husband. According to the Torah, a surviving brother of the deceased widow's husband was obliged to marry the widow so that she could bear a son who would then carry the name of the dead brother. The surviving brother was a married man and could not marry his widowed sister-in-law. This law of the Torah couldn't be circumvented by invoking the *cherem* of Rabenu Gershon, by which polygamy was prohibited. The widow had to be released by the act of *chalitzah*. The shtetl was in an uproar, and on the evening when this act was performed the entire shtetl gathered at the *beth-hamedresh* to witness the ritual. The shul was overflowing with people. The *gabbai* of the shul was a neighbor of ours, and I was permitted to enter. The ceremony didn't last long. The woman drew the shoe from the foot of her brother-in-law, spat before him, and said, "So shall it be done to a man who doesn't want to build up his brother's house."

Engagement. One of the biggest concerns for a Jew who had a daughter, especially if he had more than one, was to get them married, to find a *zywyk* (match), a *shidduch*. The mothers began to look for future husbands for their daughters when they were still as young as fourteen or fifteen.

When two friendly families had children who were born around the same time, to one a boy and to the other a girl, the parents might decide that these children would make a good match, and the conditions for a future marriage were negotiated. The children would then be considered engaged to each other. This type of engagement of small children was performed most often by Chassidim on the occasion of their meeting at the Rebbe's court. Having children of different sexes, of the same approximate age, the fathers would decide that with the blessing of the Rebbe the children could be engaged. The wives were not asked, and upon reaching the age of eighteen, and sometimes earlier, the children would get married.

Also, *shadchunim* (matchmakers), men or women, kept an eye on the rising young generation in the shtetl. Their minds were set on only one question: "Whom to pair with whom?" A matchmaker usually kept a book in which all marriage candidates were registered and all details regarding them. Some had connections with other *shadchunim* in different places. When the matchmaker was convinced that he had the right match for someone, he would appear at the house of the family, usually bearing his big umbrella, and would propose the *shidduch*. The *shadchen* had to be a good broker, able to smooth out the differences which evolved during the negotiations. The question of *yichus* (pedigree) was taken into consideration, then the amount of the dowry, and so on. The girl, also, shouldn't have the same name as the mother-in-law to be. For a *cohen*, a widow was not a match. It was said that a good *shadchen* could bring together *himmul un erd* (heaven and earth), and *ken anreden a kind yn boukh* (was able to convince you that you bore a child in your belly). They were clever people, good at flattering and exaggerating.

A *shadchen* might sometimes have his business made easy for him. A mother might have her eye on a boy in the shtetl, who she felt was a suitable match for her daughter. She then asked a *shadchen* to go to the family and propose a *shidduch*. If there were no differences in the *yichus* and financial standing of both the families, the deal was concluded smoothly.

Normally, however, after the preliminary conditions were discussed, a so-called *beshow* (get-acquainted meeting) was arranged either at a neutral place, usually midway between the city of the girl and that of the boy, at a friend's place, or at a restaurant. However, in most cases, a *beshow* took place at the house of the girl's family. The boy arrived at this meeting escorted by his parents and the *shadchen*. The boy was examined by the girl's father to find out how well-learned he was and whether he understood a *blatt Gemara*. If the father himself was not sufficiently learned to examine the boy and to find out how conversant he was in Jewish studies, he would have a learned man present to do the job. In the meantime the boy's mother observed the girl to assure herself that she was indeed handsome and knew everything a young housewife should know to run a household. She was also tested with regard to *kashruth*, mending socks, embroidering, and so forth. Later the question of the dowry was brought up, the type of trousseau she had, and what would be acquired by her parents before the wedding. The preliminary conditions were agreed upon by a *tkias kaf* (handshake). The fathers each held the corner of a large handkerchief, usually a red one, and the deal was sealed. A date for the official engagement, the *tnaim* (conditions), was then set.

At the engagement ceremony all the conditions previously agreed upon were written down. Sometimes the young man, if he was a good talmudist, was promised *kest essen* (board and lodging) with the in-laws for a specific time. This might run for a period of two or three years.

At the *tnaim* the conditions were put into writing, a plate was broken, the parties wished each other *mazal tov*, and the date of the wedding was set. On the next *Shabbes*, a *kiddush* was given at the *klouze* where the girl's father davened and a reception of close friends and family members took place. After the engagement the groom received gifts from the bride's father, usually a golden pocket watch with a golden chain, or a silver cigarette case. A learned boy would receive a leather bound set of the Talmud.

Able and learned *yeshivah bocherim* were in demand, and very often a father would go to a *yeshivah* and ask the *rosh yeshivah* to choose the best student as a match for his daughter. He would care for him and his family's well-being, and the young man would have to do nothing but study and study.

More progressive parents sometimes chose a bright high school student from a good family, but not so well-to-do that the boy could have the means to carry on his education at a university for a professional career. They then sent a *shadchen* to the boy's parents, proposing that they send the boy to a university, pay for his board and lodging there, and be responsible for all costs in connection with his studies. Upon agreement the youngsters were engaged, and during the time the young man was away the girl's parents engaged good tutors for their daughter so that, when the fiancé returned as an educated professional, she would not be far behind in her education.

As the bridegroom received his gifts from the girl's parents, the girl received hers from the boy's parents, usually a nice set of golden earrings, a diamond ring, and a necklace. The bride and groom now bought each other a *briefshteller* (correspondence book) which contained samples of form letters to be written in any possible situation.

At the home of the bride a hectic rush began. To prepare the trousseau seamstresses were hired weeks or months ahead of the wedding, working in the home of the bride. Two or three weeks before the wedding a caterer came to the home and baked different kinds of cakes, cookies, and other sweets. The roasting and frying of fowl and many other sorts of meat and the cooking of fish began at least one week before the wedding.

An engagement was seldom broken. *Uplosen a shidduch* was a shame, and besides, a proper match is arranged in heaven.

On the Sabbath preceding the day of the wedding, a *foreshpiel* (small reception) took place. A *kiddush* in the synagogue or *shtibl* where the bride's father belonged was served; and at the home a reception for family members and close friends was given.

Before the wedding the groom received from his father-in-law a *talles* and from the bride a velvet *talles* and *tfillin* case which she embroidered and prepared for him. Only married men had to put on *tallesim* at prayer. Although a boy was considered mature at thirteen, he reached manhood only upon his marriage. On meeting a young man, one might ask, *"Zu bist di a bocher oder hot eer a waayb?"* ("Art thou a bachelor or are you married?")

Before the wedding the bride went to the cemetery to beg at the graves of her relatives for their presence at the wedding. On the day of the wedding the groom and bride fasted.

The *kalah* (bride) prepared herself for the bridal night. She went to the *mikveh* (ritual bath), and the nails of her fingers and toes were cut short and burned together with a piece of wood by an attendant, the *bayderin* (a profession which was not held in high esteem). The girl immersed herself completely three times in the *mikveh* and was now kosher. The attendant went out first and looked to be sure that there were no men on the bride's way out of the *mikveh*.

The parents met, and the *ktubah* (marriage contract) was prepared and written by a *soifer* (scribe). The dowry had to be paid in accordance with the stipulations of the *tnaim*. If the dowry or a part of it was to be paid before the *chuppah* and the bride's father didn't have the full amount, the *khosen*'s father might decide to postpone the wedding or to break the engagement entirely. This was something that actually happened only seldom.

A wedding was normally celebrated at the home of the bride and at the expense of her father. If, however, the house was not large enough, then a room at the Jewish hotel was rented for the occasion. The groom, his parents, and their invited guests (if they were from out of town) used to arrive a few hours before the *chuppah*. The groom lodged with a family friend and was escorted by his party with an orchestra to the wedding place. There, the *kalah*, in a white wedding dress, with a veil and a wreath of myrtle as a symbol of innocence, often crying, awaited the bridegroom, ready to go to the *chuppah* (a canopy made of embroidered cloth, or a *talles* stretched over four poles). The groom approached the *kalah* and lowered her veil. This could have been the first time he saw her face. The groom went under the *chuppah* escorted by the *unterfeirers* (escorts) and then the bride followed, escorted by her *unterfeirers*.

Guests with lighted candles encircled the couple under the *chuppah*. The *rav* or the bride's father, if he was a learned man, officiated. The *ktubah* was read, and the groom placed a ring on the bride's finger, pronouncing the *haaray at* ("thou art consecrated unto me") formula. The *rav* pronounced benedictions over wine, and the *khosen* and the *kalah* each took a sip. The bride tried to step on the groom's foot so that she might be the dominant one in the family. The bride and the escorts circled the *khosen* seven times. The *khosen* stepped on a glass pipe from a kerosene lamp or any other glass vessel, which made noise when broken, and everyone shouted, *"Mazal tov"* (good luck). The *khosen* and the *kalah* were united for a short while in a *cheder m'youchad* (separate room), and on the way they were showered with grain. After the *chuppah* the *kalah*'s hair was cut off and a *shaitl* (wig) was put on her head.

In a large dining room supper was served. The *khosen* and the *kalah*, sitting at the head of a long table, ate the *gildene youkh* (golden soup), chicken soup with fat globules and *rendlech* (small globes from dough fried in chicken fat), from the same bowl. After hand washing, fish, challah, and vodka was served, followed by roast fowl and meat, washed down with wine. Men and women were seated at separate tables. A separate table was also set for the poor, and *tsdakkah* money was given to them. Beggars came from all the neighboring *shtetlech* to a wedding of the rich. The *khosen* made a *drushe* (speech), and the *badchen* (jester) took over his duties as the master of ceremonies. He announced *drushe geshank* (wedding gifts given to the newlyweds) and made fun of everyone with a big dose of *chuzpah*.

An orchestra played *yiddishe shtiklikh* (Jewish wedding music). Everybody was in a gay mood. The guests started a dance holding handkerchiefs—and so it went until the wee hours. The young couple, being tired, retired earlier. The next morning the bride's mother-in-law checked the linen.

The festivities went on for a whole week, until the Sabbath of the *Sheva Broochos* (Seven Blessings). On this Sabbath morning the *khosen* was led to the *shtibl* or to wherever the father-in-law was davening. He was called up to the Torah for *maftir*, and a *kiddush* was served for all those present in the *shtibl*. At home a Sabbath meal awaited the relatives and friends, with a separate table for the women, loaded with preserves, candies, and all kinds of sweets.

Not one father became broke after having spent more than he could afford for wanting to show off for his daughter's wedding. Of course, there were families, and they were in the majority, who, not being able to afford luxuries, arranged their wedding ceremonies modestly, but all the traditions were followed.

The law of the land demanded that a marriage be performed by a rabbi authorized to perform marriages, or at the Registrar's Office. The *rav* in the shtetl was not given this authority. And Jews considered going to the Registrar's Office as performing another wedding with their own wife. Being concerned with the question of marriage from the religious point of view only, they were satisfied with the way their marriage was performed. The result was, however, that from the point of view of the law they were not considered to be a married couple. When a child was born his birth certificate read: "(Name) _____, son/

daughter born out of wedlock, (Mother's name) _____,
(Father's name) _____." This was annoying to a grown
man who bore the mother's family name and not the father's. He
was treated by the law as a bastard. In time, however, marriages
were registered after the Jewish wedding at the Registrar's Office.
In some cases, couples married for twenty to thirty years registered their marriage with the Registrar's Office and adopted their
grown children, thereby legalizing their relationship.

Taharat hamishpachah was strictly preserved. Contraception
or abortion was unthinkable. A wife went once a month to the
mikveh. During the menstrual days she didn't touch a man, and
if for some reason she was not able to go afterwards to the
mikveh, she stayed away from her husband until she could go.
Usually the beds were placed at some distance from each other so
that they wouldn't be together when the wife was impure.

There were some families with an abundance of children, and
bearing twelve children was not rare. But mortality in infancy was
high. As soon as the bride became pregnant she avoided working,
and everybody tried not to irritate or scare her lest it influence the
well-being of her baby. A midwife was engaged, and a week or so
before the expected delivery the midwife moved into the house in
order to be on hand when she would be needed. Delivery took
place at home as a rule, and a doctor was called in only in the case
of an emergency. After the baby was delivered it was bathed and
swaddled in a long pillow and then rolled around with a wide
ribbon, keeping the legs and the back straight like a mummy. The
swaddling was changed a few times each day, and once a day the
baby was bathed. The mother was kept in bed for at least ten to
fourteen days.

Breast-feeding was common, but if a young mother didn't want
or couldn't breast-feed her baby, a wetnurse was hired. A wetnurse, preferably a Jewish woman, had to be healthy, and had to
have shortly before weaned her own baby so that she would be
able to feed the new one. She moved into the home of the family,
leaving her own baby in the care of her family. She was paid well
so that she would have no worries about the well-being of her
family. She was given plenty of milk, meat, and cream. Nothing
was spared her. Care was also taken not to upset her lest the milk
should spoil, or even worse, she would quit. She stayed with the
family for about two years until the baby was weaned. She was

treated and felt herself a member of the family, calling the baby "my child," even when it was grown up. Bottle feeding and formulas were not in use. After the first child was born the husband's father bought a baby carriage.

Giving a name to a child was not as simple as one would think. Between the two mothers-in-law haggling went on as to whom the child should be named after. *Yiches* was brought up. They argued about who from the deceased ancestors was most worthy to have his name preserved in the family (a child should never be named after a living person). If no agreement was reached there might be a compromise for two names, one after a member of the husband's family and one after someone from the wife's family, or a name from the Torah was given.

Giving a name to a girl was a simple ceremony. On a Shabbos after the birth the father was called up to the Torah, and after a few *misheberakhs*, with a pledge for *tsdakkah*, the name was pronounced. After *davenen*, a *kiddush* was served for the congregation at shul (*laykakh* and *shnaps*, honeycake and vodka). A reception at home concluded the ceremony.

With the birth of a boy, however, another procedure was followed, the *brith milah*. The circumcision was performed on the eighth day after the birth of the child. Shabbos is not excluded, and to perform a brith milah on Shabbos is not a *chilul shabbos*. The mitzvah of a *brith milah* is greater than Shabbos. Only in the case of sickness of the child may the *bris* be postponed.

On the eve of a *brith milah, krishma laynen* was done. The *bris* took place at the home of the parents of the infant. One of the grandparents, or a *bekuveter* (honorable) Jew was asked to accept the honor of being *sandek*. He sat on a comfortable chair and another chair was set aside for the *kissay shel Eliyahu* (the chair of the prophet Elijah). The father brought in the baby. The *quater* took the baby from him and put it on the lap of the *sandek* (the functions explain the names, which have no equivalent in English). The *mohel* dipped a piece of gauze in wine, applied it to the mouth of the baby as a kind of anesthetic, and performed the surgery. Another man performed the so-called *metzitzah* (sucking the blood from the incision) and spraying the wound with powder from molded wood, after which a dressing was put on.

Despite the fact that the operation seems to lack sanitary precautions, there was never a case of infection.

The name of the baby, agreed upon previously, was announced, and after many blessings the boy was declared as having entered into the covenant. He was then returned to the mother, who soothed him with her breast. The guests were invited for lunch, and everyone received a package containing sweets, *laykakh*, *flooden* (*baklavah*, a kind of Greek strudel), and other goodies to take home.

On the eve of the next Saturday, a so-called *ben zuchor* was held. Relatives and friends visited for a while and were treated with cooked broad beans and peas, and beer was served. The next Saturday morning the father was called to the Torah and pledged *tsdakkah* at *misheberakhs* for different charities. A *kiddush* for the entire congregation followed after the service, and close friends and relatives were invited to the parents' home for a light lunch.

With all the ceremonies behind her, a Jewish wife resumed the tasks of housekeeping, the care of her children, and helping at the business.

If the firstborn child was a boy he belonged, according to the laws of the time of the *Beth Hamikdash* (the Holy Temple), to the *kohanim*, to be a servant in the Temple. He could, however, be redeemed by paying to a *kohen*, on the thirty-first day after his birth, a token amount of money. The ceremony took place at home where a supper was served, and a *kohen*, any *kohen*, received the ransom money. This act of redemption was called *pidyon haben*. No children of *kohanim* or levites, or those who were born by caesarean operations, had to be redeemed.

At thirteen, a boy reached the age of Bar Mitzvah. No big and lengthy preparations were needed for the Bar Mitzvah ceremony. In most cases the boy was very well prepared for this day due to his studies. He studied the *Shulchan Aruch*, and he even knew how to put on *tfillin*. But he was still shown by his rebbe how to do it as a form of rehearsal. It was a simple chore and caused no excitement. On a Monday or a Thursday, whichever followed the birthday first, the father took the boy to the shul, where he put on the *tfillin* and was called up to the Torah. After the morning prayer the father opened a bottle of vodka and unwrapped a package with *laykakh* (honey cake). The *yidden* drank, had a bite of *laykakh*, and wished each other *l'chayim*.

The following Saturday the boy was again called up to the Torah for *maftir*. The father pronounced, *"Baruch sh'patranu m'onshe shelzay"* ("Blessed art Thou, for I am no longer responsible for his transgressions"). From now on the responsibilities for his deeds lay on the Bar Mitzvah boy himself. The boy chanted the *Haftorah*, of which he understood every word, and held a *drushe*, showing how well learned he was. The congregation was treated with a *kiddush*, of course, *laykakh yn bronfen*, and sometimes with fish and challah. Friends and relatives were invited for a Shabbos dinner which took place at home. Usually the Bar Mitzvah boy received a watch from his father and an embroidered *tfillin* sack from his mother. As a matter of fact, a Bar Mitzvah was not celebrated in the shtetl as a swaggering and lavish event or with so much ado as they are nowadays.

In the life of a boy in the shtetl, not very much changed with his reaching the thirteenth birthday. He prayed every morning and evening as before. Now he put on *tfillin* for the morning prayers, except on Saturdays, holidays and *chol hamoed* Pesach and Sukkoth. From this time on he would be counted as a member of a *minyan* and fasting became obligatory. Actually, nothing has changed in the life of a Bar Mitzvah boy in this country either. The one who prayed every day before the Bar Mitzvah continues to do so, now with *tfillin*. The one who didn't pray up to this time and who didn't know how to *daven* also continues as before. Nevertheless, he will remember his Bar Mitzvah as a bond with the Jewish nation and this, in itself, is not too bad.

Love of and caring for children was a characteristic quality of Jewish mothers, who usually applied it, exaggeratedly—the "Yidishe Momma." Living mostly under unsanitary conditions and spending the whole day in the unventilated *cheder*, the kids looked sickly and pale. As a remedy, prescribed by the doctor, they were, as a rule, given cod liver oil every morning. Cod liver oil has a bad taste, and the kids didn't like it. They had to be bribed or forced to drink the oil.

Living cramped in the shtetl, running after *parnusse* from the early morning until late in the evening, and usually looking after a large family, brought stress on the housewife, who, after the harsh winter and the load of work in connection with Pesach, deserved a rest. During the summer months, with the unbearable heat arriving and businesses slowing down, Jews sent their wives, with the children and a servant, to villages in the nearby

Carpathian Mountains. Whoever could afford it left for spas such as Karlsbad, Marienbad, Franzensbad, and Bad Ischl, where the Austrian Emperor Franz Josef used to spend the summer. Others would travel to Vichy and other spas in France and also to Italy or Rumania. Those who had rheumatism, as well as some who did not, went to Pieštany or Trentschin Teplitz. Husbands wealthy enough to be able to afford it, and having trustworthy personnel on whom they could rely, accompanied their families.

Concern for the good health of the family was one of the main characteristics of Jews in the shtetl. In the case of sickness in the family the barber was called first. However, if his recommendations didn't work and the patient didn't improve, a doctor was called. Only in extreme cases and as a last resort did a Jew decide to go to the hospital. The doctor there, they said, was a butcher, and the only thing he knew was to cut. Besides, in the hospital one would be in a ward with other patients, non-Jews, who would make fun of him, especially when he would put on *talles* and *tfillin* for prayer.

The womenfolk didn't rely on doctors only. In the case of a serious sickness they hired a *minyan yidden* to recite psalms (*thillim soogen*). They also ran to the synagogue, opened the ark, and cried in a sing-song voice, begging the Almighty for *rachmunes* (mercy and help). They would also run to the cemetery (*kvoorim raassen*) begging the relatives to go before the *Ribboyne Shel Oylam* (the Creator) and *maylitz yoysher zaan* for a *refuah shlaymah* (and beg for a complete recovery). A family member was also sent to a *tzaddik* (a rebbe) with a *quittl* and a *pidyon*, a slip of paper with a written petition and a donation for the rebbe.

The rich people weren't concerned about money in the case of a sickness and would invite a professor from Vienna to come to see them, regardless of the cost. The professor's diagnosis and advice were regarded as infallible. The local doctor who took part at the concilium was pleased when the professor stated that actually he didn't know why he was needed, as his colleague, the doctor, was an excellent one. Having a professor in the shtetl was a big event. Everyone who was sick or did not feel well made all possible efforts to consult the professor.

Death. An elderly Jew who was sick and felt that his end was near prepared himself for the unavoidable and said his *avowal* so that when the *malech hamoves* (Angel of Death) arrived, he would be ready. The close family members gathered at his home, and if he was still conscious he repeated his last will, giving advice to the children and requesting that they, first of all, take care of his widow. His last will was always kept as though it was a holy commandment.

Women prepared their shrouds while they were still alive, so that if they died without means for *tachrichim*, they would be buried in their own shrouds. This was done even by the wealthy women, because one never knew what could happen; today you are rich, tomorrow you could lose everything you possess.

A widowed father or mother was taken for the rest of his or her life to a daughter or son and was cared for, honored by the children. They were treated with great respect and love by the entire family and by the grandchildren. It didn't matter how poor the living conditions of the children were; a place for the *bobbe* or *zayde* was always available.

When death occurred a feather was put under the nose of the dying person to be certain that the person was not breathing. If this was the case, the eyes were closed by a close relative. The body was taken off the bed and put on the floor with its feet in the direction of the door and covered with a sheet. Two candles were lit in candlesticks and placed on the floor at the head of the corpse. The mirrors were covered with black cloth, and the water containers were emptied into the gutter. Also, the neighbors in the three houses on the left and right sides of the house where the death occurred had to pour out their water and empty the containers.

Members of the *Chevrah Mishnayis* came to read chapters of the Mishnah and to recite psalms. When a person heard of a death, he said, "*Baruch dayan emeth*" ("Blessed be the Righteous Judge"). The rule was that the burial had to be done as soon as possible, and it was even done on holidays, but never on Shabbos. However, if a son, a *kaddish*, was away from the shtetl, the burial could be postponed until he arrived, but never for too long.

The *Chevrah Kadisha* came to the house with the *taarah brett* (cleansing board) and the *mitah* (stretcher). If the place was too small to perform the rites, the corpse was taken to the *taharah shtibl* at the cemetery. The corpse was washed and cleansed, *tachrichim* were sewn and put on. The men had their *kittl* and *talles* put on over the *tachrichim*. The corpse was ready to be buried and was laid in a coffin made of simple boards. Women were permitted to cleanse male corpses, but only women could cleanse female corpses.

Family and friends came to ask for *mechillah* (forgiveness). A small sack which contained earth from *Eretz Yisroel* was put under the head of the corpse, a piece of a branch was put into his hands, and the eyes were covered with shards. The coffin was put on the stretcher and was carried on the shoulders of relatives and friends, who often changed places on the way, and the *levayah* (funeral procession) left for the cemetery. Hearses were not used at all. If the deceased had been a learned man or a well-known one, the funeral procession might stop in front of the *klouze* or synagogue and a *hesped* (eulogy) would be made. Wherever the procession passed, the stores were closed and everyone, whether he knew the deceased or not, joined the procession, even if only for a short time. Members of the *Chevrah Kadishah* clanked their tin *pushkes* (boxes), proclaiming "*Tsdakkah taatzel m'maaveth*" ("charity helps avoid death"). Everyone placed some change into the *pushke*. After arriving at the cemetery, where the gravediggers were already waiting by the dug-out grave, the coffin was taken off the stretcher and put beside the grave. The bottom of the coffin was taken away and the body lowered into the grave. Burying without a coffin was against the law, and this was done in disobedience of the law. *Kohanim* didn't enter the cemetery grounds but waited outside. The cries of the womenfolk, in a shrieking sing-song, were heartbreaking. Clothes of close relatives had been rent, and the son or sons said *kaddish*. If there was no son, a close relative said *kaddish*, and for the next eleven months a man was hired to say *kaddish* every day and to learn *mishnayis*. Before the participants of the *levayah* left, everyone tried to throw a shovel of earth into the grave. On the way out of the cemetery the *beth hakvooroth*, the *heilige ort* (holy place), the *beth chaim* (place of life), beggars sat on the ground and aggressively asked for alms. After washing their hands, the people went home by another route than that which was used for the *levayah*.

At the home of the bereaved family, hard-boiled eggs sprinkled over with ashes, peas, and lentils were eaten, and *shiva* began. The close relatives sat on the floor, or on very low chairs or boxes.

Businesses were closed, and even the cooking was left undone. The mourners were supplied with food by friends and relatives. Throughout the seven days of *shiva* prayers with a *minyan* were held at the mourners' house in the morning and in the evening, everyday, with the exception of Shabbos. On entering the house of the mourner, no greetings were exchanged and sympathy was expressed, *menachem oovel zayin*, saying, "*Hamakom yenachem otchem b'toch shaaray avaylay Zion v'Yerushalaim*" ("May the Lord have mercy with you as with all the mourners for Zion and Jerusalem").

Shiva was the first period of mourning, the next being the *shloshim*, thirty days during which one was supposed to have no haircut, and the third was the eleven months of saying *kaddish*. During the first year after the death mourners did not attend places where music was played or where entertainment was involved. Marriages not arranged previously were not permitted. During the first year a *matzevaah* (tombstone) was erected. For a *rav* or just a *talmid chacham* (a sage), a mausoleum was built. On the first and all subsequent anniversaries of the day of death a *yourzaht* took place. At *davenen* the surviving family members said *kaddish* and pledged donations for charity. Also a *kiddush* was given and everyone wished the *neshoomeh soll hooben an alyiah*. On the following Shabbos the family sent treats to the *klouze* for the *shalosh seudah*, such as *shnaps*, challah, herring and fish. If the sons were not learned enough to learn *mishnayis* themselves, somebody was hired to do so. The grave of the departed was visited, as it was also done later every year, in the month of Ellul. Upon leaving the cemetery a small pebble was placed on the grave. On the day of the *yourzaht* candles were lit at home and were also given to the shul. The surviving members of the family remembered the deceased whenever *mazkir* was said on holidays.

8

Religion and Tradition

JEWISH LIFE IN the shtetl was based on religion and tradition. Nothing was done which would not be in accord with religion and tradition.

The first thing to do every morning was to say the prayer *modeh ani lefanechoo* ("Thank Thee, eternal King of the Universe, that Thou hast graciously restored to me my soul. Thy faithfulness is great"), then one had to wash his hands by pouring water alternately, three times, on the fingers of each hand, *naygel upgyissen*, and then one washed his face and said the benediction. After the *naygel upgyissen* the water had to be poured out so that it would not be used for any other purpose.

Purity was observed by everyone. Hands had to be washed on many occasions: upon coming from the lavatory or bath, after cutting the nails or hair, after putting on or taking off the shoes, after having visited a home where a corpse lay, after attending a funeral, and after touching anything unclean.

Before a man began his daily work, but not before dawn, he *davened* (said the morning prayer).

In order to enable everyone to pray with a *minyan* at a time which would not conflict with one's daily work there were on weekdays two or three *minyanim* at different times in a *klouze*. If there were not enough people for the quorum of ten, as required for a *minyan*, one of them would go out and ask a passerby to come in and be counted toward the *minyan*. Nobody would bar a Jew from attending a service in a *shul*, be it on a Sabbath or any *yom tov*. To sell admission tickets to a house of prayer was considered improper.

One of the many blessings a male had to recite was to thank God for not being made a woman. In many cases this blessing was well justified if the man spent all his time in the *beth hamedrash* studying Talmud, sniffing tobacco, or smoking his pipe, or being involved with others in a *pilpul* (a hairsplitting explanation of a chapter in the Gemara), while his wife had to bear all the troubles in connection with the household. These included raising the children, who arrived one after another every year with regularity, and most of all, making *parnusse* for her husband and family.

Deviation from a commandment was an *avayrah*. Should a member of the community leave the faith, he was declared dead and *shiva* was observed by his close relatives for an hour. His name was never mentioned: *Yemach sh'mo w'nimmach zichro* ("May his name be erased out forever"). A father would say of a son, "I would rather die than see him turn his back on the faith of our forefathers." A *shmad* never occurred in our shtetl, as far as I can remember. A Jew would do everything possible in order to avoid being in the situation where he would be forced to do an *avayrah*.

Being drafted into the army involved *chilul Shabbos*, a desecration of the Sabbath, and eating *trayfe* food. Therefore, a boy who reached the age of nineteen, when he would have to appear before the draft commission, had to think about how he could be declared unfit for military service. Some parents were farsighted, and when a boy was born they went to the Registrar's Office and declared that they had neglected to register a son who had been born three or four years earlier. They paid a fine, but when the boy was called before the commission, being nineteen according to the official list, he was actually only fifteen or sixteen, and not fit to become a soldier.

Boys who were scheduled to appear before the draft commission, which was normally held in the spring, got together after Sukkoth and formed a gang of draftees (*shtellers*), also called *plahguers* from the German word *plagen* ("torment"). They banded together, went on a diet which was close to fasting, didn't sleep, spent the evenings learning, drank vinegar, ate lemons, swallowed many aspirins, tried to force out hemorrhoids, and often with success. There were even some who cut off a finger from the right hand, and with a little bribing, the commission declared them unfit. If there was a poor boy who could not pay enough money for a bribe, a rich man, fearing the poor boy might point a finger at his son, paid the bribe for both of them. There were also cases when a rich boy was declared fit for the service and not wanting to be drafted paid another boy to serve in the army in his place. Another method used to avoid serving in the army and not be forced to transgress the tradition was to leave for America.

Some boys got away with playing the role of a *meshuggene* (crazy person). Another played the role of a completely deaf person. He played this role excellently. He didn't react to any sound, not even the loudest, and didn't blink when the captain, a member of the commission, shot his gun into the air behind his back. He still kept his composure. The decision was then unanimous, *untauglich* (unfit). The boy, who was listening attentively to the deliberations, heard this verdict and became so excited that before the decision was announced he started to run right out of the room. Needless to say he was called back and the proper decision was pronounced, *tauglich* (fit).

A Jew had to observe all the rules concerning eating habits, clothing, and conduct towards others, all of which were founded and depended upon a lot of do's and don'ts. It was not enough to avoid transgressions. One was bound to fulfill the *taryag mitzvoth* (the 613 commandments).

A Jew in the shtetl would never leave or enter a house without kissing the *mezuzah*. To ride a vehicle on Shabbos was unthinkable, and it was the same with smoking. The worst, however, was considered *chilul Shabbos befarhessia* (desecration of the Sabbath in public). Such a person would be treated as though he were under a ban. Only a doctor who was rushing to a patient was permitted to ride in a vehicle on Shabbos. A patient was excused for consuming *trayfe* food if it was prescribed by a doctor. A sick person was also excused from fasting if ordered by a doctor to eat. In this case, not obeying the doctor's orders and fasting was considered an *avayrah*. The rule was that *pikooakh nefesh dokhek Shabbos* (the saving of life overrules the Sabbath).

Eating habits were ruled by tradition and customs. *Haymishe machulim* were: *pitsyeh, varenikis, kishke,* and of course, on Shabbos, fish, chicken soup with noodles, *tzimmes, tshulent, kugel,* stewed prunes, stewed carrots, dairy foods on Shavuot, cabbage rolls on Sukkoth, and latkes on Chanukah, sweets on Purim, and so on. All very fattening and richly spiced. There were not many occasions for making a *shehechjanooh* during the year, such as eating some fruit brought to the market for the first time in the season. Now, when we have all kinds of fruit the entire year round, nothing is a novelty anymore.

Other customs, not so much in use nowadays, which should be mentioned are: *toyvlen* (rinsing new dishes and pots and pans in a creek before using them); thrusting a knife into the ground if it was a *flayshig* one and had been used by mistake to spread butter, or vice versa.

The traditional Jewish garb was a white shirt, a vest from under which the *tzitzis*, the *arbah kanfas*, dangled, a black, long caftan for weekdays and a silken one, a *zhipitze*, for Shabbos, black pants, a wide-brimmed velvet hat for weekdays, and a *shtraymil*, a fur hat, for Shabbos. A *yarmulke* worn under the hat or under the *shtraymil* was always protruding. Hanging from both sides of the face were long, curled *payes*. The *yarmulke* was never removed from the head, even in bed. The caftan was bound with a black, silken, nicely twisted sash. From one of the pockets in the back of the caftan a corner of a huge red handkerchief jutted out, as a rule. Socks were traditionally white, and boots might be kid leather shoes with elastics, or low knee boots. In winter, woolen boots with galoshes were worn, also black, woolen fur-lined coats with fur collars and fur hats. Depending on the means of the wearer of the clothing, the fur in use ranged from the cheapest to the best.

Women used to wear all kinds of dresses over corsets which were tightly pulled in at the waist. They wore black silken coats in the summer and fur-lined coats in the winter. The *shaytel* (wig) was covered with a black laced shawl, or a wide-brimmed hat with a lot of artificial flowers and a plume of ostrich feathers. Elderly women all dressed alike, wearing black usually. Younger ladies, however, were in favor of fashionable clothing, and some models were brought from Vienna or Paris. One could often see a *chussid* in his traditional garb with his wife following him at a distance of a few feet, dressed up like a beauty queen from Paris. This presented a striking contrast.

It was strictly observed that no *shatness* (a mixture of linen and wool) was used.

During the years before World War I, some Jews, mostly the ones who had a business which brought them in touch with authority, or who had to travel abroad, shortened their caftans, or did away with the caftan completely, choosing to wear suits, albeit in dark colors, such as black, dark brown, navy blue, or dark gray. They started to wear hats which were the same shape as those the Gentiles used to wear, or homburgs, and kept the *yarmulkes* in their pockets instead of under their hats. When entering an office they would take off their hats and put the *yarmulke* on. They even went so far as to trim their beards and comb back the *payes* (earlocks) behind their ears. Although they were pious and adhered to tradition they were called *daytschen*, which stems from the German *deutsch*. Not wanting to commit an *avayrah* (sin) they used chemicals to get rid of their facial hair but let their *payes* grow.

For high school students, uniforms and caps similar to the uniforms worn by officers of the Austrian army were compulsory. No chassidic *shul* would permit a student to enter its sanctuary in this attire.

Chasidim outside a house of prayer on Saturday, Cracow, 1938

Reprinted by permission of Schocken Books, Inc., from Image before my eyes by Lucjan Dobroszycki and Barbara Kirschenblatt-Gimblett. Copyright © 1977 by Schocken Books, Inc. Photographer Roman Vishniac

Palace of the Tshortkever Rebbe, Moshe David Friedman, of the Chassidic dynasty in Czortkó

9

Chassidism

THE HORRORS OF the massacres perpetrated by Chmielnicki in the seventeenth century and the subsequent persecutions inspired by the church left the Jews in despair. Many turned to mysticism.

If was then that Shabsai Zvi, a Turkish Jew, proclaimed himself the Messiah. He would redeem the Jews and bring them out of their misery. Many Jews believed in him, and he won thousands of followers, not only in Poland but also in Palestine and Turkey. After being jailed in Turkey, he accepted the Islamic faith to save his own skin. Nevertheless, remnants of his followers in Poland still waited for the redemption to come and continued to toy with the messianic hope.

Seventy years later another Messiah appeared. He was Jacob Frank, a native of Korolówka, a village in the vicinity of our shtetl. His education consisted of attending *cheder* in our shtetl and later in Tshernowitz. He studied Zohar and went to Turkey, where he became familiar with the teachings of Shabsai Zvi.

Back home in Poland he declared himself to be the incarnation of Shabsai Zvi. Reviving the sect he won masses of followers, especially in Pokucie. He preached that impurity would bring redemption. The more sins one committed—eating *chazer*, arranging sexual orgies, etc.—the sooner redemption would arrive. He also recommended renunciation of the Talmud.

In response, the rabbis issued a *cherem* on the renegades. Frank, however, in order to win recognition from the authorities, accepted the Holy Trinity and brought accusations against the

75

Jewish religion. The Polish authorities, especially the church, pleased with these happenings, ordered a debate between rabbis and the sect. The debate resulted in new repressions against Jews. In order to win more support from the Polish government, Frank and the majority of his followers accepted Christianity and were baptized.

However, the Frankists, soaked in mysticism, practiced a mixture of Christianity and Jewish tradition which didn't please the authorities, and Frank was jailed in the monastery of Częstochowa. After his release he went to Moravia, and his followers dwindled away from the sect.

Between the talmudic scholars and the *prosti Yidden*, the Jewish masses, there was a wide intellectual rift. This contrast brought a new movement, Chassidism, into life.

The root of the term *chassidism* is *chaysed* (righteousness). It involved goodness, kindness, charity, and piety.

The founder of Chassidism was Reb Yisroel ben Elieser, born in 1700 in a village in southern Poland. He preached that one need not be a scholar in order for his prayers to be heard by God. He was well learned in Torah and Mishnah and understood the Kabbalah. With his wife and two sons he settled in a village in the foothills of the Carpathian Mountains.

His wife, who rented and kept an inn, was the *parnussegeberin* (the one who earns the livelihood for the family). Reb Yisroel withdrew to a cave which he found in the mountains, near the town of Kossów in the vicinity of our shtetl. He lived in seclusion, (except for the Sabbath, when he would return to his family). He worked wonders, curing the sick who came to him from great distances, Jews and Gentiles alike, but never asked for payment for his help. The peasants, the *hutzuls* (mountaineers), revered him, and he was known among them as the Saintly Srul. They were the ones who were responsible for spreading the tales about the miracles he performed. He became the *Bal Shem Tov* ("the man of the good name") and as a result is known as the Besht, abbreviated from the first letters (*roshay tayvos*) of *Bal Shem Tov*.

The Besht insisted that not the letter but the spirit of the Law was important. What counted was sincere prayer, with emotion, devotion, ecstasy, and strict observance of the commandments.

The unlearned Jews were speedily attracted by the teachings of the Bal Shem Tov, and Chassidism became a brotherhood. A *chussid* could always count on help and hospitality from his brotherhood. The Bal Shem Tov became the leader of a cult which soon spread throughout Poland and the Ukraine. One of his most influential disciples was the Magid from Mezeritsh, whose descendant, Reb Yisroel of Rizhin, was the founder of the Rizhiner line of Chassidim. Reb Yisroelke's sons, grandsons, and disciples founded the well-known Chassidic lines of Sadagora, Wizhnitz, and Czortków.

Chassidism began as a democratic movement. But it changed, and some *tzaddikim* became hereditary bureaucrats claiming they were born with magical powers derived from their ancestors. Dynasties of *tzaddikim* arose, each with their own followers.

Nearly every shtetl in Pokucie was the site of a rebbe and, of course, the *shtetlekh* surrounding Śniatyn were each the site of a *tzaddik*. Beginning with the famous Czortkower court, there were courts in Sadagora, Wizhnitz, Kossów, and Boyan. Each of these rebbes had his followers in our shtetl who built their own *shilechel* or *klouze*. Followers of other rebbes, such as the Sandzer, Zhidatshover, Nadwornaer, Ottynier, Belzer, Husiatyner, and Kopitshintser, were also in our shtetl, but they were not able to afford to build a *klouze* of their own.

A rebbe was not a *rav*. He had no *smicha* but was looked upon as an intermediary between the Chassidim and God and the *maylitz Yoisher* (the solicitor at the Upper Court).

Tales of miracles performed by the rebbe were told and retold by the Chassidim. Each one praised the supernatural power his rebbe possessed. Quarrels between the adherents of one rebbe and those of another have not been a rare event.

A *chussid* would often tell about the miracles performed by his rebbe: how he exorcised a *dybbuk*, how many sick people he restored to health, how an amulet given by him saved the life of the person who wore it, how many barren women gave birth to sons after having received his blessings, how a young man who was drafted into the army was turned back as unfit after only two days in the barracks because he blessed him and promised that God would help, how a business belonging to a man who was broke and was about to become bankrupt started to flourish after he was taken into partnership with this businessman, and so on. To which another *chussid* would reply, "Never mind, what you are telling me are *boobe mayses* (fairy tales). What your rebbe can do in a year, my rebbe can do in an hour. No, not in an hour, but in only one minute!"

Even the *nigun*, the melody of the songs, differed from court to court. The *nigun* a *chussid* hummed served to indicate to which rebbe he was attached.

Chassidim used to go to the rebbe for advice before concluding a transaction or closing a deal. It often happened that he asked the rebbe to accept a partnership in a deal he was going to close, or in a business he was going to start. Of course, no payment was requested for his share.

As a rule Chassidim traveled to the rebbe, especially when they had problems, any kind of problems, to be solved. It happened, however, that a rebbe would come to visit the shtetl. This, of course, was a big event for his followers. A cavalcade of bearded Chassidim in their long caftans, on horseback, met the rebbe on his way and escorted him in his carriage into the shtetl. The Chassidim quarreled among themselves as to who would have the honor of hosting the rebbe. In this case it didn't matter which rebbe's *chussid* one was. Everybody tried to see the rebbe and give him *sholem* (a handshake), which the rebbe answered only with the tips of his fingers. A *pidyon* (some money) and a *quittl* (a slip of paper outlining the problems) followed. The *pidyon*, of course, was not as large as the one he would have given to his own rebbe. The same thing happened to a rebbe who didn't have enough followers with their own *klouze*. The only difference was that the rebbe davened on Shabbos in the *beth hamidrash*, and not in the *klouze* of his followers, but Chassidim from all other clans tried to see the rebbe.

There were also rebbes who lived in poverty, led an ascetic life, aimed for *oylam habah*, *Yene welt* (the other world), fasted every Monday and Thursday, studied the Torah *yomam w'laaylah* (day and night), especially at midnight (*chatzoss*), and refused to accept a *pidyon* (a donation from petitioners for help). The rebbetzin (the rebbe's wife) had a hard time to make ends meet but the rebbe's followers didn't let him down. They supported him with anonymous donations.

There were, however, rebbes who lived in luxury, residing in the so-called courts, furnished with antique furniture, oriental rugs, crystal chandeliers, and vast living space for the family, with bathhouses, kitchens, a *beth hamidrash*, and *mikveh*. The *gabbai*, the *shames*, the cantor, the servants, and the coachmen were all housed in a separate building in the courtyard. Further back in the yard there was a large coachhouse with stables for the horses. When the rebbe or members of his family went out for a ride, the coach was drawn by a team of four horses. The court was ruled by a strict protocol.

In the summer the rebbe and his family left the court, going to famous spas such as Karlsbad, or the like, making the trip in a private, rented railroad car. They usually occupied an entire hotel. The wife and daughters paraded on the *corso*, attired in the newest fashions from Paris and Vienna. Of course they were of silk and velvet, although they preserved a traditional style.

The Chassidim believed in their rebbes and flocked to the courts in the thousands, especially for the High Holidays. Some even left their wives and children, and lived for months at the court. Although they had to sleep on benches in the *beth hamidrash* and there was next to nothing for them to eat, they derived *naches* from living close to the saintly man. A *chussid* arriving at the court had to first see the *gabbai*, who was also the master of protocol and the master of ceremonies. He knew all the Chassidim and also their worth—who gave lavishly, and with whom he had to haggle about the size of the *pidyon*. The *gabbai* treated the Chassidim according to the size of the *pidyon*.

The rebbe waited in his study behind closed doors. The *gabbai* held back the elbowing and pushing crowd of Chassidim. The first admitted were the rich ones, and then the *prosti oylam* (the mob). Once inside, a *chussid* approached the rebbe with humility and handed him a *quittl*, a piece of paper on which he had registered his troubles, requesting help. Together with the *quittle*, the *pidyon* was given. The rebbe listened quietly, and his advice was usually, "Go home. God will help."

Women were also allowed to see the rebbe. Before letting one in, the *gabbai* gave her instructions as to how she should behave, such as to keep a respectful distance from the rebbe and not to cry too much.

The biggest event was to be with the rebbe on a Friday evening and to listen when he *sugt toyreh*—commented on some passages of the Torah. The rebbe entered the room, which was filled with Chassidim, sometimes 200 or more in number, some sitting at long tables and some standing. The rebbe took a seat at the head of a long table in the middle of the room, made *kiddush*, washed hands, and said the blessing over the challah, a *moitze*, ate a small piece of it, and tearing off small pieces, gave them first to the members of his family, and then to the Chassidim, the richer ones, who were seated next to the family. The remaining pieces of the challah were then given to the others for as long as they lasted. Chassidim at other tables received challahs for themselves, but these challahs were not touched by the rebbe.

Male servants brought in platters with fish, meat, and later with *tzimmes*. The rebbe, who was served first, took only a small piece of each serving, and the remainder of the dish, which was called *shirayim*, was cut into small pieces and was given to the Chassidim, who fought for even the smallest crumb of *shirayim*. After the meal the rebbe chanted a hymn, and dancing and singing began. Of course, *shnaps* and wine, brought by the Chassidim, was available in abundance. The same ceremony took place at the Sabbath dinner, the *shalosh seuda*, and the *mlaveh malkah*.

Chassidism degenerated into worshipping the *tzaddikim* as demigods. No wonder, then, that opposition to this kind of idolizing of the *tzaddikim* started to emerge among people with brighter minds, the so-called *mithnaghdim*, who were well learned and no less pious than the Chassidim.

10

Synagogues

IN THE SHTETL there were the *groisseh sheil* and the *bays hamedrash,* the house of prayer, study, and assembly. The latter was a kind of secondary synagogue, where day and night groups studied rabbinic literature and Talmud. Most studying took place after the *maariv* prayer when the stores were closed.

In addition each Chassidic brotherhood had a *klouze* of their chosen rebbe, five of them in our shtetl. Some craftsmen had their own *shilechel* for the members of their guild. Also, two private *shilechels,* each on private premises, one at the house of the Jewish landowner, and one at the house of the banker, were functioning as well.

The 400-year-old main synagogue was a masterpiece of art. It was built of wood with carvings both inside and out, which were done by Jewish and Gentile woodcarving specialists. The beautifully wrought *aron hakodesh* contained more than a score of Torah scrolls, many of them centuries old, and *klay kodesh* of pure silver, the Torahs having been written by famous *sofrim.* The *aron hakodesh* was covered with a velvet *parocheth* (curtain) with a gold-embroidered *Magen David,* the two tablets of the Ten Commandments, two lions, one on each side, and the name of the donor.

The *bimah* in the middle of the synagogue, as well as the walls and the balcony enclosing the *ezrath noshim* where the women prayed, had beautiful carvings as well. Many brass chandeliers, lighted by candles, hung from the ceilings.

In the hall to the left of the entrance to the synagogue there was a room, a chapel, called the *shnaaderishe shilechel*, where the tailors used to pray. The room to the right was the *poolish*, where old prayer books and *sfarim* with torn pages and not fit for use any longer were stored; pages of Torahs spoiled by mistakes made by the *soifer* at the time of writing were also kept in the *poolish*. Torahs desecrated by vandals or scorched in a fire had to be buried at the *mookom kodesh*, the cemetery. In the hall there was also a water container fastened to the wall, with a pitcher and a towel which were used to wash the hands before entering the sanctuary. The used water was drained outside by a pipe.

Inside, in the northwest corner of the synagogue, there was a wooden box which sat on four legs like a table. The box was filled with sand. Candles were stuck into the sand and lit during the prayers.

On the bench along the *mizrach* wall, to the right of the *aron hakodesh*, was the seat reserved for the *rav*, who used to *daven* on Sabbaths at the main synagogue.

On both sides outside of the synagogue were steps leading up to the balcony to the *ezrath noshim*. The balcony was closed in, with only small windows left high up, so that the women could follow the prayers by listening without being able to look down into the sanctuary. Among the women there was always one who knew well how the prayers were conducted. She was the so-called *zugerke*, from the Yiddish *zugen* ("to tell"). She followed the voice of the *baal tfillah* (cantor and reader) and announced to the women the page of the *sidur* or *machzor*, and which prayer was just being said by the *baal tfillah*, or the page of the *chumash* when the Torah was read. From time to time she commanded, "*Waayber waynts*" ("women, cry"), whereupon all the women started to cry and repeated the words pronounced by the *zugerke*.

Unfortunately, the synagogue was built on the edge of a ravine and the soil was eroding under the eastern wall. The situation was becoming worse and worse, although efforts were made to save the synagogue by supporting the wall with countless pillars. In 1900 the community decided to build a new stone and brick synagogue. Work was started, but the funding was slow due to the fact that the majority of the citizens belonged to one or another Chassidic *shilechel*.

A Chassidic *klouze* consisted mainly of one larger or smaller room, depending on the number and the means of the members.

On a balcony over one-half of the *klouze* was the *ezrath noshim*. The entrance was from the outside, with high windows similar to the ones in the main synagogue. Here too there was a *zugerke* doing her job.

At the entrance into the *klouze* were placed the same facilities as were provided in the synagogue: water, a towel, a box filled with sand for the candles, brass chandeliers hanging from the ceiling, and so on. The furnishings inside were different from those of the main synagogue. Whereas in the synagogue the benches were placed one behind another facing east, the *klouze* had another arrangement. The walls were simply whitewashed. Along the *mizrach* (eastern) wall there was a bench with reserved seats for the members who had bought them. One seat on this bench, which was to the right of the *aron hakodesh*, was reserved for the *rav*, and a few seats were given to learned men free of charge. Another long bench was placed opposite the *mizrach* wall. Behind this bench was the *bimah*. Before each seat there was a lectern where the owner of the seat could lock up his *talles* and *tfillin*. The seats were marked with the name of the owner and passed from father to son. Along the north, east, and west side-walls were long benches with tables. There were no restrictions for seating at these tables. No *tallesim* were provided at either the synagogue or the *klouzes*. Everyone had his own *talles*. Even a stranger visiting the shtetl had his own *talles* because no Jew would leave for a trip without taking his *talles* and *tfillin* with him.

On Shabbos, *sholosh seudah* was eaten at the tables along the wall. On weekdays the Chassidim and *bocherim* studied Torah at these tables. Each day, as soon as the *maariv* prayer was over, the *bocherim* extinguished the candles in the *klouze*, collected the ends, and used them later, one by one when studying; making use of two candles would have been considered a luxury.

Some Chassidim used two sets of *tfillin*, exchanging the *tfillin* during the prayers, by putting on what were known as "Rabenu Taam's *tfillin*." In some *shtiblech* only one *minyan* was held. It took a *chussid* a long time *zikh maychen zaan*, to prepare himself for the prayer. When appearing before God to *daven* one must be clean, inside as well as out, and he would spare no effort to force a bowel movement before the prayer, hence hemorrhoids were a widespread ailment among Chassidim.

In the evening after *maariv*, the Chassidim usually discussed politics, but most of the time was taken up with telling stories about the miracles which their rebbe and his ancestors had performed. Of course, they were studying, discussing, explaining, and interpreting every word from the Talmud. All this was done by the light of a single candle.

11

Holidays

THE SABBATH. The Sabbath was the day of complete rest. Everything in the shtetl was brought to a standstill, as was also the case on all Jewish holidays. Gentiles wouldn't come to the shtetl on these days because they knew that nobody would talk to them about business. No work whatsoever was done on the Sabbath, no smoking, no riding, no cooking, and no walking farther than a *tchom Shabbat,* approximately 1,000 feet. Only *pikouach nefesh* (a threat to life) took preference over the Sabbath. The Sabbath was a holy day, and holiness was not to be disturbed by mourning, so no burials were permitted on the Sabbath and *shiva* was interrupted.

In a household, preparations for the Sabbath began on Thursday. It began in the early morning with a visit to the butcher, where there was pushing and elbowing. All the *balebustes* or their servants were there at the same time, and each wanted to be served first so that no one else could buy the cut that she wanted. The same *shtipenysh* (pushing) occurred at the slaughterhouse for chickens. The *shoychet* worked fast, killing a chicken, throwing it to the floor and, while holding the handle of the *chalef* (knife) in his mouth was already plucking the feathers from the neck of the next chicken. Some of the women who brought their chickens to be killed came out splattered all over with blood.

After the visit to the butcher and the *shoychet,* vegetables were bought at the marketplace, and the day was concluded with shopping at the grocery store. In the evening the chicken was opened up and checked to make sure that it was kosher, that there were no spots on the liver or anything else which might be suspicious. If the condition of the chicken was suspect the problem was put before the *rav* who, after examining the part of the chicken brought to him, and looking up the case in a *sayfer*, decided whether the chicken was kosher or *trayfe*. In the latter case it was sold for close to nothing to a Gentile.

The kosher chicken and the meat had to be koshered, meaning, it had to be soaked, salted, and rinsed. Later in the evening the dough was left to rise. The one for bread, leavened with sour dough, left for this purpose from the previous week's baking, or with yeast for the challahs *kichlech*, and knishes. Friday was the busiest day in the household. The wife rose in the wee hours, preheated the oven with wood, kneaded the dough, took a piece of it and burned it in the oven while saying the appropriate blessing. Then she nicely twisted the challahs and put the dough for the dark bread on cabbage leaves, prepared cookies, honeycake, spongecake, *kichlech*, and knishes, and put them all into the oven.

Fish was bought on Friday morning only, because they were brought in a vast water-filled tank by train from Galatz, Rumania, and the train arrived early in the morning. Only carp was imported, and it was available live from the tank. It was first come, first served. Cheaper fish were bought from Gentile fishermen, who delivered their catch from the Prut River, peddling from house to house in the shtetl on Friday. Whoever couldn't afford to purchase carp or the cheaper fish bought herring.

Challahs were made in large quantities, and the surplus challahs were given to the women who collected them in the shtetl for the needy families. The bread and sweets were intended to last for the whole week, but large families had to repeat the baking again during the week.

When the baking was finished, cooking and roasting for the Sabbath meal began. Also, the *cholent* and the *kugel* were prepared and put into the preheated oven, which was sealed with clay, to have the *cholent* ready and hot for the Sabbath. A clay jug was also filled with hot tea and put into a niche made especially for this purpose on the oven. It was covered with pillows so that on Saturday morning the tea was hot and ready, with no need to be warmed up. Some housewives brought their *cholent* to the baker on Friday afternoon and picked it up on Saturday after *shul*.

The house was thoroughly cleaned, the floors were scrubbed and waxed. Those who did not have wooden floors plastered theirs with a mixture of clay and cow dung and spread fine sand over it. Shoes were cleaned and polished so as not to have to do it on Shabbos. The children washed in a washtub, the girls' heads were rinsed with kerosene, then the wife washed herself, and all changed their clothes.

The husband closed his store early, as did all the Jews, and he went with his sons to the *shwits* (steambath). To enjoy the *shwits* fully, the people slapped each other on the back with a broom made of birch twigs. Before leaving the *shwits* three immersions in the *mikveh* were made. Underwear changed, they headed home, where a roast with fresh challah was waiting.

Preparation for the *klouze* began with putting on *shabesdike beguddim* (Shabbos best clothing), which was totally different from what was worn during the week. Then the father and sons left for the *klouze*.

Women didn't go to the *shul* on Friday evening. After the menfolk left for the *klouze*, the wife covered the table with a white tablecloth, then put on the table, at the end where the father sat, two challahs, covering them with an embroidered napkin or some other white cloth. She put on the table the silver or brass candlesticks, or a candelabrum which had been handed down in the family from generation to generation, or had been received as a *drushegeshank* (wedding gift). (A poor woman who didn't have candlesticks used two empty bottles instead.) Then she covered her head and face with a shawl or a large kerchief, kindled two candles, and if she could afford it, for each member of the family, one more candle was lit. She said the blessing, and while moving her hands over the flames of the candles she whispered the prayers and, as a rule, was weeping bitterly.

Before *lecht bentshen*, she put some change into the *pushke* (the box), mostly for *Reb Meir Bal Haness*. Finally she sat down, tired after all the work she had done, and relaxed, awaiting the return of her husband from the *shul*. The husband arrived in high spirits after having enjoyed the *l'chou doydi likrass kallah* ("let's meet the bride, the Shabbos"), sang the *Eshes chaayil* ("A good wife who can find?"), and in a high spirit of the holiness of Sabbath all was set for the Sabbath meal.

He brought with him an *oyrakh* (guest) who was usually a poor Jew stranded in the shtetl and could not afford to stay at the hotel. Supper began with *kiddush* over wine. First, the father made *kiddush* and let the wife and the children have a sip, then the *oyrakh*, and the sons who were over thirteen made *kiddush*. Hands were washed and the father said the blessing *hamoytse lechem min haaretz*, and sliced the challah for all those present at the table. If something had been forgotten, for example, salt, the father only said "*nouh, nouh*" because after he said the *broukhe* he was not allowed to speak *oysreden* before he had eaten the challah, and without dipping the challah in salt he couldn't take a bite of it.

First fish was served, and it was washed down with *shnaps*. A chicken broth with noodles followed, then came the cooked chicken and/or roast beef, and *tzimmes* (stewed carrots or stewed prunes with figs and raisins). Between meals *zmiros* were chanted by all present. Lights were not put out; they had to burn down by themselves, and the candlesticks must not be touched. After supper there was *mezoumen bentshen* (thanking God for having enjoyed the supper) if there were at least three men participating.

After supper one might go over to a neighbor's house for a chat, or the neighbor might drop by. Broad beans with a lot of pepper were eaten and beer was served.

On Sabbath morning the clay jug was taken from the nook and everyone drank a glass of hot tea. Nothing was eaten before *davenen*. The father went to the *mikveh* and after he came back, he and his sons were *maaver the sedrah* (going over the portion of the Torah for the week), chanting according to the markings in the *chumash*.

The Gentile servant, if there was one—and if there wasn't one, a Gentile called the *Shabbos goy*—took the candlesticks from the table, since they could not be touched on Sabbath. In the wintertime he heated the oven, for which he received a piece of challah and a *shnaps* and some change on Sunday.

The father and sons put on *shabesdike* clothing and left for the *klouze*. They checked to see if there was anything in their pockets, because it was not permitted to carry even the lightest thing on Shabbos in a public place. By means of an *eyrev*, a wire spanned on poles and encircling the shtetl, it was transformed from a public to an enclosed place. Nevertheless, a *chussid* would take no chances. Therefore, the handkerchief was knotted around the neck or around the wrist so that it was made a part of the clothing. The wife chose her nicest dress, put on her jewelry, covered her head over the wig with a lace scarf, or put on a hat with ostrich feathers (in the winter she wore her fur coat) and left for the *ezrath noshim* at the *klouze*.

Upon returning home from the *klouze* there was *kiddush*. The oven was opened, the *cholent* taken out, and the second Shabbos meal was served. After *zmiros* and *bentschen* the father lay down for a nap.

During the summer the boys recited *Pirkay Avoth*, the "Ethics of the Fathers," and in winter *Borchu Nafshi*. The boys were quizzed and examined, usually by the grandfather, about their studies during the past week. If the boy did well he received a *k'nipp in backl* (a pinch on the cheek), and the grandmother gave him *Shabbos oybs* which she prepared for him regardless of whether he passed the exam or not. The bag he received contained cookies, fruit, nuts, candies, and sweets.

The womenfolk read the *Zeenah u reenah*, written in Yiddish and pertaining to the appropriate portion of the Torah for the week. It was interwoven with miracles and legends about the mystical river Sambation, the Leviathan, and others. Descriptions of how the Holy Temple was destroyed made them weep. Some read *maaseh bichlech* (tales in Yiddish).

In the late afternoon the father and the boys returned to the *klouze* for *minchah davenen*, after which *shlosh seudah*, the third meal of the day, was eaten in the *klouze*. Usually whoever had *yourzat* during the past week and was called to the Torah during the morning prayer served *kiddush* after the prayer, and in the evening *shlosh seudah*. He brought to the *klouze shnaps*, beer, challah, fish, herring, and pickles. Everybody ate and sang the songs and melodies of the rebbe, the *tzaddik*. Then the *maariv* prayer was said, and if there was a new moon the Chassidim went outside for *mechadesh zaan the lehvouneh* (thanking God for the past month and praying for a good next one).

At home the women didn't kindle any light before the appearance of at least three stars in the sky, and having noticed the stars they said, "God *fun Avruhum*" (thanking the God of Abraham, Jacob, and so on, for the past week and begging for a good coming week for the people of Israel).

Upon leaving the *klouze* for home everyone wished each other a good and happy week. The father made *havdalah* over vodka, a child held a twisted candle high, and father smelled spices from a special box and, spilling a little alcohol on the table, ignited it. Then he passed his hands over the flame, as though he were catching the flames and putting them into the pockets so that money might flow into them during the coming week.

After the *havdalah* the *mlaveh malkah* (escorting the Queen Sabbath out) followed. This was another supper consisting of borsht on bones and meat with hot cooked potatoes and a plate of roast. After the *mlaveh malkah* the family, the married sons with their wives, the daughters with their husbands, and the *mechutunim* (in-laws) visited. Partners and/or clerks also came. Business was discussed and plans for the next week were drawn up. Innumerable glasses of tea with lemon were drunk, some of the men smoked good cigars or a pipe, and some sniffed tobacco from a silver box.

Late at night, after bidding each other a *gute woch* the company left. The next morning was business as usual.

Pesach. Passover falls on the fifteenth day of Nissan, the month of the spring, which is the first month of the religious year and the seventh month of the civil calendar. It is celebrated for eight days, of which the first and last two days are feast days and the four days between are the days of *chol hamoed,* the intermediate days on which work is not prohibited.

On the first day of Pesach, a prayer for *tal* (dew) is included in the *mussaf* prayer, and is repeated daily until Shmini Atseret, the eighth day of Succot. It is a prayer for dew in Palestine for the plants during the hot summer season when no rain falls at all. It shows how our people, although in dispersion, feel themselves attached to the land of our ancestors.

A housewife began the preparation for Pesach immediately after Purim. First a barrel which served for this purpose year after year was koshered. The barrel was half-filled with water, stones were heated until they were red-hot, and then they were thrown into the barrel, and the water began to boil. The best available beets were bought, washed, cut, and set to sour in the barrel. The barrel with the beets was put into a corner of a room, and everybody in the household was warned to keep *chumetz* away from the borsht-to-be.

Then the purchasing of staple food to be used on Pesach began: eggs, fruits, potatoes and other vegetables, chickens, turkeys, ducks, and/or geese were bought and put into cages or let loose to run in the backyard so that they would be fed and fattened for Pesach. Wine and slivovitz, *Kosher shel Pesach* was ordered from pious Chassidim in Hungary who could be trusted that it would really be kosher. Poorer people made their own wine by setting raisins to ferment.

Everything was bought in larger quantities than was needed for the family. It was kept in mind that there were many people who could not afford to buy what was needed for Pesach and that one must help them. One had also to think of his employees. It was customary to distribute among the employees before Pesach a few liters of wine, a bottle of slivovitz, dozens of eggs, and some money. This was done to respond to the *kol dichfin* ("let those who are hungry come in").

Starting well before Pesach, the *moes chittin* committee collected money for distribution among needy people so that all in the shtetl would be able to enjoy the *yom tov*.

A week before Pesach the great and thorough cleaning began. Furniture was moved outside and was cleaned and polished. Walls inside and out, if one lived in a log cabin type of house, were whitewashed or painted, and the houses were made *pesachdik* room after room, restricting the use of the rooms already cleaned and being careful not to bring in any more *chumetz*. The *klouze*s also received a cleaning, and the walls were whitewashed. The tables, lecterns, and the benches were taken outside, where they were cleaned and washed.

There were two types of matzos, *shmira* matzos and regular matzos. The latter were white and round in form, whereas the former were light brown in color. A bakery in the shtetl was koshered under the strictest supervision of the *rav*. Later, it was watched by a *mashgiach* appointed by the *rav*, so as not to allow the slightest change from the rules during the process of baking the matzos.

A second bakery was also koshered, *k'das w'kdin*, according to the rules of the law. The first bakery was for the baking and selling of matzos. The second bakery was used by families who considered matzos made by others not kosher enough for them. They would pay for the use of the bakery by the hour. An appointment had to be made weeks before Pesach because the majority in the shtetl liked to bake their own matzos.

Flour was purchased from a miller who was a pious man. The

flour which he sold was ground with all precautions to make it fit for baking matzos. Then it was delivered from the mill to the bakery by a trustworthy Jew so that nothing could happen on the way which might make the flour unfit for the baking of matzos.

In the bakery, a team of bakers and helpers were ready and waiting to do the job. There was a flour measurer, a water pourer, a kneader, and behind long tables with new wooden tops, girls waited for a piece of the dough to roll it out flat and round. After which the so-called *shtipler*, a perforator, made holes with a piece of broken glass or a toothed wheel. Everything was done quickly and was passed to the baker with the minimum of delay so that the dough would not leaven during the process of baking. Challah was taken and the matzo was shoved swiftly by the baker into the oven.

The woman whose matzos were being baked ran around and watched to be certain that no water, God forbid, should be spilled during the rolling of the matzo or on its way to the oven. The baked matzos were put into a wicker basket, usually a conical one, which was stored in the attic from Pesach to Pesach, and was never used for any other purpose. Before putting in the matzos, the basket was lined with a clean, unstarched sheet. At home, the basket with the matzos was covered with a clean sheet and put in a corner of a room with the least traffic and watched that *chumetz* would be kept away. Matzos weren't to be eaten before the Seder, i.e., before the blessing of *achilas matzos* was made.

A similar procedure was followed when baking *shmira* matzos, the only difference being that beginning from harvesting of the wheat all was done by the Chassidim themselves. The harvest must have taken place only after a reasonable period of time with no rain. The threshing and the grinding of the grain on stones with no prior shelling was all done by the Chassidim involved. The flour was kept in new sacks, and the baking was done by pious teenagers (no girls). Whoever could not make *shmira* matzos himself would try to get at least three *shmirah* matzos for each of the two Seders. Some Chassidim in good standing with the rebbe, the *tzaddik*, received a package of *shmira* matzos, which were baked at the court and, therefore, had double value; one was the assurance that they were strictly kosher, and the second that coming from the rebbe's court they had the *tzaddik's* blessing.

The house, spic and span, was ready for Pesach. The dishes which were used during the year were put away till after Pesach. The *pesachdik* dishes, which had been tucked away for the year in the attic, including a wooden mortar for making *matzo* meal and the fat stored since Chanuka, were brought in. A true *chussid* would never allow matzo meal to be used in his household except for the last two days. What's more, a *chussid* wouldn't eat at another *chussid*'s home although the other may have been just as pious. *Aych mish mich nisht* was the saying.

If new pots and pans or dishes were bought they had to be taken to the creek for immersion. Some pots were koshered by pouring water into a big vessel, then putting a stone, which was heated until it was red-hot, into the vessel. The stove, which was, as a rule, wood-fired with cast iron plates, was koshered by firing the stove and covering the plates at the same time with burning embers until the plate became red. The oven was koshered by firing wood until the lining of the oven was red-hot.

The day before *erev* Pesach all the *chumetz* in the house was stored in one place, preferably outside the house. A Gentile was asked to buy the entire amount and a *shtar m'chirah* (bill of sale) was written and signed. The buyer deposited a down payment on his purchase and became the legal owner of the *chumetz*. After Pesach he was asked to finish the deal. Since he was not ready to pay the balance of the purchase price, a settlement was reached; he canceled the purchase and received a double refund of his down payment. The seller then regained ownership of the *chumetz*.

After *maariv* on the evening before the eve of Pesach the man of the house had to make sure that not even the smallest quantity of *chumetz* was left in the house. He performed a search for *chumetz*, the *bdikath chumetz*. For this purpose he used a wooden spoon and a wing from a goose or a chicken and collected all the crumbs, which were purposely laid out by his wife, into the spoon. With the search completed, he wrapped the spoon and the crumbs together with the wing in a linen cloth, fastened it with thread, and the next morning at nine o'clock, he and his neighbors made a bonfire and burned the *chumetz*. From that time on *chumetz* was not to be eaten.

On *erev* Pesach all the firstborn males were required to fast.

The housewife grated the potatoes for *chremzlech* (potato

latkas/pancakes), cooked the fish, roasted the meat, and prepared everything needed for the Seder, the three matzos, *muror*, the *charosoth*, an egg, parsley, and a shankbone.

The menfolk left for the *klouze* and the wife prepared the table for the Seder. Covering it with a nice white tablecloth, she put on the candelabrum, the goblets for each person, for the *arba kosyoth* (the four cups of wine) the goblet for Eliyahu Hanavi, the plate with the *charosoth*, and the three matzos in a nicely embroidered bag with three compartments. She dressed and bejeweled herself. She was a *malke* (queen), and waited for the return of the husband with the sons from the *klouze*.

The father put on a white *kittel*, sat down on a chair upholstered with pillows, and conducted the Seder. After *kiddush* the telling of the Haggadah began, and everything was done the same way as it had been done for 3,500 years, and as it is still done today. The same *shehechyanu* blessing, the same old Haggadah, the four *kashyot*, the singing of *chad gadyah*, the ransom for the *afikomen*, and ending with the *l'shanah habaah b'Yerushalaim*.

The children had a school holiday, played with nuts on *chol hamoed*, and ran around in the narrow streets of the shtetl.

After Pesach the *pesachdik* dishes were cleaned and stored cautiously in the same place as usual until the next year.

Shavuoth. On Pesach, the *sefirah*, the counting of the *omer* for seven weeks started, and at the end of it Shavuoth was celebrated.

During *sefirah*, weddings did not take place, haircuts were forbidden, and bathing in the river was not allowed. An exception to these rules was the thirty-third day of the omer, Lag B'omer. On this day weddings were allowed, hair could be cut, and the *melamdim* took their *kinderlach* from the *cheder* into the woods and forests out of the city on an excursion.

Bathing and swimming in the crystal-clear water of the river was the only sport pursued by Jews. Men and women bathed in full-length underwear at different locations and at quite a distance from each other. On Fridays the entire shtetl went to the beach.

Shavuoth was a sublime holiday, the festival of giving the Torah on Mount Sinai. Synagogues and homes were decorated with green plants and branches. The feeling of the people in the synagogue was one of loftiness and one can never forget the sweet melody of *Hakdamot meilin*.

It was customary to eat dairy food on Shavuoth, such as butter on *babkahs*, blintzes with cheese, sour cream, cheese cake, fish, and so forth. Poor peoples' menus, however, consisted mainly of dairy foods throughout the year. For them there was the so-called *mamalyga*, or *polenta*, or *kulesha*, a cheap dish made of corn meal, cooked to a hard consistency and eaten with milk or cheese, or a potato soup with sour milk.

Tisha B'Av. Eating dairy dishes was also customary on the *najn tayg*, the nine days of the month of Av before Tisha b'Av. Tisha b'Av was a day of fasting, and prior to it was the seventeenth day of Tamuz, *shiva assar b'Tamuz* another fast-day. Tisha b'Av was the day of mourning the destruction of the first Temple in Jerusalem by the Babylonians two and a half millennia ago. Not only was the first Holy Temple destroyed on Tisha b'Av, but on this same day of the year the second Temple was also burned by the Roman Emperor, Titus *Harashah* (Titus the wicked). On this day during the Bar Kochba uprising Betar fell. The expulsion of Jews from Spain also took place on a Tisha b'Av. The murders perpetrated by the Crusaders also started on Tisha b'Av. Nevertheless, when marking the day with the solemnity of mourning, only the destruction of the first Temple was remembered. The fasting started on the eve of Tisha b'Av and the Jews gathered in the synagogues and *shtiblech*. The cover of the ark was removed, lights were dimmed, and the congregation sat in stockinged feet on overturned lecterns and chanted the *Aychou Yoshvou Boudod Ha'ir* (the Lamentations of Jeremiah), bewailing the destruction of the *Beth Hamikdash* in a sad melody and reading elegies composed by famous poets during the centuries. On Tisha b'Av morning the *Aychou* was chanted again in the synagogue, but at the morning prayer no *talles* or *tfillin* were put on. Tisha b'Av was a working day. On Tisha b'Av one was not supposed to study Torah. Outside the synagogue, boys used to throw burrs and musk thistles at each other. On the following Sabbath, the Sabbath Nachmi, Isaiah's *Nachmou, nachmou ami* was read as an exhortation not to lose hope. For what was left to a Jew was hope—nothing else but hope.

Rosh Hashanah. The civil calendar begins on Rosh Hashanah, the New Year's day on the first of the month of Tishray, which is the seventh month of the religious year. Elul, the month following Av and preceding Tishray, was the month of *din v'cheshbon*, when in heaven stock was being taken and everyone's good deeds were weighed against his bad deeds and judgment was passed. Elul was devoted to preparing for the High Holidays. One searched his soul, so that he would be ready and in good standing when the balance sheet of his *mitzvos* and *avayros* would be closed.

This is the time of *Slichoth*, prayer and repentance. In the wee hours of the morning, the *shames* made his rounds in the streets of the shtetl, banging with a wooden hammer on doors, calling out, *"Shtayt oyf fahr avoidaas haboray"* ("Get up for divine worship").

People visited the graves of relatives, begging them to plead on their behalf when their case came up for judgment.

Throughout Elul the *shofar* was blown every morning except on Saturdays and on the day before Rosh Hashanah.

On Rosh Hashanah, although working and riding were not allowed, smoking and lighting fires and cooking were not forbidden.

The synagogues were full on Rosh Hashanah. Nobody was barred from joining the congregation in prayer and no tickets were needed. For the services on the two days of Rosh Hashanah and for Yom Kippur the best available cantor was hired. He began with the humble prayer *Hinneni Haouni*, begging the Almighty to recognize him as a worthy beseecher for the congregation with his prayers before the Highest Judge.

The highlights of the special prayers on this day were the *al chet*, the *ounesahnay toykef*, *dichenen* (the blessing by the *kohanim*), *maskir*, and the blowing of the *shofar*. During these prayers, heartrending weeping was heard from the *ezrath noshim*. Wishing each other, with a handshake, *L'shanah tova tikatayvou* ("May you be inscribed for a good year"), a happy New Year, the congregation left for the *yomtovdikke* dinner.

First they had *kiddush*, then a rare fruit, for example, a pineapple or grapes (which up until Rosh Hashanah were not yet ripe) was eaten in order to have the opportunity to make a *shehechyanou*. The *moytse*, usually from a round challah, was dipped in honey, not in salt as was done throughout the year. Apples were dipped in honey and eaten as well. A tradition was also to serve chicken soup with *kreplach*. After a short rest the menfolk returned to the synagogue. From the synagogue the congregation went to the nearest creek for *tashlich*. There, while saying the suitable prayers, pockets were turned inside out and any crumbs which were there were thrown into the river. As they were carried away, the sins of the people went along with them.

Yom Kippur. Yom Kippur is the day of atonement, the most solemn of all the holidays. During the *asayret yemay tshouvah,* the ten days from Rosh Hashanah until Yom Kippur, another chance for repentance is given. Repentance and charity may avert a bad sentence, when the lot of every human being is decided. People, on these days, repented and gave *tsdakkah.*

A few days before Yom Kippur, the housewife made candles which were to be lit on Yom Kippur eve, one at the synagogue, where it was placed in the sandbox kept there for this purpose, and where, during the year candles offered to the *shul* were kindled. The other one was kindled and left at home. The candles were made of pure beeswax. Warmed wax was rolled out into two flat rectangles for two candles, a bigger and a smaller one. The bigger one was for the well-being of the members of the family. The smaller one was in memory of those who had passed away. For each member of the family a piece of cotton yarn was laid on the wax to make a wick. When the yarn was laid on the wax the name of the person on whose behalf this was being done was pronounced and a prayer was said. Laying a yarn on behalf of the soul of a dead relative was accompanied by a lot of crying. After the wicks were laid out, the wax was rolled up to form a nice, smooth candle. Such a candle was expected to last for at least twenty-six hours. This procedure was called *knaytlach laygen,* hence the saying *er laygt im tsou a knaytle* ("he is adding some more to his *tzoures* [troubles]").

Before Yom Kippur, chicken and roosters, preferably white ones, were bought and kept for *erev* Yom Kippur for *kapoures shlougen.* Men used roosters and women chickens. The man had one rooster for himself, and the woman had one chicken for herself, but several children might collectively use one bird among themselves. The bird was swung above the head three times while the person recited *"Ze kapourousi, ze chalifousi, ze hatarnegol yelech l'missah w'ani l'chaim toywim,"* meaning, "This is my sacrifice, my offering, let this bird die and I shall have a peaceful life instead." The birds were then taken to the slaughterer, and then cooked.

In the forenoon of *erev* Yom Kippur the life in the shtetl ground

Shlougen Kapoures—a rite performed on the day before Yom Kippur. A person's sins are symbolically transferred to a fowl, which is slaughtered on his behalf.

Reprinted by permission of Schocken Books, Inc., from Image before my eyes by Lucjan Dobroszycki and Barbara Kirschenblatt-Gimblett. Copyright © 1977 by Schocken Books, Inc.

to a halt. One could feel in the air that something special was taking place. The men ran for a *toyvel* (an immersion in the *mikveh*). Back home they put on the *shabesdike malbishim* (Sabbath clothing) and went to the *klouze* early in the afternoon. There, after *minche*, a *chussid* laid down on a bench and the *shames* lashed him with a leather belt, counting thirty-six *malkes* (lashes) on his back in order to afflict the soul. On a long table, plates for collecting charity were placed and funds needed for the upkeep of the *klouze* were also collected. Each plate was marked with a slip of paper, showing the organization; and there was not one organization in the shtetl which did not have a plate on the table. The *gabbai* watched over the donors to be sure that nobody got away with giving a smaller donation than he could afford according to his assessment. And he knew everything about everyone in his *klouze.*

On *erev* Yom Kippur, grandfathers placed their hands on the heads of children and blessed them, *"Yesimchou Aylohim k'Ephraim w k'Menasseh"* ("May you, with God's help, be like Ephraim and Manasseh").

Old quarrels were forgotten and forgiven. People begged each other for forgiveness. How could one ask for forgiveness for himself if he didn't forgive others their offenses?

After *farfasten,* having consumed an opulent supper which should keep one full for the next twenty-four hours, the father put on the *kittl* and the family left for the *klouze*, the *beth hamidrash,* the synagogue, or wherever one belonged. Only girls and small children could stay at home. On the way people wished each other, whenever they met, a *chtimah tovah.* At the *klouze* the wax candle was put into the sand-filled box and was lit. Shoes were removed and the men remained in their socks. The floor had been strewn with hay with the fact in mind that when one fell *koreyim* (face down) he would not touch the bare floor.

The prayer began with the *b'daas hamokom ou b'daas hakohol* and the Kol Nidray. After the prayers only the women and boys went home, and the Chassidim remained at the synagogue overnight, studying Torah.

On Yom Kippur everybody—men, women, and boys—spent the entire day in the synagogue with only two short interruptions, after *laynen* (reading the Torah) and before *minchah* (the afternoon prayer) to catch outside a little fresh air. Everybody, including boys over thirteen, fasted. Younger boys fasted as long as they could. They showed their tongues to each other as proof that they were still fasting, in which case their tongues had to be white. Fasting was very tough for some people, and with the day passing slowly, they became very weak. In order not to fall asleep and to remain attentive, liquid ammonia was sniffed from a small bottle, or a pinch of snuff was taken from a silver box. A sick person was forbidden to fast if a doctor disapproved. It would be a sin not to obey the doctor's advice.

After *maariv*, with the blowing of the *shofar* and repeating seven times, *"L'shanah habaah b'Yerushalayim,"* the women hurried home to prepare the *offasten*, the breaking of the fast (with coffee and a piece of cake) before serving supper. The men remained at the *klouze* and gathered outside for *mechadesh zaan* the *levouneh*. After thanking God for ushering in a new month and praying for a good new one, they left for home, wishing each other *"Ihr zolt zych houben oysgebayten a chsima toyve"*—that their prayers should be accepted and that they should be inscribed with good marks.

Sukkoth. Immediately after Yom Kippur hammering was heard all over the shtetl as the construction of *sukkahs* began. Every household, or two neighbors jointly, as well as each *klouze* and the synagogue in the shtetl built their own *sukkah*. The building of a *sukkah* didn't in most cases, require any skill or hard work. From year to year, the walls of the *sukkah*, which consisted of boards nailed together, were stored behind the house. If a wall of the house could be used for the *sukkah*, only three other walls were needed. If not, then there were four walls to be put together and a room was ready. On top of the walls, laths were laid out crisscross. Some houses had closed-in verandahs from which the roof could be lifted, leaving an open ceiling which was already lathed. For both kinds of *sukkahs* only *skhakh* was needed. The peasants knew that Sukkoth was coming and brought to the marketplace lots of reeds and corn stalks for sale.

Having laid out the *sukkah*, the chairs and tables were brought in and the children took over the job of decorating the *sukkah*. Artificial flowers, garlands, and papier-maché lanterns were hung from the ceiling. Red apples and small decorative melons were also part of the job of decorating.

The *etrog* (citrus fruit) and the *loulav*, consisting of the palm branch, the myrtle, and the willow was bought. To buy an *etrog*, which had to be imported from Genoa, Corfu, or Morocco, one had to be an expert. The main problem was to choose one without any blemish, *pgam*. The price varied a great deal, according to the quality of the fruit and whether it had a good *pitom*. Each congregation and nearly every *chussid* bought an *etrog* and a *loulav*. The *etrog* was kept in a silver box padded with cotton or wool. It was taken out carefully every day during the holiday, with the exception of the Sabbath, to make a *bruche* (say a blessing). The families who didn't have their own *etrog* had one brought home by the *shames* for the women to say the blessing. The male members of such a family used the congregation's *etrog* for this purpose.

No *chussid* would eat outside of the *sukkah* during the Sukkoth holidays, even if it was raining a little. The women didn't eat in the *sukkah*.

On Sukkoth an auction of honors for the coming year was held at the *klouze*. The receipts from the auction were the main source of income for the *klouze*. Other funds came from collections on the plates on *erev* Yom Kippur and also from donations pledged at various occasions. These included *misheberachs*, when one was called to the Torah on the occasion of his celebrating a *simchah*, or when there was a sickness in the family, or for having avoided injuries when in an accident, *goymel bentshen*.

The days of *chol hamoed*, the four intermediate days, were working days (*tfillin*, however, were not put on) but the Chassidim, nevertheless, used to wear *zhippitzes* and *shtraymlich* on these days.

After *chol hamoed* came Hoshanah Rabbah, the day when the sentences meted out to every individual received final approval, the *gmar* at the High Court. On this day the last plea was entered, begging for help and mercy, *hoshanah*. At the morning prayer the floor was struck five times with a bunch of willow twigs, also brought to the market by the peasants. As the leaves fell from the twigs, so may our sins fall from us.

The last two days of Sukkoth are Shmini Atzeret and Simchat Torah. On Shmini Atzeret, a prayer for rain, *birchat geshem*, for a good crop in Eretz Yisroel during the winter season, was introduced in the *mussaf* prayer and repeated daily until the first day of Passover. This again shows how attached the Jews felt to our

ancient land. On the eve of Simchat Torah, already on the afternoon of Shmini Atzeret, the Chassidim returned to the *klouze*.
Since these were the most joyful days in the year, drinking,
dancing, and singing began, and the gaiety was carried on until
late in the evening. Children came to the *klouze* with paper flags
on tiny flagstaffs, with red apples in which candles were inserted.
All Torahs were taken out of the *aron hakodesh*, into which a
burning candle was placed, and the *hakafoth* procession began.
Everyone was honored with carrying and dancing with a Torah.
Of course, the sequence of being called to take up a Torah had
previously been auctioned off. For the first rounds more generous
pledges were received. Only the last rounds of the *hakafoth* were
offered free. Regardless, everybody present received a *hakafah*
whether it was paid for or not.

On Simchat Torah, the completion of the yearly cycle of the
weekly Torah readings was celebrated. Everyone, without exception, was called to the reading of the Torah, but boys under
thirteen years of age could be called as a group. Boys over thirteen
were lent a *talles* by the father, but the younger ones stayed at the
Torah under one *talles*. The concluding portion of the Torah was
read and the one who was called to this reading was the *chatan
Torah*. As the Torah scrolls were rolled back the reading started
from the beginning, and the one honored with the call for the
reading of this portion was the *chatan Brayshit*.

The remaining *etrogim*, which had not been sold before Sukkoth, were bought for the making of preserves, which were excellent. Besides, the fall was the time for making all kinds of preserves. Since the shtetl and the surrounding villages had an
abundance of every kind of good fruit, the housewives made a lot
of plum jam, *powidle*, and many other kinds of preserves and
jams. A housewife, when asked why she made all these preserves,
used to say "*M'soll nysht b'darfen*" ("Ready if needed, but better
not to be needed"). Preserves and various juices made from fruit
were offered as a medicine at *bikkur cholim* (visiting a sick
person), so it was better not to have to use them.

Chanukah. As soon as Sukkoth was over, provisions were
made against the winter. Produce and staple food were bought in
larger quantities, such as potatoes, cabbage, carrots, cucumbers
for pickling, and apples and pears which would not ripen until
late in the winter. Also, wood was piled up for heating and
cooking purposes during the winter.

Right after Sukkoth with an eye to the future, and thinking about the coming Pesach, when a lot of fat was needed, geese were purchased, put into cages, and fed very well in order to have them fattened at the time of Chanukah. When Chanukah arrived, the geese were slaughtered and plucked, then skinned. From the skin, fat was melted down and put aside, locked in special containers which were not to be touched until Pesach. The meat and the *greaves* were gradually consumed, the latter was used mostly for making *vareniki*, dough stuffed with mashed potatoes, fried onions, and *greaves*, and then cooked. Of course, *latkes* were also eaten.

During the long winter evenings goose-feathers were plucked from the quills, and new pillows and eiderdown were added to the daughter's trousseau.

The eight days of Chanukah were, with the exception of the Sabbath, working days, and at the same time a kind of feast. It was an event in the history of the Jewish people, elevated to a religious tradition.

After the victory of the Hasmoneans over the Greco-Syrians who desecrated our Holy Temple in Jerusalem, only a small bottle of sacred oil was found which should have lasted for not longer than one day. Miraculously it lasted for eight days, hence the tradition of the lighting of candles during the eight days of Chanukah, beginning with one candle on the first day, and adding one candle on each consecutive day. The candles were lit in menorahs, some of which were beautiful works of art. They were made from silver or brass and kept in the family from generation to generation. Poor people who didn't have such menorahs used self-made ones. Four large potatoes were each sliced lengthwise. In each of the halves a cavity was scraped out and filled with oil. Cotton rolled into a wick was put into the oil, with one end sticking out, and the menorah was ready.

Children traditionally received gifts of some change, *chanukah gelt*. There was no *cheder*. Self-made cards (*quittlich*) were played. Older children used to cast *draydlach* by splitting a thick wooden rod lengthwise and carving out on each side the form of one half of the *draydl*. Then, both halves were put together, leaving one end, for pouring in the melted lead, open. The lead was cooled, and the *draydl* was ready. It showed on each of its four sides the letters, *nun, gimmel, hay, shein*, meaning *Ness gadol, hayah sham* ("a big miracle happened there").

Christmas and Chanukah often fell at the same time. Jews used to pass their evenings in seclusion behind closed shutters in order not to be subjected to excesses from drunken carolers. Although the Jews wanted only to be left alone, most of the carolers had the temerity to knock at the Jewish doors, and when allowed in performed anti-Semitic plays mocking Jews. They brought in the crèche and demanded, for their carol singing, vodka and money, which they received as a form of ransom, so that they could be gotten rid of.

Tu B'Shvat. The fifteenth day of the month of Shvat, a month before Purim, is known as the "New Year for Trees." It celebrates the day in *Eretz Yisroel* when the orchards were cleaned after winter in preparation for spring and new trees planted. On this day all kinds of fruit were eaten, especially those from *Eretz Yisroel.* Children were given bags containing raisins, almonds, nuts, and various kinds of dried fruits. Children were also free from *cheder.* Although a working day, it was nevertheless considered to be a holiday.

Purim. Purim is a day of joyous celebration, but not a religious holiday. It is a workday, but the Chassidim used to put on *shtraymlech* and *zhipitzes,* and refrained from work. The saying was, *Kadukhes is nisht a krenk, un Purim is kayn Yomtov nisht* ("High fever is not a sickness, and Purim is not a holiday").

Purim celebrates the events in ancient Persia when the Jewish Queen Esther, under the guidance of her uncle, Mordechai, saved the Jewish people from annihilation when evil was decreed by Haman, Prime Minister of the kingdom, but the King reversed the decree, and Haman, together with his sons, was hanged instead of Mordechai.

On the eve of Purim and on the morning of Purim, the *Megillath Esther,* the Book of Esther, was read in the synagogue and *klouze* from a scroll. Kids had fun using their noisemakers, the *gragors,* whenever the name of Haman or his sons were mentioned during the reading of the *Megilla.* Women seldom went to the *shul* for this occasion. The *shames,* however, went to their homes with the scroll and read the *Megilla* for them. One might mention that none of them understood a word of what was being read.

Days prior to Purim the women were busy baking a lot of goodies, cakes, cookies, pastries, and so forth. According to an old established tradition, people sent each other sweets as a gift, the so-called *shlachmoones*. The size of the gift indicated how highly in esteem the recipient of the gift was held by the sender. *Hamentashen*, a cookie in the form of a triangle, stuffed with poppy seed, plum jam, or nuts and honey, was a must.

Purim was a day of giving *tsdakkah*. The man of the house was at home all day, sitting behind a table on which change was set. Whoever came in received a suitable donation. Beggars ran from house to house. There were also respectable men who collected donations for some worthy purpose, and they were always given an adequate amount of money.

In the evening the *seudath* Purim was held and the revelry began. Purim *shpielers* arrived, playing the story of Esther and Haman, *Akaydas Yitzchak*, and the story of Joseph and his brothers. They were treated with *laykakh* and *bronfen*, and were given some change. Kids used to masquerade themselves, girls as boys and boys as girls, or as Cossacks, Arabs, and soldiers. It was a big issue if one of them was recognized. Families gathered at the house of their oldest member, and there was feasting and more drinking than usual. Purim was one of the two days in the year when a Jew may get drunk. The other one was Simchat Torah.

Fasting. Fasting, which Jews practiced, and still practice today, as a sign of repentance, mourning, or petition for God's help when in distress, should be mentioned.

Pious Jews seeking forgiveness of sins, even those committed unintentionally, fasted every Monday and Thursday. Also, after each of the two festivals, Passover and Sukkot, on Monday, Thursday, and Monday.

Fasting on Tisha b'Av and Yom Kippur has already been mentioned, and there were other fast-days during the year, such as Tsom Gedaliah on the third of Tishray, the day following Rosh Hashanah, commemorating the assassination of the governor of Judah appointed by the Babylonians; Assarah b'Teveth, the tenth of Teveth, the beginning of the siege of Jerusalem by Nebuchadnezzar; Esther Taaness, the thirteenth of Adar, the day before Purim when the Jews fasted in Shushan, praying that the catastrophe planned by Haman would be averted; the fourteenth of Nissan, fast of the *bkhor* (firstborn), on the day before Passover, commemorating the sparing of the firstborn Jewish children when the tenth plague was inflicted on the Egyptians; Shiva assar b'Tamuz, the seventeenth of Tamuz, when the walls of Jerusalem were breached before the destruction of the first, as well as of the second, Temple; and finally the fasting by the bride and the bridegroom on the day of their wedding. Fasting was also practiced if one had a bad dream.

12

Political and Social Life

THE POPULATION OF Eastern Galicia was composed of Ukrainians, Poles, and Jews. The Ukrainians, who were the overwhelming majority of the population, lived mostly in the villages, with only a small percentage in the cities. The Poles lived exclusively in the cities, with the exception of some Polish families who worked in the rural areas as administrators on the estates belonging to Polish landowners. The Jews, occupying the center of the city, the shtetl, lived as though they were on an isle surrounded by a sea of Gentiles. Only a few Jewish families lived in one or another of the neighboring villages as *kraytshmers* (innkeepers) or farmers. Some were administrators or leaseholders of estates, and often also owners of estates.

In Galicia, there were no restrictions against the Poles. Moreover, although a minority in East Galicia, the Poles were the actual rulers of the land. They occupied nearly all the positions in the governing bodies at all levels, except those of the local government in the villages which remained in Ukrainian hands. Even here the decision maker was the Polish landowner on whom the peasantry was entirely dependent. Galicia was ruled by a *Sejm* (governorship) in Lwów, the Governor usually being a Pole.

In the Austrian Parliament in Vienna, nearly one-fifth of the total of the deputies were Poles who were organized in the *Kolo Polskie* (the Polish Club) and so were in a position to obtain from Austria the widest possible autonomy for Galicia.

The political activities of the Poles in our city were concentrated in two organizations, the T.S.L. *(Towarzystwo Szkoly Ludowej)*, the Society for Education, to which quite a few Jews belonged, and the *Sokól* (the Falcon), an exclusive club to which Jews were not admitted except for the two or three assimilators who were, anyhow, living beyond the pale of the Jewish society.

The first mentioned organization, the T.S.L., was devoted to the promotion of Polish culture and history by way of lectures and festivities arranged on the anniversaries of special events in the history of Poland.

The second organization, the *Sokól*, functioned formally as a gymnastic club. The club was located in a fine building, surrounded by a beautiful park with tennis courts, and equipped with its own generating station for electricity. It was built in part with government subsidies from taxpayers' money and in part from private donations. The fund raisers didn't hesitate to solicit money from Jews. The building had a well equipped gym hall and a large auditorium. As a rule the auditorium was never rented to Jews. The club members, when at the club or on other occasions, for example, parading through the streets of the city, wore special uniforms. They went through special military training, as was the case in almost every city in Galicia, and later formed the nucleus of the Polish Legions fighting during the First World War under Pilsudski against the Russians.

In many other cities in Galicia, the Polish workers were organized in a socialist party, the P.P.S., (the Polish Socialist Party). Our city had no noteworthy industry and no need for such an organization.

The Ukrainians, the majority of the population in East Galicia, felt frustrated and embittered for not sharing in the governing of the land and for being treated as second class citizens. They were organized in many political parties, all of which tried to shake loose from the influence and burden of the Polish rulers.

There was the *Sicz* (pronounced Sitsh), an organization named after the Cossacks in the Eastern Ukraine with whom Chmielnicki started his march on Poland in 1648. Their aim was the separation of each part of the Ukraine, the eastern part from Russia and the western from Austria which was ruled by Poles, and uniting these two parts in one independent state, the *Samostiyna Ukraina* (an independent Ukraine).

There were the *Russophiles* (friends of Russia), whose aim was to sever East Galicia (the Western Ukraine) from Austria and to unite it with the East Ukraine under the reign of the Russian Czar. They feared that it would be impossible to launch a simultaneous uprising against Russia and Austria and considered it better for the Ukrainians to be under the Russian than under the Austrian oligarchy where the Poles were the factual rulers. Both these parties put their members through rigorous military training.

There was still another Ukrainian organization, the *Slavophiles*, whose dream was the achieving of an empire of Slavs united in one federation and composed of Russians, Ukrainians, Bulgars, Serbs, Bosnians, and Croats.

After World War I such a mini-state of Slavs, Yugoslavia (*youg* meaning south), was created to which some Slavic nations, except Russia, the Ukraine, and Bulgaria, belonged.

The aim of all the Ukrainian parties was to free themselves from the Polish hegemony. They asked for adequate representation in the *Sejm* (the Governorship in Lwów) and for better education for Ukrainians.

The Ukrainian language, for example, was taught only up to the fourth grade in public schools, whereas the Polish language was the dominant one. In the high school, in our city the Polish, German, and French languages were obligatory subjects, whereas the Ukrainian language could be taken only on a voluntary basis as was English. The only university in East Galicia, in Lwów, was a Polish one. The struggle to also have a Ukrainian university in Lwów culminated in the assassination of the *Namiestnik* (the governor of Galicia), the Polish Graf Potocki, by a Ukrainian student named Siczinski.

Now, about the Jews:

At the turn of the nineteenth century and the beginning of the twentieth century there was no organized political activity in the shtetl. The Jewish population was composed of an overwhelming majority of Chassidim, adherents of different "courts," and a few *maskilim*. There were *talmiday chachumim* (scholars for whom everything beyond their studies was *hayvel havoolim*, meaningless, nothing but empty talk). The world beyond their studies didn't interest them at all. There were also simple people immersed in their businesses and nothing else. Then came the so-called *am haaratsim*, the simple, uneducated people, who were usually poor and hard working, and whose only worries were how to make a few cents. There were also other groups, such as socialists; the tailors', shoemakers', and other artisans' apprentices. The intelligentsia were split, with a few assimilators calling themselves "Poles of the Mosaic faith," and the remainder being Zionists. There were also individuals with no convictions whatsoever, the *Moshkes.*

Most of the Polish landowners had "their Jew"—a Jack of all trades. The Pole called the Jew, regardless of his name, "Moshko," hence they were nicknamed *Moshkes.* They usually treated the *Moshkes* with contempt and made fun of them. But the want was terrifying, and *woos teit men nisht far parnusse* ("to make a living one has to suffer"). So, the Jew when humiliated could only grin. For a small favor some sold themselves to the devil, siding always with the authorities even on issues detrimental to the interest of the Jews, for example, voting and campaigning for anti-Semitic candidates against a Jew.

In the shtetl everyone was busy with his own way of making *parnusse* (a living) and didn't, wouldn't, or rather couldn't care less if there existed a world beyond the marketplace or the store. The big question was whether or not a Jew should take part in politics at all. The Poles were the rulers of the land, and acting against them would be considered a *mored b'malchoos* (revolt against the crown). It was no wonder, then, that life in the shtetl was sleepy, with little opportunity for entertainment.

From time to time, maybe twice a year, a tight-rope walker came to the city to show off his acrobatics. The whole population of the city filled the marketplace, usually on a Sunday, to watch, for a few *kraytzer* (the equivalent of a cent), the artist walking and balancing, with a pole in his hands, on a rope which was stretched tightly between the tops of two posts installed on opposite sides of the marketplace. Another attraction was when a wandering entrepreneur from as far away as Prague used to come to the city with a merry-go-round. Mothers couldn't refuse their children who wanted to mount the horse for a ride.

One could take a trip around the world without leaving the shtetl when he visited the photoplasticon which came to the shtetl for a few days. In the center of the ballroom of the hotel a big circular booth was set up. At certain intervals there were holes in the wall of the circle in which lenses were installed. For a few *kraytser* one could sit in front of a hole and watch the three-dimensional pictures with all the wonders of the world: people from different races, animals, huge buildings and even the Kaiser in his palace. The pictures were moved by turning a manual crank.

People who were music lovers had the opportunity to listen to the newest songs, that is, the newest in the shtetl, although they were already forgotten elsewhere. In the hotel, a family of singers, father, mother, and their talented offspring, usually ranging in ages from six to sixteen, presented their talents and played old scratched records (his master's voice) on a phonograph, a novelty at that time in the shtetl.

Wandering organ grinders and Yiddish folksingers were often visitors to the shtetl. Their songs and plays were sentimental and sad, and unlike the singers with the phonograph, touched the people, especially the womenfolk. They described the details about the Dreyfus affair, about the terrible cruelties during the pogrom in Kishinev, and lamented the fate of the poor people. Also, how the rich man eats, everyday, the best roast, whereas the poor only know *suntig bulbes, muntig bulbes, dinstig bulbes, mitwoch bulbes, donershtic bulbes, fraaytik bulbes oon och unway Shabbes a shtik broyd oon a shwants foon a herring* ("Sunday, potatoes, Monday, potatoes, . . . and so on, and on Saturday, a slice of bread and a tail of a herring").

One of the common events was the showing of a big brown bear by a *Hutzul* (a mountaineer from the neighboring Carpathian Mountains). This tame animal was kept on a chain. The bear danced to the music of the flute played by his master. The children were even allowed to touch the bear.

A Yiddish theatrical group only rarely came to the shtetl because there were no facilities available in which to present a good play. The only adequate space, which belonged to the Polish Sokól club, wouldn't be rented to Jews.

The shtetl considered it a great honor when Sholem Rabinowicz (Sholem Aleychem) visited it on his way to Czernowitz and everybody could hear the writer himself read some of his works.

To see a good play one had to go to Czernowitz, where an excellent German theater with good actors, some of them visiting from Vienna, presented a repertoire of the best plays. It was only a forty-five minute ride from the shtetl to Czernowitz by bicycle. Usually a group of five or six students mounted their bicycles in the late afternoon on Saturdays and went for the forty-five-minute ride. However, in order to hide the fact that they were riding their bicycles such a short time before the Sabbath was over, the bicycles were taken on Friday to the house of a non-Jewish colleague, who lived outside the city on the way to Czernowitz. The same thing occurred when a Yiddish theater presented there a play which happened quite often.

Once a wandering circus tried its luck in the hope of making some money. A large tent was built on a meadow outside the city. Posters with pictures of the artists and the animals were posted all around the city. A few days before the première, the elephants, bears, ponies, and monkeys were paraded through the streets of the city. All the children of the city accompanied the procession of the animals through the streets, and on their way back to the tent. Even the *rebbes* allowed their students to go to have a look at the animals, the wonders of the *Riboyneh shel oylom* (the Creator of the world). Alas, on the opening day and also on the next two evenings, nobody showed up to buy a ticket. The children were told that they had already seen the animals and that it might be too dangerous to be locked up with them in the tent. And so the big tent remained empty except for a few urchins who gained entry by crawling in under the canvas. The owner of the circus decided to leave the city.

In order not to compete with each other when supplying fodder for the animals and whatever else the circus needed, the *Luftmenshen*, or agents, had formed a *yad achad*, or cartel, upon the arrival of the circus. When they heard about the decision of the circus owner to leave the city empty-handed, they came to the conclusion that a way must be found to make some profits by keeping the circus in the city for at least one more day. Indeed they worked out a plan which worked very well.

They approached the owner of the circus with a proposal that he stay in the city for one more day. All three of them guaranteed, with all the properties they possessed(!), a complete success. The proceeds from the evening were to be divided equally among the four of them. The owner of the circus had nothing to lose and could only stand to gain. No alterations to the circus tent were required. Only a small booth with an entrance and exit would be placed a few steps inside, behind the entrance to the tent, which was to be kept in darkness. The entrance price of a ticket was to be cut in half. All agreed, and new posters were distributed announcing that on the final day a spectacle at the circus, something which had never before been shown, would be presented. Nobody should lose this once-in-a-lifetime opportunity to witness a spectacle about which they would talk for generations to come.

Before the opening hour of this last performance a large group of curious onlookers gathered at the entrance to the circus. The barker urged the gapers to go in and find out for themselves what a surprise awaited them. When nobody responded, he announced that he would admit one man, but only one, at no charge so that he could tell the rest of the people whether or not it was worthwhile. One man stepped forward and volunteered. When he was let into the dark tent, he was guided to the booth where a strong man was waiting. As soon as the volunteer entered the booth, he was slapped, first on the right side of his face, then on the left. Before he was aware of what had happened he was kicked out with the advice, "Go and tell your friends how stupid you were to enter the tent, but it would be better if you let them have the same surprise." When he left the tent everybody asked him how it had been and he said that it was a real surprise. So all present went through the booth, and all were ashamed, but wanting the same thing to happen to the others did not warn them of the surprise. When the circus left, the wives of our agents had enough for *Shabbes tsu machen,* to prepare everything for Sabbath.

Finally, one event which should not be forgotten and should be mentioned is the following: A teacher in Cracow had made a replica of the *Beth Hamikdash* (Holy Temple) retaining all the forms, details, and proportions of the original. He traveled with it from shtetl to shtetl until he came to ours. Nobody missed the occasion to admire the masterly work. Even elderly Chassidim came to the display looking for some point to criticize, but finding none, commended the artist, who had worked on this model for five years.

After *maariv* (the evening prayer), the men usually remained in the *beth hamedresh* (synagogue) and the many *klouze*s (the Chassidic places of prayer) for a talk. There the Chassidim told and retold the miracles which had been performed by their rebbes and bragged about the splendor displayed at the court of the rebbe.

Other groups discussed wars which were going on in different corners of the world at that time, or wars which had taken place not so long before. They criticized the commanding generals of one or the other side as if they knew better what this or that general should have done. The Boer War in South Africa, the wars in the Balkans against the Turks, and, of course, the annexation of Bosnia and Herzegovina by Austria were discussed in every detail.

The most heated debates, however, were ventilated when the war of 1905 between Russia and Japan was brought up. Every detail was analyzed and digested, and everyone was familiar with the names of the generals, the ships involved, and the ports which were attacked. Rejoicing was in evidence whenever the Russians took a beating. The debates always ended by expressing the hope that *Fonyeh* (the nickname used by the Jews in Galicia for Russia) would have a *mapooleh shlayma* (crushing defeat).

The terrible pogrom in Kishinev, took place in 1903 after a blood-libel. Fifty Jews were killed and wounded, bellies of pregnant women were cut open and the unborn babies thrown into the streets. All this was discussed in horror and awe, not only in the after evening-prayer hours in the *shtiblech*, but in every home as well. Bialik's "City of Slaughter" was read with ardent devotion, the same as was the *Aychoo yoshwoo* (Jeremiah's Lamentations) on Tisha b'Av, when we mourn the destruction of the Holy Temple in Jerusalem.

Another subject much talked was the Dreyfus affair. Dreyfus, a young, very able officer on the French General Staff, was charged with treason, having allegedly sold some French military secrets to the Germans. In fact, another officer, Count Esterhazy, of Hungarian origin, was the one who passed the military secrets to the Germans. On the basis of fake documents Dreyfus was accused of having carried out the act of treason. Dreyfus maintained that he was innocent and that the charges against him were made up to cover up the crime of the real culprit. But anti-Semitism prevailed over justice. Dreyfus was sacrificed on the altar of anti-Semitism; he was stripped publicly of his rank as an officer and sentenced to life imprisonment on Devil's Island in French Guiana, where he languished for more than four years. Dreyfus had nothing in common with the Jews of the shtetl except for the fact that he was Jewish. The shtetl was convinced of his innocence and that he was the victim of an anti-Semitic plot, the waves of which, if successful, could have repercussions on Jews all over Europe. When Dreyfus was acquitted in 1906, the Jews felt that a load had been taken off their hearts. People who defended Dreyfus and helped to prove his innocence, such as Clemenceau and especially Emile Zola, who attacked the French injustice with his publication of *J'accuse*, were revered in the shtetl as though they were saints.

Alfred Dreyfus, a French army captain, spent four years on Devil's Island after being falsely convicted of spying for Germany, here shown at his reinstatement.

There was not much of entertainment but there was no lack of *tsores* (distress) for our Jews to grieve over. The Beilis case attracted much attention. Mendel Beilis, a poor Jew, was arrested in Kiev in 1911 and charged with having killed a Christian boy for Jewish ritual purposes. In the tradition of the Middle Ages, Jewry as a whole was placed in the prisoner's dock. It was well known that a Russian was the murderer and that the accusations against Beilis were unfounded, that the crown witness, Tsheberiak, a receiver of stolen goods, herself a thief, had been instructed by the *pops* (Russian priests) as to what lies she should tell on the witness stand. Jews were therefore afraid that the court in Kiev would follow the dictate given by the anti-Semites from the highest level in Petersburg, the reigning hierarchy, and that a guilty verdict would follow. The experts, Russian priests, explained to the jury how the Jews murdered Christians for ritual purposes and asserted that they were convinced that the boy had been murdered as prescribed by the Jewish religion.

In the shtetl, the non-Jewish population as well as the Jews followed the news from the court proceedings in Kiev. For the Jews the only question was what new lies could be brought up at the hearings. The non-Jewish community was split concerning the innocence or the guilt of Beilis. The majority of the Christians believed that the accusations were false, but there were some who were ready to believe that what the priests said was true.

One day, when a class of students on a *majówka* (a school outing, usually held in the month of May) was sitting around a bonfire in a clearing in a forest which was not far from our city, two Christian students were talking about the Beilis trial. One asserted that the whole thing was built on a false accusation and that his parents had discussed the matter with the Polish parish priest, who understood Hebrew. They were told that the whole thing in Kiev was a trumped-up story. He was convinced that Jews didn't use blood in the making of matzos. The other boy said that he was not so sure and that he awaited the outcome of the trial.

The relationship between Jewish and non-Jewish students in our school was a friendly one. Jews and non-Jews visited each other's homes and very often did their homework together. On Pesach the Jewish students gave their non-Jewish colleagues some matzo and received from them pisanki (colored eggs). At Christmas time the non-Jewish students treated their Jewish colleagues to *kutyiah* (a traditional meal) made from boiled wheat with honey, nuts, and poppy seeds.

The teacher, an ardent anti-Semite who had been listening to the talk of these two students about the Beilis trial, decided to conduct an investigation of his own. With an insidious grin he turned to a Jewish student and said, "You are an excellent student in my class and you know that I like you very much. I am sure that you also do very well in your studies with the rebbe at your synagogue and that you, therefore, know all the Jewish religious rituals. Tell me then, please, is there much blood needed for matzos?" The student, a sixteen-year-old boy, blushed dark red and after a while, when he found his composure replied "*Panie Profesorze* [Mister Professor, Sir], you know very well that the accusation of using human blood for ritual purposes was first invented against the early Christians and that later these libels took a full turn and through the centuries were leveled by anti-Semites against Jews. You certainly know, also, that some Popes and cardinals condemned the libel, so why are you asking such questions? Knowing the Jewish ritual I must tell you that Jews are forbidden to eat any blood. Before meat can be consumed it must be drained of any blood it contains; it must be soaked, salted, and rinsed in order to drain any blood that remains after the slaughter. Jews don't make *krwawe kiszki* [sausages stuffed with blood and *kasha*—buckwheat]. Two years ago the corpse of a Christian peasant was found in this forest where we are now sitting. He was murdered by his own brother. Only five years ago in a village just 4 kilometers from this city the Jewish innkeeper was hacked to death with an axe by his Christian neighbor, and how many Jews were murdered only nine years before by Christians during the pogrom in Kishiniev? No, Jews don't perpetrate murder, not for matzos, and not for any other reason. No, Jews don't murder as Christians do. Why, then are you playing the role of a Sherlock Holmes with your tricky questions? There is no lack of anti-Semites in Kiev." This said, the student left for home, not waiting for an answer.

The next day the student was brought before the principal and asked to retract his remarks made in a state of undue irritation slandering Christians before the class. The student said that he had been provoked by the professor, who had showed his anti-Semitic feelings not only on this but on many other occasions. It was true that he had been angry, but what he said was the truth, and the truth could not be wiped out by simply retracting what had been said. At the conference of the board of professors the student was suspended from the school. Although he was later reinstated, his parents took him out of this school and sent him to school in another city.

How happy the Jews were when, in 1913, the jury in Kiev reached a verdict of not guilty for lack of evidence.

As we see, the Jews of our shtetl were concerned first and foremost with events appertaining to *klal Yisroel* (the Jews as a whole). The Chassidim, led by the rebbes, were opposed to any kind of political activities. On the other hand, the *maskilim*, adherents of the *Haskala* (derived from *saychel*, meaning "intellect") movement, the Enlightenment, only a few in our shtetl floating in a sea of Chassidim, kept to themselves and didn't engage in political activity. But in other cities of Galicia the *maskilim* were very active in politics.

In Western Europe the *maskilim* believed that to be treated as equal citizens Jews should adapt to the manners of non-Jews. After the pogroms in Russia and the continuation of anti-Semitism, even against the enlightened Jews, the *maskilim* realized that their hope to attain civil rights through emancipation was an illusion. They then became convinced that the solution of the Jewish problem was the establishment of a Jewish national home in Palestine and not by assimilation.

Our shtetl had only a small number of *maskilim*, but some of them were highly educated, great scholars, and talmudic sages with encyclopedic brains. On the shelves of the study of a *maskil* one could find not only the *Bible*, the *Zohar*, the Talmud, and many other Jewish books, but also the *Brockhaus Lexikon* (encyclopedia), *Brahms Tierleben* (*The Life of Animals*, by Brahms), the works of Schiller, Goethe, Nordau, Ibsen, Heine, Peretz, Bialik, even Renan and Spinoza. They subscribed to Hebrew, German and Yiddish newspapers, the *Hazefira*, the *Neue Freie Presse*, where Herzl was a correspondent, the *Lemberger Tugblat*, and others.

The *maskilim* studied languages, astronomy, and mathematics. Whenever a student from our high school working on an assignment had a problem in mathematics which he couldn't solve, he went to Reb Leybush, who showed him a simple way in which to solve the problem.

Many cities in Galicia had their active Zionist organization from the beginning of the movement. Delegates were sent from these cities to the first and to all subsequent Zionist congresses. The Zionist organization in our shtetl, however, was anemic and dormant due to the opposition of the Chassidim. They represented the majority and held the upper hand. Herzl's *Der Judenstaat* (*The Jewish State*), for example, was circulated secretly from hand to hand. The Chassidim asserted that the Zionists were following the path of the *maskilim*, and with all the doctors and the *daitshen* (germanized Jews) at the helm of the organization were paving the way to assimilation and were a threat to Judaism. Zionists in our shtetl had to go underground with their activities. The youth, boys and girls, had to hide the fact that they were interested in Zionism. They couldn't keep any Zionist literature at home, for it was anathema to their Chassidic parents.

In order to learn what was going on in the movement and to study Zionist literature, boys and girls met secretly in a forest not far from the city, usually on Saturday afternoons. There, the geography of Palestine and Jewish history were studied, and plans were made on how to join a *hachsharah* (a collective farm, preparing for *aliyah*—going to Palestine).

Among the girls attending the secret meetings was the daughter of a *shoychet* (ritual slaughterer). A neighbor of the *shoychet*, who accidentally heard something about girls meeting boys outside of the city, and that one of the girls was the *shoychet's* daughter, said to the *shoychetke* (the *shoychet's* wife), who was her friend, "Watch your Surtsiele—*Sken foon daym kayn gits nisht aroyskoomen* [it might end up badly]." The *shoychetke*, frightened to death, started to check her daughter's underwear every month. After a few months, however, she lost track of the counting and mistakenly assumed that the so anxiously awaited period was a few days overdue. When the daughter came home in the evening from the store where she was working as a salesgirl the mother didn't say anything to her. However, when the *shoychet* came from the *klouze* after *maariv* she called him into the kitchen, broke into a terrible cry, and told him what had happened.

Upon hearing this, the *shoychet* grabbed a stick and without asking any questions yelled, "I will kill her and her *mamser* [bastard]." He began to mercilessly beat his daughter, who couldn't understand what was happening. The *shoychetke* was crying all this time, encouraging her husband by saying, "*Git azoy. Ich wel zi sammen*" ("That's right. I will poison her"). Suddenly the *shoychet* looked down to the floor where his daughter was lying in a pool of blood. He then realized what he had done. He turned to his wife and started to beat her with all his strength yelling, "*Nadir for a bilbel of a kusherer yiddisher tochter*" ("That's for your libeling a good Jewish girl"), and the *shoychetke* pleaded, "*Shoyn genig, ekh hob mikh toye gewayn*" ("Enough, enough! I made a mistake!"). The next day in the wee hours the girl left home for the Jewish agricultural farm in Slobódka Leśna, founded and funded by the Baron Hirsch Foundation. There she went through the *hachsharah* (preparation for *aliyah*) and not long afterwards went up to *Eretz Yisroel*. Her parents came to learn about her whereabouts only after they received a letter from her from Jaffa.

As a result of the pogroms in Russia at the end of the nineteenth century and in the years 1903 and 1905, Jews began to flee that country in masses.

After crossing the river Dniestr, which at some points formed the border between Austria and Russia, the refugees were only a few kilometers from our shtetl. So it was the first stop in their wandering. The homeless brethren were met with hospitality. A committee was formed with the aim of extending a helping hand to the refugees, securing jobs and a roof over their heads. Some of the refugees decided to stay and make their home in the shtetl. Others moved on to other cities. The majority, however, left after a short time for America.

The journey to America at that time was, relatively speaking, not a difficult undertaking. The crossing of the border from Austria to Germany, passport or not, was not a big problem. Whoever had enough money made his way straight to a port in Germany and then had only to pay for the passage to America. Those who did not have the means to pay for their passage worked in Germany at different places on the way to a port, saving money. With the help of the local Jewish communities, who looked askance at the *Ostjuden* (Jews from the East) and didn't want to see them settled in Germany, they were able to pay for the passage to America. Others, having reached a port city without money for the ship's ticket, hired themselves as hands on the ship, doing the most dirty job, and thus they were able to see their dream of reaching the shores of America fulfilled.

The Russian Jewish newcomers were a blessing to our shtetl. Most of them were first-class artisans, and the ones who decided to stay in the shtetl were in no time able to open their own shops. In general, the refugees were very well educated people who could learn a *blat gemara* (understand the Talmud). They also knew foreign languages and possessed secular knowledge. The intelligentsia, mostly students, installed themselves as Hebrew teachers, and many married daughters of respectable families in the shtetl.

From the political point of view they were a mixture of *maskilim*, Zionists, socialists, and even some revolutionaries. The latter didn't observe any religious rules but had to keep their behavior secret because they knew that otherwise their stay in the shtetl wouldn't be a long one. They didn't even fast on Yom Kippur, but because they lived with Jewish families there was no way to get any food on this day. Therefore, on Yom Kippur they went for lunch at the Christian butcher-delicatessen shop which was located far away from the Jewish sector of the city. They could be sure that no Jew would see them going there because every Jew was at the synagogue. At the restaurant they ate *chazer* (pork). Some time later the butcher asked a Jew to tell him what day of the year it was that Jews were allowed to eat pork. And so the secret of these *trefniakes* (those who didn't care for *kasruth*) became known and an uproar ensued in the shtetl. The *parnassim* (the board of the Jewish community organization) supplied the Polish authority with a list of the unwanted immigrants, insisting that all the revolutionaries be ordered out of the shtetl. To speed things up the Jewish community supplied the few men with money and tickets, and the revolutionaries left for America.

When an elderly *chussid* asked for and received an explanation of what being a revolutionary meant he said: "A *pushit narishkayt* [it's simply stupid] to seek to overthrow the Kaiser, who resides in his castle behind seven locks and has a *machne of meshorsim* [troop of servants] at his disposition. What most amazes me is that they want to make Ivan for a *pan* [master] instead of Froim Josel [Kaiser Franz Josef]."

With help from the Zionists among the Russian immigrants, supported by the *maskilim*, new vitality was brought into the political life of the shtetl, and after only a year or two a Zionist organization was formed. A flat consisting of a few rooms was rented and a library was installed.

High school students became a strong factor in the organization. Although not allowed to take part in any political activities, and in spite of the fact that students were compelled to wear special uniforms and so were recognizable when attending political meetings, they managed to attend lectures delivered mostly by out-of-town lecturers.

People were encouraged to drop in at the local organization for a talk or to read a newspaper, a book, or to play chess or dominos, and so on. Every Saturday night lectures were given. On other days, courses in Hebrew were introduced, and the geography and the history of *Eretz Yisroel* were taught.

The *shekel* (membership fee) was sold, and money for *Keren Kayemet l'Yisrael* was collected at all possible occasions, such as engagements, weddings, *brith milahs*, and other festivities. Stamps and telegrams for conveying congratulations were sold, garden parties with lotteries were held, and *Keren Kayemet* boxes were placed in many households and businesses, where they were kept along with *pushkes* (boxes) for *Reb Meier Bal Haness*. In many houses the youngsters kept the boxes hidden from a *chussid* father. Donations for planting trees in *Eretz Yisroel* and for inscriptions in the Golden Book (Roll of Honor kept at the *Keren Kayemet l'Yisroel* in Jerusalem) were collected. Zionist literature, which the Chassidim called *trayfe pussel* (not kosher and illegitimate) because it led to assimilation, was distributed.

The Zionists, for their part, asked the Chassidim to join ranks with them because Zionism was the ideal for which Chassidim were praying three times daily, repeating: *"V'sekhsenah aynaynoo b'showkha le Zion berakhamim"* ("May our eyes behold the return to Zion in mercy"), and pronouncing so often *"Le shanah habaah b'Yerushalayim"* ("Next year in Jerusalem"), which is the essence of Zionism.

Nevertheless, it took years for the local organization to grow strong enough to send a delegate to the Zionist Congress. The first delegate was sent from the shtetl in 1911 to Basle for the Tenth Congress.

The activities of the Zionist organization evolved and expanded, especially at the time of elections to the Parliament in Vienna. Even some younger Chassidim joined the Zionist organization.

As for the elections to the municipality, the Jews always managed to have their representatives elected, but the *Buergermeister* (mayor) was in office for many years. The election of the mayor had to be confirmed by the *Bezirkshauptmannschaft* (the administrative body of the district), and it would never approve anyone who was not put up by the Poles. Anyway, he was no anti-Semite, knew everyone in the shtetl, spoke Yiddish fluently, and even dispensed medicines to poor Jews at no charge. He was the pharmacist in the city.

Around the middle of the first decade of the twentieth century a new democratic method of voting to the Austrian Parliament was introduced. Two elections based on democratic principles were held before the First World War, one in 1907 and the other in 1911. As it was said in our shtetl, "Democracy-schmocracy, if you will not fight for your rights you will be the loser."

The fight was a really hard and hectic one in both elections, and although other cities in Galicia were able to elect a Jewish representative to the Parliament in Vienna, our shtetl lost both times. First of all, the voting lists were falsified. The authorities put all types of pressure on the Jewish voters to induce them not to vote for the candidate of the Zionist party. The rebbes asked the Chassidim to vote for the candidate favored by the authority and not by the Zionists. One shouldn't go against the will of the government but should try to achieve relief only by requesting, petitioning, and asking.

Taxes of persons known or suspected of voting for the Jewish candidate were suddenly raised, with no installment payment granted. The health department displayed vigorous activity inspecting shops, stores, and *chederim.* Some voters were called in to the authorities and were promised favors in the form of concessions and licenses if they would vote for the Polish and not the Jewish candidate.

In the election of 1907 the central Zionist Organization put up Dr. Osias Thon as a candidate in the electoral district to which the shtetl belonged. Dr. Thon was rabbi in the progressive synagogue in Cracow. He was a known Hebrew writer and a friend of Herzl. The Poles started a campaign of terror. At a meeting where Dr. Thon came to speak, a representative of the district government appeared and declared that he was closing the meeting because no permission for holding the meeting had been received. Although the meeting took place in the synagogue and permission for gatherings in the synagogue was not required, protesting his decision didn't help. His reply was: "So what, the meeting is now closed because the building is not fit to hold such a large crowd." The audience left the synagogue, but when Dr.

Thon started his speech outside of the building, gangs of hooligans appeared and started to beat up the assembled group and forced them to leave the scene. The Zionists arranged smaller meetings and went from home to home explaining how important it was to have Jewish representatives in the Parliament who would be able to fight for rights for Jews.

On election day there were gangs watching the line of voters at the polling stations. They simply pushed out of the line anyone they suspected of wanting to vote for Dr. Thon. At once a gendarme would appear, and under the pretext of disturbing the peace these people were arrested and kept locked up until the polls closed.

Inside the polling station voters were screened once again. If some of them managed to get in they were asked for identification, although no identification cards were in use. Some of them were told that they had already voted and it would be wise for them to disappear immediately if they didn't wish to be charged with the crime of attempting to vote twice. In fact, however, before the doors of the polling stations were opened a large number of ballots for the Polish candidates were thrown into the boxes, and on the voters list the names of voters who were supposed to vote for Dr. Thon were checked off as already having voted. On the other hand, the *moshkes* were led into the stations without any obstruction. Unfortunately, Dr. Thon lost the election to the Polish candidate, but other cities in Galicia succeeded in electing Jews to the Parliament in Vienna.

How could the authority know who was going to vote for Dr. Thon and who would vote for the Polish candidate? It has to be mentioned with a feeling of shame that the authorities had their informers among the Jews. It was nearly impossible to find out who the informers were in connection with the elections and also who the denunciators on other matters were. But one of them was not careful enough and exposed himself by openly agitating for the Polish candidate. He was the owner of an inn which was licensed for the sale of beer only and who had been trying unsuccessfully for years to have his license extended for the sale of alcoholic beverages. Suddenly at the time of the election he finally received his desired license. When confronted by the president of the Zionist Organization, who surprisingly asked him if a pious Jew should pay the price he paid for receiving a better license, he was taken aback, and losing his equanimity, said, "I am no *mooser* [informer], but I have a *shtib mit kinderlakh* [many children to support]."

This was not forgotten and vengeance was planned. In the evening of the next Simchas Torah, when wine was drunk in abundance at the *klouze*, a few young men innocently joined the group where the informer was sitting and started to ply him with more and more wine, later adding vodka to the wine, and it was not very long until he was drunk and unconscious. The young men then said that he needed fresh air, took him outside, and put him into a casket-like box which had been prepared for this occasion. His home was not far from the *klouze*, and the casket was put on the doorsteps to his home. On the top of the casket was placed a nicely written note which read, *"V'lamalshinim al tihyeh tikvah"* ("May the slanderers have no hope"). A pebble was then thrown against the window of the house, and one can imagine what happened when his wife found him snoring in the box. The informer was too ashamed to talk about what had happened to him and the means by which he had come home. But the lesson was not forgotten, not by this individual, nor by any other *moshke* informer.

In 1910 another problem in connection with the census-taking evolved. Austrian law didn't recognize Hebrew or Yiddish as a language. Hebrew was considered a dead language, the same as Latin. Yiddish was regarded as a jargon, kind of a corrupt dialect of the German language. Since belonging to a nationality was determined by one's mother tongue, the Jews were not recognized as a nationality by Austrian law and were not allowed to declare Hebrew or Yiddish as their mother tongue, nor Jewish as their nationality. They were forced to register other languages as their mother tongue, and those who registered Yiddish or Hebrew had their registration changed from Yiddish or Hebrew to Polish by the authority.

The Poles wanted to achieve greater autonomy from Austria for a decentralized government of Galicia. In order to prove to Vienna that Galicia was Polish they needed to present the central government in Vienna with statistics showing that the Poles were really the majority. This could have been done only by registering the Jews in Galicia at the census-taking as citizens whose mother tongue was Polish.

In a decentralized Galicia governed with great autonomy from Lwów by the Polish *Staathalter* (governor) the Poles would gain the upper hand and would even short-cut the use of the German language. The Jews, however, were against decentralization of the Austrian government, as well as against more autonomy for Galicia, fearing that they would lose any protection against the Poles they could expect from the government in Vienna.

In order not to let the Poles get away with using Jews as a tool for political aims favorable to them, high school students volunteered as enumerators in the census and we were able to register German for nearly all the Jewish population by explaining the reason for doing so, and persuading them that while Yiddish was not allowed they would commit a sin by signing false statements declaring Polish as their mother tongue, since they didn't know the Polish language and their mothers didn't know Polish either. Contrarily, Yiddish is similar to German, and therefore declaring German as their mother tongue was stating the truth.

At the next election to the Parliament in Vienna, which was held in 1911, the Jewish candidate put up by the Zionist Organization was Nathan Birnbaum. He was one of the first Zionists, a friend of Herzl, but at the time of the election he was known as an ardent Yiddishist, proclaiming Yiddish as the national language of the Jews. The Zionists chose him for the candidacy and hoped that he would be supported by the entire Jewish community. In later years Nathan Birnbaum became an adherent of Orthodoxy and somehow removed himself from political Zionism. He was known as Matatyahu Acher.

As during the election of 1907, the acts of terror repeated themselves, not only before the election but especially on election day. All the tricks which had occurred four years earlier were used again. In addition, an innovation which was invented for this election should be mentioned. At six o'clock the hands of the clock on the tower of the city hall were moved ahead by two hours to indicate that it was eight o'clock, the time when the polling station had to be closed. The crowd of voters waiting in line to vote were told that the voting time had passed and the gendarmes dispersed the voters. When protesting that it was not yet eight o'clock, they were told that the time shown on the clock on the city tower was official regardless of what other watches showed. In fact, the voting time was not over, and the people who were known as voters for the Polish candidate were let in by the rear door. No wonder then that the Polish candidate was the winner.

Still worse things happened in another city in Galicia, in Drohobycz. When voters who were waiting at the entrance of the polling station saw that only those people who it was known would be voting for the Polish candidate were permitted in, they started to push through the cordon of police. The army was called in, shots were fired at the crowd, and a heavy toll was taken in lives and injuries.

After the election a new term was coined, *Galizische Wahlen* ("Galician elections"), which was a synonym for something done by means of fraud and terror.

We lost the election again, but the Zionist organization in our shtetl came out stronger than ever, gaining more and more members.

13

The Outbreak of World War I

AFTER GERMANY SEIZED Alsace-Lorraine from France, there were no major wars in Europe during the forty-three years prior to 1914. People hoped for peace and that disputes between states would be settled by arbitration. People trusted the Hague Convention, the International Red Cross was brought into existence, and the use of *dum-dum* (soft-nosed) bullets and poison gas was outlawed, although these prohibitions were later ignored when war came.

In recognition of people who distinguished themselves in preserving peace, the Nobel Prize was established, ironically by a man who made a fortune through his invention of more deadly explosives. Esperanto, invented by Dr. Ludwig Zamenhof, a Jewish physician in Warsaw—a language which could be mastered in two to three weeks—would serve, as was the general belief, as a means for breaking the barriers of mistrust and misunderstanding between nations and would serve the cause of peace.

However, the main powers of that time in Europe were divided by serious disputes and rivalries. Each of them, although proclaiming peaceful intentions, at the same time, armed themselves under the motto: *Si vis pacem para bellum.* ("If you wish peace, prepare for war"). In the skies over Europe hung an overcast which clouded the hope for peace.

The popular belief was that the bullet that killed Archduke Franz Ferdinand on June 28, 1914 in Sarajevo, was the first shot of the war, but this incident was not the reason for the outbreak of the war. With or without the killing of the Archduke, war in

Ludwig Zamenhof (1857–1917), philologist and creator of Esperanto
Reprinted by permission of Schocken Books, Inc., from Image before my eyes by Lucjan Dobroszycki and Barbara Kirschenblatt-Gimblett. Copyright © 1977 by Schocken Books, Inc.

The Royal Library of Copenhagen Collection

Europe would have broken out. There would have been no difficulty in finding a casus belli.

The fear of a possible war weighed heavily on the minds of the Jews as the political situation deteriorated after the assassination. Solace was found in the belief that the Emperor Franz Josef needed a war like a *loch in kop* (a hole in the head). He did not want a war at his age, the best proof of which was that he left Vienna for a quiet vacation in Ischl.

During this period a group of five students, including the author, home in the shtetl for a vacation, had worked out a plan for a five-day-long excursion over the Carpathian Mountains, descending on the west side of the mountains into Hungary and returning home by train. The news of the assassination of the Crown Prince and the threat of a possible war delayed the departure. However, after the good news that Serbia had accepted the Austrian ultimatum it was decided to go ahead with the excursion as planned. No persuasion or reasoning could make us change plans. The more we were urged not to leave home, the more obstinate we became. After all, we understood better what was going on in politics, didn't we? "Even if war broke out, *woo shtayt es geshriben* [where is it said] that the Russians will come to us? Why not go to them, and how far is it to Kamenetz Podolski? Our cavalry would be there the day after the war started. Are we wiser than the Kaiser? He left for the mountains, and why shouldn't we? After all, it is already a month since the shooting in Sarajevo occurred, and the tempers have already calmed down."

We left the shtetl on July 27. Apart from a change of underwear, and some toiletries, everyone filled his knapsack with a good supply of pipe tobacco. The group as a whole had a compass, field glasses, and a detailed map of the terrain. No food or tents were needed. The *Hutzuls* (Ruthenian mountaineers), who were in the mountains for the entire summer tending their sheep in the *poloninas* (pastures) were very hospitable people, and anyone who came up to them was always welcome to find shelter in their *coliba* (hut), to sleep on fresh hay alongside the *watra* (watchfire). Whoever came to their hut was also invited to share in their meal, which consisted of *mamaliga* (corn meal cooked in salted water to a hard consistency) with *bryndza* (sheep cheese) and milk. They didn't ask for payment but were more than happy if they were rewarded with pipe tobacco, which they couldn't afford to buy.

We had a good time, hopping around in the *Czernohora* (the eastern Carpathian Mountains), climbing the Hoverla, the highest mountain in that area, enjoying the beauty of the sunrises, and the fresh air, drinking the crystal-clear water from the springs, many of them containing healing qualities. The evenings were spent with the *Hutzuls*, listening to their tales about Dobosh (a kind of Robin Hood), and the miracles performed by the *sviaty* Srulko, the Saint Israel, i.e., the *Bal Shem Tov*, whom even Dobosh revered and admired.

We enjoyed the excursion very much and were singing when we descended the mountains on the Hungarian side, heading for the village of Koeresmezoe, the railroad station on the border between Hungary and Galicia.

At the railway station, while we waited for the train, a Hungarian gendarme with a huge plume of feathers on his shako, and a rifle with a mounted bayonet, started to ask us questions. However, since he didn't know any language other than his native Hungarian, he sent a peasant for the village Jew to serve as a translator. In the meantime he ordered us to empty our pockets and lay out the contents of our packs. He was horrified when he saw the field glasses, the compass, and the map, and was convinced that he had just caught a gang of spies.

Soon a Jewish boy, about twelve years of age, with long *payes* (earlocks), arrived, and the questioning began. The gendarme wanted to know where we were coming from, what we were doing in the mountains, and so on. Then he declared that he didn't believe our story, and that we were spies whom he had caught red-handed. There was a war going on, martial law had been decreed, and he had the right to shoot us on the spot. He then started to handcuff us, binding our hands behind our backs.

The Jewish boy, sensing what was going on, ran home and soon returned with his father, an elderly Jew with a graying beard, who knew from his son of the threat uttered by the gendarme, and was frightened. He knew how stupid a man the gendarme was, and tried to convince him that what the boys had told him was true. Nothing could change the mood of the gendarme, who normally would have listened to the Jew in whose inn he received a free *schnapps* anytime he wanted. This time, no, he would not be a traitor and let these spies go. It might cost him his head. He might be better off to finish off the spies right on the spot and be sure to get his reward.

After a heated debate between the gendarme and the Jew, the gendarme finally made a concession and agreed to take the spies to the district command of the gendarmerie in Marmaros Siget.

The train was scheduled to leave in approximately thirty minutes. From the money which the gendarme took from us, he bought tickets for himself and us. When the train arrived, the stationmaster emptied a compartment for the spies and the escort, and we were on the way, in the opposite direction from home. The Jew from Koeresmezoe didn't go home but instead boarded the same train, and in Marmaros Siget followed the group, so that he would know where the gendarme had taken us.

As soon as the Jew from Koeresmezoe knew which prison we were being detained in, he ran to the office of the Jewish Community and alarmed the president, who, not losing time, called a lawyer and went with him to the office of the gendarmerie. There they didn't have to deal with a simple-minded gendarme. The officer in charge asked a few questions only, and said that the previous year he had been on the same excursion, with the difference being that he went in the opposite direction, i.e., starting on the Hungarian side and returning from the Austrian side of the Carpathians. He reprimanded the gendarme for having left his post. He ordered him to escort the boys, not as prisoners, but as their guardian, and to see to it that they had no trouble when boarding the train for the trip home, because the trains were now full of soldiers.

This was a show of solidarity by a Jew to fellow Jews unknown to him and, moreover, from a foreign country. We wanted to reimburse him for the cost of his railway tickets from Koeresmozoe and back, but he firmly refused, saying that he shouldn't be robbed of a mitzvah (good deed).

When, on July 28, Austria declared war on Serbia, events began to move at a hectic speed. On August 5 Austria-Hungary declared war on Russia. The day before, a manifesto over the signature of the Emperor Franz Josef was glued onto the walls of the shtetl. It was in German, Polish, Ukrainian, and, wonder of wonders, Yiddish, a language which was not recognized. In it the Emperor asked his people for unity, loyalty, and sacrifices in defending the honor of the fatherland.

The next morning a policeman mounted a stall in the market-place and started to beat a drum. When people filled the square he announced that war with Russia had broken out and that from now on martial law was being decreed. All men belonging to the reserve were to report for further orders at the town hall, and were to bring their military books with them. All owners of horses were to bring the horses and wagons to the marketplace for cattle. A commission would choose the ones fit for the army, and would pay cash on the spot for the accepted horses and/or wagons.

At the town hall the reservists were told where to go and which units they were to join, and were directed to appear two days later at the railroad station to be sent to the appropriate unit. There were some exemptions from military service for people who received certificates from the local authority which stated that they were *unentbehrlich* (indispensable) because their businesses or services were of vital importance to the government and/or the army. Not called up yet were the Landsturm (reservists over 45 years old).Later, during the war, a decree was issued stating that everybody except the person in the army was dispensable. At the railroad station, when the men were leaving, there were heart-rending scenes. All who had a member of their family leaving were there to say goodbye. Everyone cried, not knowing whether they would ever see their beloved ones again.

14

The Russians Occupy the Shtetl

AFTER THE MEN left, mourning hung over the shtetl. It was the mood of Tisha b'Av, but not just for one day.

Hungarian infantry, artillery, and cavalry units passed the city on their way toward the Russian border, which was not too far away. They were singing and in high spirits proclaiming that the *Russki* would be beaten and that the war would be over in a few days.

The Jews, however, asked each other, *"Un tomer nysht?"* ("What if not?"). Approximately five days later the answer to this question was written on the wall when the Hungarian units which had been so sure of a quick victory passed the shtetl in the opposite direction, in a big hurry and without all the cannons, machine guns, and other equipment which they had carried with them when going eastwards to beat the Russians.

Now a terrible panic befell the Jews of the shtetl. From experiences of their fathers sixty-six years earlier, they knew what it could mean for them, should the Russians occupy the shtetl.

In 1848 when Austria couldn't suppress the Hungarian uprising by herself, she turned to Russia for help. The Tsar sent into Hungary a division of Cossacks, who were well experienced and skilled masters at battling rioters. Since the shortest way from Russia to Hungary was via our city, over the Carpathian Mountains, the shtetl saw the Cossacks hurrying through the city on their way to Hungary.

The Cossacks quickly succeeded in breaking the back of the Hungarian uprising. On their way back, the Cossacks stopped in our city, and the Tsar declared that, for his help in the suppression of the Hungarian uprising, and also because he wanted to have a border with Hungary, he intended to annex the district of Pokucie, which included our shtetl. The Cossacks made themselves at home in the shtetl. Robbing, beating, raping, and plundering began at once. Foodstuffs and fodder was requisitioned. The Cossacks chased the Jews out of their houses, some of which were burned, and moved into others, often together with their horses. Furniture was broken and used for heating purposes. The Jews fled into neighboring Bukovina, leaving everything behind. Only after many months of haggling, and the payment of compensation for her intervention in Hungary, did Russia withdraw the Cossacks.

Around the twentieth of August, nearly two weeks after the declaration of war on Russia, our city was surrounded by Cossacks, who entered it without meeting any resistance whatsoever. The Cossacks were given three days of freedom by their commander to do whatever they pleased with the population. At once pillaging and robbing began. The Christians marked their houses by hanging crosses or pictures of saints at the entrances, and so they were spared. Houses were burned, but only Jewish ones. A Cossack broke into a Jewish home and seeing a Jewish girl there, wanted to rape her. Her father begged the Cossack to leave her alone and offered him money. When the Cossack showed no intention of leaving, the Jew became enraged, grabbed an axe, threatened the Cossack, and chased him out. However, another Cossack appeared from nowhere and killed the Jew. The girl escaped through the back door and ran to a Christian neighbor for shelter. Many Jews hid with Christian families and in other places which they thought were safe.

Luckily the three days given to the Cossacks for free pillaging ended abruptly after only one day. The detachment was ordered to leave the city for the front in pursuit of the Hungarians who were retreating westward. The one day of sojourn of the Cossacks in the shtetl left the Jews victimized mentally and physically and with extensive material damage.

After a few days a military command took over the city and some order was restored, but again not for the Jews. Jews had to pay contributions, goods were requisitioned for the army, and although the military paid for the requisitions, they didn't pay in cash but with worthless receipts. Jews were restricted in their movements, and to leave the city one had to apply for a *propusk* (pass), which was not easy to obtain, and if granted was due to payment of a fee. Hostages were taken and sent to Russia. Some of them returned after the Russian Revolution. Some died there, succumbing to maltreatment. Those who were detained in places where Jews lived were lucky. The Russian Jews extended a helping hand to the Austrian hostages. The Russian occupation forces didn't give a damn about the well-being of the civilian population, especially Jews.

The wealthier people who still had money could buy or barter some valuables for food. However, if it were not for the help and generosity of a Jewish purveyor on war contracts to the Russian army, Jews in the shtetl would have starved to death. With each delivery to the army the purveyor was able to set aside a few sacks of flour, sugar, some tea, and even, from time to time, a cow for the Jewish community. The Jews welcomed even lard and bacon, which was promptly bartered for chicken, eggs, potatoes, and other vegetables. The generous purveyor who helped the Jews was himself, oddly, a *trefnyak* who did not observe *kashruth* and whiled away the nights eating and getting drunk with the Russian officers whenever he was in the city.

For Pesach, the Jewish community in Kamenetz Podolski, not far away from the border on the Russian side, sent to our shtetl a quantity of matzos, wine, eggs, and goose fat which was distributed so that everyone in need got some food for the holiday.

The shtetl was in despair because, as we learned from the Russian newspapers, the all-out offensive launched by the Russians was steamrolling westwards almost without letup. They captured Lwów, and, while they couldn't take the fortress of Przemyśl, they laid siege to it, and still advanced farther west. The Austro-Hungarian forces were badly beaten and fell back almost to the outskirts of Cracow, but were holding the line along the Carpathian Mountains. The Russians captured Tarnów and before the end of 1914 the front was running from Czernowitz, which was close to our shtetl, to the Baltic in the north.

The northern part of the front was held by the Germans and the southern part by Austro-Hungarian forces, but the Russians advanced far west and the picture was very somber. The shtetl feared that it would have to bear the yoke of the Russian occupation until the end of the war. And who knew how long the war would last, or whether they would leave Galicia after the war at all?

Luckily the Austro-Hungarian army, with the help of the Germans, launched an offensive in the spring of 1915 on the whole length of the Galician front and broke through the Dukla pass in the Carpathians near Gorlice and Tarnów. At the same time, the Germans attacked in the north and occupied Poland. The Russians were beaten on the whole length of the front. Our shtetl, which lay close to the Carpathians, was freed in May 1915 after nine terrible months of Russian occupation.

The entry of the Austrian army was celebrated with joy. Soldiers were met with flowers and the people danced in the streets. A week after the Austrians retook the city civilian administration was restored, and two days later an order was published stating that all men between the ages of nineteen and forty-five years were to appear before a recruitment commission. The commission was not choosy and drafted just about everybody, including the writer of this book. Even those who normally wouldn't have been drafted due to some incapacity were declared fit, fit for *Kanonenfutter* (cannon fodder), unless they were blind or totally invalid. The draftees were sworn in, promising to defend the Kaiser and the Fatherland on land, sea, and in the air. After two more days the recruits left for Hungary in cattle cars.

15

In Wartime Austria

AFTER THE THRASHING the Russians got at the Dukla Pass, people believed that there would be no more occupation of the shtetl and began to rebuild the ruined houses and businesses. However, fortune is fickle, and the freedom from the Russians lasted no longer than about a year, for they started a new offensive against the Austrian forces in Galicia in 1916.

This time, however, the Jews of our shtetl, remembering the experience of the previous Russian invasion in 1914, didn't wait for them. As soon as the front began approaching the city, everyone fled westwards, leaving everything behind. They fled by whatever means they could find; railroad, horse and wagon, and even by foot over the Carpathians. The Jews did the same thing from all other cities in Galicia and the Bukovina. Hundreds of thousands were on their way, heading for an unknown destination with no prospect of what lay ahead of them. Although there was a shortage of transportation the refugees were given preference.

Some were sent to relatives in other parts of the Austro-Hungarian monarchy who were willing to accept them. The ones who had no relatives were sent to various places all over the country. Wherever the refugees arrived they received a warm welcome from the authorities. They were given apartments for which the rent was paid by the government. They also received all the social services they needed. Each one received a certain amount of welfare. When a family had a member in the army it received an allowance above the amount of the welfare which they were getting. The majority of the refugees found refuge in Vienna, where some of them even started up businesses, remaining there after the war. My parents and some of the other members of my family were sent to Bohemia, to the Sudetenland, close to the world-famous Karlsbad spa.

Consider the care taken of the refugees by a country at war fighting its enemies on two fronts, and then compare it with the treatment of the Palestinian refugees. The latter were forsaken by their Arab brethren, leaving them at the mercy of the international relief agencies for help. It brings to mind the beggars who came to the *shtetl* for the yearly fairs. They uncovered the wounds on their legs or arms, which were always kept open by scratching them constantly so that they would arouse compassion. Now after thirty years, the problem of the Palestinian refugees still remains an open wound which has not been allowed to heal. Their compatriots, the Arabs, are in a position to solve the problem of the refugees with little effort. They have the money and the immense tracts of land on which to settle the refugees, but they prefer to keep the wound open.

The Russian offensive, although successful at the beginning, was brought to a halt by the Austrian army, and before the end of 1916 the Russians were pushed out of Galicia.

All the efforts of the economy were geared to meet the needs of the army. Raw materials which could be of any use for the army were subject to requisition. Metal of all types, church bells, door handles, household items, and so forth, if of bronze or copper, were requisitioned to be melted and used in the manufacturing of weapons. Shortages of nearly everything were felt. This was made worse by the effective Allied blockade.

The population at home was dependent on what was left over after the army was supplied. Rationing of nearly everything was introduced. As the war years dragged on, rations were drastically reduced, especially those of foodstuffs, to about a 1,200-calorie diet daily per person. Most of the time even these meager rations couldn't be obtained. A black market was born, and those with money could buy everything. Money lost its attractiveness, and bartering became popular. To acquire some food, people were ready to give away everything: household items, clothing, objects of art, jewelry.

Those who were relatively better off were the farmers. One could find on a farm pieces of the best modern or antique furniture and even grand pianos which the peasants got in exchange for flour, potatoes, or fruit. By law, the farmers were obliged to supply cattle and most of their farm products to government-authorized purchasers for the needs of the army. The farmers, however, managed to set aside a substantial part of their deliveries, which they then sold on the black market. Bakers and merchants who were distributing rationed products also knew how to save a part of the stuff by giving short weight and selling the merchandise saved at inflated prices. Ration cards, mostly counterfeit, were also traded on the black market.

To describe what was in short supply is easy, namely everything. However, as we know, need makes the old wife trot. People helped themselves as best they could.

The so-called *ersatz* (replacement) was invented. Synthetic chemistry was in universal use. Nettles were used as an additive in the manufacturing of textiles for the army. However, the uniforms made of the textiles mixed with nettles had the habit of falling apart when they got wet. New recipes for food were in use; cornmeal and potatoes were added to flour for baking of bread. Coffee was replaced by roasted barley, if one could get barley. Tea was replaced by blossom tea, and the leaves of some plants were used as ersatz tobacco.

Restaurants served meals only against coupons cut off from the ration cards. So-called *fleischlose Tage* (days without meat) were introduced. Another method of conserving food was the introduction of *Eintopfgeruechte* (one-dish meals) on some days. No separate servings of soup, noodles, potatoes, fish, or whatever were allowed. All the ingredients had to be cooked in one pot and served in one bowl. One never knew what kind of *ersatz* was added. It could be turnips, which had been saved from cattle fodder, or bran.

Due to a shortage of coal, railway service was reduced to a minimum. Trains ran with substantial delays and with no light or heat in the coaches. People used candles when on a trip. The overcrowded cars had most of the windows broken, and there was no glass available to replace them. The lack of panes induced the people to board or leave the overcrowded cars by way of the broken windows.

The cities all around the country became drab looking. Clothing was remarkably shabbier because there were no new textiles available. Old clothing had to be remodeled or turned inside out, and dresses were dyed anew.

In Vienna the streetcars, run by women, were overcrowded, and their running time was reduced by more than one-half. Hotels were filled, and unless the receptionist was bribed, there were no rooms available. Soap was scarce, and most of the houses were infested with bedbugs.

Coffeehouses were, as in the good old days, always full to overflowing. People grumbled but were happy that they could have their coffee as usual. They tried to forget that it was *ersatz*. Speculators conducted their suspicious business in coffeehouses.

Shortages or not, the people danced, sang, and drank. The mood which prevailed was that of "I don't care! Maybe tomorrow will never come, so let's have a good time today." Theaters and shows were always sold out, and to find a table in a cabaret was a problem.

Industrialists made fortunes on supplies for the army, and black-marketeers made large profits on their tarnished deals. A class of *nouveaux riches* was born who had plenty of money but inflation was eating away the substance.

People were enticed to buy war bonds, which, after the war, became a complete loss. They were asked in the name of patriotism to donate jewelry and objects made of gold and silver to the treasury. This was done under the motto *Fuer Kaiser und Vaterland* ("For the Emperor and the Fatherland"). In lieu of the donated jewelry the donor received a simple ring of steel with the engraved inscription *Gold gab ich fuer Eisen* ("I donated gold in exchange for steel"). Whoever had no such ring to show was considered a bad patriot. As another sign of patriotic feeling, people wore buttons in their lapels with the inscription *Gott strafe England* ("O Lord, punish the English"). I couldn't understand why England, the enemy who was so far away from Austria, was singled out for punishment and not the enemy who was closer to home, Russia, who was devastating our lands. It was probably because of the blockade of the Central Powers on the seas. Propaganda or not, the shortages weighed heavier on the minds of the people than patriotism. It was up to the tsars of the economy to find ways to overcome, at least to some extent, the burden of the shortages. They, however, didn't succeed, and that, among other reasons, led to the defeat.

16

My Adventures as a Soldier

MEANWHILE, AS MENTIONED already, I had been drafted into the army. All of us draftees, filled with grief and sorrow on being torn away from our beloved ones, were starting a new life—the life of a soldier, i.e., a life directed by others. In the army men became puppets; all their thinking was done for them by their superiors. They had to obey orders, with no questions asked, and be ready and willing to sacrifice their lives, which actually ceased to be their own.

Before the train loaded with draftees left the shtetl, rations consisting of bread, a small package of butter, and a sausage were distributed among the soldiers. Jews exchanged the sausages with Gentile soldiers for butter, trying to avoid eating *trayfe*, as long as possible. For that reason they carried with them a cooked or roasted chicken, or meat of some sort, which had to last for at least a few days. There were some Jews who never ate any meat from the army kitchens during their entire war years.

Our transport headed for Gross Wardein (Nagy Varad), Hungary. On arrival, we were marched into barracks on the outskirts of the city. There, after having received the necessary equipment, those who had previously served in the army were dispatched to the cadres of their regiments. The greenhorns were assigned to units to which they were best suited, such as the infantry, cavalry, or artillery. I was assigned to the infantry.

Then once again a swearing-in ceremony took place. The recruits repeated the oath word by word, and swore to defend with their lives, on land, in the air, and on the seas, the Austro-

Hungarian fatherland and his Apostolic Majesty Franz Josef I, Emperor of Austria, King of Hungary and Bohemia, and so on and on. To list all his titles would take more than a full page.

The Making of a Soldier. After Italy switched sides and declared war on her former ally, Austria, the time for melting the raw material of a recruit and remodeling him into a soldier was reduced to only two and one-half months. Normally this training would have taken up a whole year.

The drilling of the recruits was very harsh, and the drill sergeants did everything to squeeze out the last drop of sweat from the men. Especially for the *Einjaehrigfreiwillige* the drill yard was a hell and plenty of torture. Before the war university students and high school graduates were liable for only one year of active service. They went through schooling and training for future officers and were released as cadets (reserve). They were called *Einjaehrigfreiwillige* (one-year volunteers), although one seldom volunteered. The sergeants knew that these young men would be sent to a school for officers and in another three months would become cadets, their superiors. The sergeants were angry that they needed twelve years of active service in order to reach the rank of sergeant and that these young men would be promoted to officer aspirants after only three more months of schooling. The recruits, they said, had no experience whatsoever, some even didn't know right from left. At the command "turn right" they turned to the left, and vice versa. Therefore, as long as we have the upperhand we should teach them a lesson and show them who is the boss.

Any offense by a recruit against discipline and the rules was severely punished. A rifle not cleaned properly, the blouse or coat not buttoned up as it should be, the bedding not folded on the cot as prescribed, shoes not polished glossy enough, any moving when at attention, returning to the barracks later than allowed according to the pass, not saluting properly when meeting someone on whose collar were more stars than on your own, and many other such actions were considered offenses.

The punishment could be *Kassernarrest* (ban on leaving the barracks) for a certain time except for duty purposes. It could be *Wacharrest* (detention in the guardhouse) or even imprisonment. It could be worse, *Spangen* (clasping)—a six-hour penalty during which the hands were handcuffed behind one's back and clasped together with the feet. And, horror of horrors, it could be worse still: *Anbinden* (the tie-up)—which was a real torture. The hands were fastened to a rack above the head, and the rack was raised to a height where the feet no longer touched the ground. Maximum time for this cruel punishment was three hours, and a doctor had to be present. If the delinquent fainted he was taken down until he regained consciousness and then the procedure was repeated until the prescribed time of the punishment expired.

There was seldom a doctor who would allow a soldier who came to see him complaining that he was not feeling well to stay in the barracks for a day or two and not take part in the drilling exercise. If his body temperature was not over 38° Celsius, no matter what the complaint was, the only remedy prescribed was one or two small packages of aspirin. At that time aspirin was dispensed in powder form, tablets were not in use.

After approximately two and a half months of basic training and drilling, *Marschbatallions* (field battalions) were formed, ready to be dispatched to the Russian or Italian front. The soldiers were equipped with new uniforms, new rifles with live ammunition, gas masks, iron rations of canned meat and biscuits sufficient to last for three days. One could not touch these rations without a special order. This was given only in the case of an emergency when food couldn't be brought to the front line. There were many other items, all together making up a total weight of 28 to 30 kilograms, which one had to carry on his back.

For communication with his family, each soldier received a few postcards with preprinted contents in all the languages used in the Austro-Hungarian monarchy. *"Ich bin gesund und es geht mir gut"* ("I'm fine and in good health") was printed in German along with the same text in the Polish, Ukrainian, Czech, Hungarian, Slovakian, Croatian, Rumanian, Slovenian, Serbian, and Italian languages. Not one more word could be added. The return address didn't show the whereabouts of the sender; only his name and fieldpost code for the return address was permitted. Letters had to be submitted to the censor, who would cut out a part of the contents, or would even destroy the entire letter, if he thought it suspicious.

Before leaving for the front a priest celebrated a field mass for the Catholics, blessing the soldiers, who were being sent out to kill other Catholics in the ranks of the enemy. On the other side, priests in competition with our priests begged the same God for the well-being of the soldiers on their side of the front.

A *Feldrabbiner* (chaplain) held a service for the Jewish soldiers who were being sent out to kill other Jews, soldiers of the opposing armies. He, at least, didn't have any competition, because there were no rabbis in the armies on the Russian side of the front who would pray for the well-being of their Jewish soldiers.

After the basic training, the *Einjaehrigfreiwillige*, with very few exceptions, were usually promoted to the rank of underofficers, and then sent to a school for further training and schooling. The school to which I was sent was in Moravia. Among the approximately 200 aspirants for the rank of officer, about thirty Jewish boys from Galicia qualified. At the beginning of December we graduated from the school; some became sergeants, and others, I among them, became officer aspirants. The graduates were then sent to the cadre of the regiment to which they belonged to await the formation of a *Marschbatallion*, to be dispatched to the front.

When I arrived at the cadre a new *Marschbatallion* was just being assembled, and I was given the command of a platoon. We received field equipment and were shipped to the Russian front. The trip took us ten days, and we disembarked in Bóbrka. We advanced by night marches closer to the front line in the direction of Tarnopol, which, at that time, was still in Russian hands. Our assignment was to replace another battalion which had suffered quite a number of casualties in wounded and killed. It also suffered from the desertion of our soldiers of Czech nationality who made up the majority of that battalion.

Die Feuertaufe (First time under fire). We stopped in a village where the command post of the battalion was located and had to advance, platoon by platoon, marching carefully and quietly in order not to draw the enemy's attention to our movements. However, after the first platoon moved out, the Russians seemed to have noticed that something extraordinary was going on behind our lines. They began to bombard our trenches and the terrain behind the front with artillery. As my platoon was the last to go to the front line, I was resting in a peasant's hut, awaiting the order for my platoon to start moving. Suddenly, all hell broke loose when the Russians directed their fire at the village.

Before I could get out of the hut it received a direct hit. I was

The *uhlan* in this picture, Ernest Ekstein, was a relative of the author's. .

A group of Jewish soldiers (landslajt) from the 24th Infantry Regiment, the author's unit

thrown to the ground and a beam from the ceiling fell upon me. I felt a warm wetness inside my clothing and realized that I was losing blood and that my legs were under some heavy load which I couldn't lift or move. I became muddled and blacked out.

Luckily I was not left alone for long. A medic who was looking for the injured noticed my head protruding from under a heap of rubble. He hurried for help. When I finally regained consciousness, it was at the field hospital.

I noticed a cast on my left leg and was told that it was broken and that it was a miracle that I was alive. All the wreckage had fallen on my legs, and the rest of my body was free and covered with dirt and dust only. The extensive bleeding had come from a deep wound in my buttock which had been caused by a piece of glass from the icon over the bed on which I had been resting when the wall and ceiling collapsed. I never knew which Ukrainian saint from the icon intended to kill me. That was my *Feuertaufe* even before reaching the front line and not having seen one Russian soldier.

Two days later I was put on a Red Cross train, which brought me to a hospital in Vienna. There a doctor found that my leg had been incorrectly set, and gave me the alternative to either leave the leg as it was and spend the rest of my life with one leg shorter than the other, or to have the leg broken again in the hospital and put back together as it should be. Everyone in the ward considered me a fool when I opted for the operation instead of grabbing the opportunity to get out of the mess of the war. As a matter of fact, there were times when I regretted my decision. Instead of being in the hell at the Isonzo front, I could have been back in Vienna finishing my education.

With a new cast on my leg, and the healing process proceeding well, I was given crutches, and a short time later I was released from the hospital and transferred to a convalescent home near Vienna. A couple of days after my arrival at the home, I was called in to the head doctor's office and was given a medal which had been waiting there for me, the Bronze Medal for Bravery. Relaxing on a bed behind the front was considered bravery. However, never look a gift horse in the mouth.

As soon as the cast was removed, although still on crutches, I was sent back to the cadre of my regiment in Hungary, to wait, once again, for a *Marschkompanie* and to be shipped back to the combat lines.

Not yet ready for a *Marschkompanie*, I was sent to a nearby village as commander of a camp with nearly 200 interned alien citizens. Some of them were there with their wives and children. They were Russian citizens who prior to the war lived in Austria.

When I went to the camp to inspect the men before they left for work, to my surprise I heard calls of "Chaim, Chaim." Soon three men came up to me. They were Russian Jews who had lived in our shtetl, having left Russia after the pogrom in Kishinev. Their work was collecting nettles in the fields and along the roadsides. Nettles were used as an additive in the manufacture of textiles for uniforms for the army. My *landsmen* had no complaints about the treatment or the food.

Around the middle of April, I was ordered to appear before a medical commission which consisted of one doctor, and he found me recovered enough to be sent back to the front. However, in view of my being wounded in battle (that's what was to be read in my personal file) I received fourteen days furlough.

I left for my furlough, heading home to see my parents and the rest of my family. It took me three days to arrive at the shtetl. I cannot describe my joy when I saw my parents after being away from home for about a year. I enjoyed only five days with my family when my furlough was cut short by a wire received by the military command of the city from the cadre of my regiment ordering me to return at once. Sad as it was, I had to obey orders and on the same day boarded the train for my return to the cadre.

The Italian Front. Immediately I was assigned to a new *Marschbatallion* which had just been formed and, once again, I was in command of a platoon. After only two days of travel we arrived at the Italian front, where our forces were to start an offensive at the Trentino.

The Austrian border with Italy ran in the form of a horseshoe from the Adriatic in the east along the Isonzo River and then along the Julian and Carnic Alps and Dolomites to the Trentino plateau. It was a mountainous obstacle along which Austria had built strong fortifications with artillery posts on the mountains.

The first Italian attack at the Trentino took place in June 1915, and resulted in a few gains for the Italians. They also attacked on the east side of the front along the Isonzo River. They made some minor progress but couldn't break through the Austrian defense lines. The Italians made three more attempts during 1915 on the

Italian Front

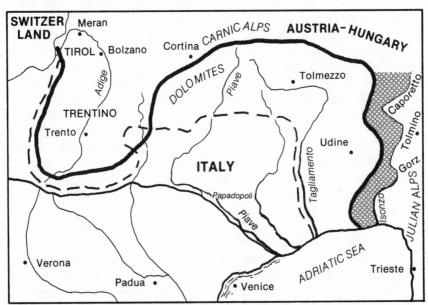

Peacetime borders ▬▬▬▬
Line after Caporetto ──────
Italian Gains in Isonzo Battles ░░░░░
End of Battle Nov. 2 1918 ── ── ──

The Italian front

Isonzo section with no success. They tried five more times in 1916 and two more times in 1917, but with no noticeable success. The on-again, off-again Italian attacks and the Austrian counterattacks, known as the eleven battles of the Isonzo, brought only heavy losses in manpower and material to both sides, with no considerable gains or progress for either one. Between the offensives, activities slowed down and a trench war was fought. The Italian forces exceeded the Austrians, in some cases, by as much as three to one, but their losses were usually in the same proportion.

In May 1916, as soon as most of the snow melted and the weather turned favorable, our forces started an offensive at the Trentino, and it was there where our *Marschbatallion* was rushed to. Our forces had already taken the first Italian defense line but suffered heavy losses and could not carry on with the push. They were halted by the Italians at their second defense line. To replace the men on the front line, we moved forward in a single file with some distance between the men. We luckily arrived at the former Italian first line, which became our first line. We repaired the trenches, and for a few days relative tranquility prevailed. Supplies could be brought to us only in the dark of the night. Before the food reached us the soup and tea became cold, but the men received enough rum to warm up and to fill their flasks for the next day. On their way back, the porters took casualties from the sporadic shooting during the previous day to the rear. The tranquility lasted for about five days and was interrupted by our artillery, which started a heavy bombardment on the Italian lines.

My first hurrah. One night we received the order to be ready the next morning for an attack on the Italian lines.

Expecting a hand-to-hand battle in the Italian trenches, we put our bayonets on the rifles. The men in the platoon next to mine, composed of Bosniaks, put their daggers between their teeth, ready to stab the enemy to death. Before sunrise we jumped over the ramparts of the trenches and ran toward the Italian line. The short run, from our trenches to the Italian defense line, their former second line, brought us many casualties from machine-gun fire and exploding mines which were laid out in front of the line we were attacking.

After having cut the barbed-wire barriers, we jumped into the trenches, the officers with their fingers on the triggers of their revolvers, the men with their fixed bayonets, and the Bosniaks with their daggers, ready to stab and kill the damned enemy. Everyone yelled like crazy from the depth of his lungs, a deafening "Hurrah, hurrah, hurrah!" but there was nobody waiting there to be killed. Before we had attacked, the Italians had fallen further back by a couple of kilometers. This was my first "Hurrah," a war cry, but without an echo. Instead of finding Italians to kill, we found, in their trenches, a good supply of cigarettes, chocolate, and different types of canned foods which we immediately "killed."

We tried to rearrange the conquered Italian trenches, which previously had been facing our line, so that they would now face their side. But if someone tried, during the daytime to look over the ramparts, a sniper's bullet was waiting for him, and the helmet was no protection. Only by periscope was it possible to have a look at what was going on in front of our line. The terrain was rocky, and it was impossible to dig in deep enough to provide good protection, and we suffered many losses. After two weeks of inaction we were taken back to a reserve position and a detachment of another regiment was sent forward to replace us. A few days after our battalion left the front line, the Italians attacked, and our forces retreated to a strong, fortified position. The situation on this part of the front had not changed, and a relative calm began with the return to trench war.

After our abortive offensive at the Trentino, our losses were replenished and our battalion was moved to a new section of the Italian front in the Carnic Alps. The positions we took over on the Carnic Alps were on a relatively small plateau on the bald top of a high mountain with not one single blade of grass or a trace of moss. This was the *Mrzli-Vrh*, which was covered most of the time with snow. Here and there on a rock the rare Edelweiss flower could be found. Some of our men, particularly the Austrians from the Tyrol and Steiermark provinces, were crazy about plucking Edelweiss flowers for souvenirs. They risked their lives scanning the terrain by periscope in order to find and pinpoint the place where a couple of Edelweiss could be seen and then risked them again during the night by crawling out to pluck a couple of these flowers. Life was the cheapest commodity on the front line, and this may be one of the reasons why there were heroes.

The Austrians and the Italians were facing each other in trenches blasted out in the hard rocks. Between the trenches was a narrow strip of no-man's land. The trenches of both the opposing forces were fortified by many rows of barbed wire, with land mines laid out in front of them.

Our side of the mountain was very steep, and to reach the top a narrow way was blasted out in the form of a close serpentine in the sturdy rock. The infantry marched up, as well as down, in single file. Every 30 to 40 meters the path was widened so that when two columns, one heading up and the other down, met at the same time, there was space for one of them to step aside to let the others pass by. Accidents were common, and it was not unusual that an animal bearing a heavy load slipped on a wet rock and rolled down into a seemingly endless abyss. Sudden avalanches also took their toll.

Supplies, ammunition, equipment, and even guns had to be brought up by hand and/or on pack animals, mules, and little horses which were specially bred and brought from the Carpathians in Galicia. The traffic on these ways had to be conducted only at night, marching as quietly as possible in order not to trigger an artillery barrage.

There was also an electrical cable railway used for bringing up supplies. For this, one terminal was blasted out at the bottom of the mountain and the other at the top as a cavern just below the trenches. By using this ropeway, material and supplies could be moved up faster and safer, although it too could only be operated at night.

As command posts and resting places for the men who were not on duty in the trenches, deep caverns were blasted out which provided secure shelter against the enemy's bombardment. We were leading the life of cavemen, not being able to emerge from the bunkers during the day to catch a little fresh air or to raise our heads above the ramparts. In addition to the everyday bombardment by artillery which occasionally erupted into a *Trommelfeuer* (drum fire), sometimes lasting for hours, we got unexpected bombings from airplanes and gas shelling.

On this part of the front not only exploding shells which sent fragments of steel and rock in all directions were against us, but it appeared that Mother Nature was also against us because of the strong winds and the avalanches. A concise description of the Italian front would be: an inferno when an offensive was underway, and a hell during the time between the offensives.

The possession of the peak of the mountain, the plateau with the trenches, was the most important matter. Whoever was in control of this highest point in this section of the front could look from that location to far behind the lines of the enemy and, as a result, could direct the artillery which disrupted the enemy's movements.

The Himmelfahrt (the assension). Both sides were safely entrenched in bombproof shelters with two or three lines of trenches, rows of barbed wire, and barriers of land mines. Each side tried not just one, but many times, to overrun the trenches of the other side in order to win control of the plateau, but neither the Italians nor we were successful. The Italians, therefore, invented a new method of ravaging our position, intending to send us together with the whole top of the mountain straight up into heaven.

Deep below the mountain they started to blast out a tunnel leading straight under our lines to a large chamber which was to be filled with enough dynamite to blow us up together with a part of the mountain.

One day when I was assigned to observation duty from a balloon high above the mountain, from which there was a very good view of what was going on behind the Italian lines, I noticed through my field glasses that from a point on the slope of the mountain on the Italian side gravel was flowing down the hillside. Such observations were dangerous and were ordered only on days of sunny weather and clear air. It was not done very often and for not longer than ten minutes at a time, which was just enough to check whether there was any abnormal army traffic behind the enemy lines.

When I was brought down I reported that I had noticed no abnormal movements of the enemy and that everything seemed to be quiet. There didn't seem to be anything worthwhile to mention but, hesitatingly, I added a note about the flow of gravel which I had spotted. When this routine report reached the general staff of the regiment, the engineering department became alarmed, and sappers with listening devices were sent up to the front line immediately. The sappers came to the conclusion that the Italians were tunneling their way in the direction of the cavern where the command post of our battalion was located and that their work was near completion.

A plan was worked out to outsmart the Italians. Countertunneling began immediately, leading in the direction of their chamber but about a half-meter below it. We had not much drilling to do because they were already close to the cavern of the commander of the battalion. When it was established that they had stopped drilling, it was assumed that they were beginning to load the chamber with dynamite. Our sappers burrowed as close as possible to the Italians' tunnel. An Italian-speaking officer was brought in, and since he could hear every word spoken on the other side, we knew exactly what the Italians' plans were. When it was established that the Italians had already sealed the chamber with the dynamite, our sappers broke through into the Italian tunnel and, first of all, cut off the ignition cable.

A huge quantity of dynamite was then hastily removed from the chamber and sent down from the front lines by the cableway. Observation balloons were sent up now every hour, and as soon as the command of our regiment was satisfied that the Italians had evacuated their lines in anticipation of the spectacle when we would be raised into the sky together with the top of the mountain, our forces moved forward and occupied the empty Italian positions without any resistance whatsoever. However, since we didn't have any connecting trenches from our lines to the newly taken Italian lines, and the Italians kept us under steady bombardment, we used a part of their dynamite to blow up their lines and retreated to our previous positions.

After about one and a half months on the Mrzli-Vrh my battalion was relieved and brought down for a lengthy repose behind the lines. Down below we received a delousing, which we badly needed, and our uniforms and underwear were disinfected. Drill and exercises were nearly nonexistent, and we enjoyed the clean mountain air and the smell of the pine trees.

A confidential order was leaked to me by a typist from the office of the command of the regiment from which I learned that a request was received for three low-ranking officers to be sent for a two or three months course of logistics specializing in communication and adjutant duties.

After a week in the reserve the colonel gave, at the daily report, a fiery speech about how brave a soldier I was and pinned another medal to my breast. It was my second medal; the little Silver Medal for Bravery. I really didn't know what act of heroism I had performed. I had already forgotten my note on the report of my observations while I had been up in the balloon, and besides, I never considered it an act of bravery. I obediently thanked the commander and asked that I be sent to the communication course. The colonel promised to look into the matter and in the next day's order of the day there was the answer to my request.

I was *in sibenten himel* (in seventh heaven) when my name, along with those of two other officers who were being designated for a course in communications, was read from the order of the day. Our battalion was on alert due to another offensive started by the Italians, the sixth Isonzo battle, which was one of the fiercest. All departures had been canceled. Fortunately the Italians stopped their attacks and the front quieted down. After a few days I was replaced at the front, received my marching orders, left the boiling kettle at the Isonzo, and headed for greener pastures. My marching documents were made out to Bielitz, a city in the Silesian Beskid Mountains, about 80 kilometers west of Cracow, where the communication courses were being held.

On my way there I made a large detour via Prague to see my parents in the Sudetenland near Karlsbad. My parents were happy to see me away from the fighting. They had known all the time where I was. I had promised my father that I would never hide my whereabouts from him. We designed a secret code by which I could convey to him where I was. By substituting figures for letters of the Hebrew alphabet, and mentioning somebody's birthday, or reminding him that a debt of a certain amount should be collected, my messages went through unnoticed by the censor. My father marked the places where I was on a map by sticking pins in the designated area. The pain which was caused to my parents when I was leaving far outweighed the joy they had felt upon my arrival.

A few days after the course started a "Dr. Rabbiner" (rabbi) from the local progressive congregation visited the school and invited the Jewish participants to come on Friday to the temple. After the service there were a lot of questions. People wanted to know how things were going at the front. They wanted to know how soon the war would be over, and of course, who would be the winner.

After the discussions and the questioning, each one of us was invited for supper to one or another gentleman's home. This reminded me of the political discussions in a *klouze* in our shtetl, with the difference being that the discussions were conducted in German, and the participants wore top hats and coats instead of caftans and shtraymils. We boys from Galicia called them the *Tempeljuden* (Jews from the temple). As for the invitations for supper, it gave me the feeling of being a poor *oyrekh* (guest) who would have been invited by my father for Shabbes.

The people most eager to invite an officer for supper were the ones who had a daughter ripe for the *chuppah* (the canopy at a wedding). If this was the case, the talk at supper was aimed at information about the guest, his family, his education, his profession, and especially whether his parents were rich. If the *pater familias* thought that the angling was worthwhile, he usually extended an invitation to drop in during the week. One visit followed the other, and the mother would say one day that they had received three tickets for the theater but that her husband could not go. They would be pleased if instead, the *Herr Offizier* would accompany them. However, things didn't always turn out as intended. In any case, a friendship evolved, which usually lasted for at least the duration of the stay in the city.

At the beginning of October, after one and a half years of military service, I was promoted to the rank of second lieutenant. Being away from the front meant that I was spared involvement in two more Isonzo battles in which, in spite of the killing and the huge losses on both sides, neither one made substantial gains.

But a week after my return to the front, the Italians started their ninth Isonzo offensive. I was ordered to replace a lieutenant in the trenches who had been wounded. Our barbed-wire barriers had been destroyed, and the mines which had been laid in front of our lines had exploded when they were hit by the bombardment or by rock splinters, and ceased to be an obstacle to the storming infantry, but the Italians were beaten back by our machine-guns, flame throwers, and hand grenades and didn't succeed in overrunning our lines. They suffered heavy losses without gaining even one centimeter of the rocky terrain. Our losses were heavy as well. I was fortunate to come out of this battle without a scratch, and also from the tenth Isonzo offensive, which the Italians started after giving us only a three-week respite. But I had to mourn the loss of a good friend from a neighboring shtetl in the Bukovina who had commanded a platoon next to mine.

As soon as the offensive was over, I was appointed to the post of communications officer. In my new capacity, I was attached to the staff of the regiment, which, although usually located behind the front line, was also constantly exposed to enemy bombardment. I was in charge of and responsible for the functioning of our various means of communication, such as the telephone, the *Meldereiterabteilung* (dispatch riders) on horses, motorcycles, bicycles, and also a squad with cages of carrier pigeons.

Among other things, my duties included coordinating the incessant flow of reports coming from all the units in the front line. I had to present these reports to the colonel in a concise and edited form for his approval and forward them later to the staff of the brigade.

Snow, ice, cold, and fog made greater military activity impossible. The infantry was unable to move, but sporadic gunfire and bombardment from the air was sowing death all around. Both sides tried to make good use of the quiet period, preparing themselves for actions to be taken in the spring. It was, therefore, very important to observe the enemy in order to at least guess what his intentions were. Different types and means of observation were used; reconnaissance flights by planes, and, good weather permitting, from frequently sent up balloons.

The Tongue. One of the means for gaining information about the enemy was to catch a so-called tongue, a live Italian soldier who would talk at the interrogation. And one night, under the worst weather conditions, when a blizzard with temperatures of 30° Celsius below zero was raging, a patrol composed of a non-commissioned officer and two men, all volunteers, was sent out. Their objective was to capture and bring back to our lines a live Italian. Camouflaged in white linen coats, equipped with handguns but no rifles, with hand grenades, and wire cutters with insulated handles in the event the barbed wire on the Italian side was electrified, silently they climbed over our ramparts, cut our barbed wire, and moved carefully on wide snowshoes in order not to break through the ice, beneath which land mines could be laid. They had to deal a surprise blow to a sentry on outpost duty, not to kill him but to return him, gagged, to our lines.

They were lucky enough to escape injury and arrived back at our lines safe and sound, not only with their own tongues intact, but with an additional Italian one. For this act of bravery, they were able to show up later with a piece of metal, a Medal for Bravery dangling on a multicolored ribbon pinned proudly to the breasts. In addition, each of them got a two-week furlough.

Le Roi est mort, vive le Roi. On December 17, 1916, the order of the day which was read to every unit of the army informed us that Emperor Franz Josef had died the day before and that the successor to the throne, Archduke Karl, was now the Emperor of the Austro-Hungarian monarchy. A time of mourning was ordered, during which the officers had to wear black armbands which had been supplied to them.

A few days after the death of the Emperor Franz Josef the

ceremony of swearing allegiance to the new Emperor took place. Nobody could understand why this had to be done. "A Kaiser is a Kaiser; it was Franz Josef before, and now Karl is the Emperor." Nobody thought of leaving the front because his oath to Franz Josef was no longer valid, so why should one risk his life going down on the icy, slippery path kept under enemy fire, and then climb up the same way back?

The Jewish officers sincerely mourned the death of the humane monarch. Discussions started about how it would be after the war under the new Emperor. There were among us colleagues from a city near our shtetl where the new Emperor had been stationed a few years before the war as the commander of a cavalry regiment, and the Jews liked him. He used to go for walks through the streets of the city. With good grace he engaged the people he met in a chat, asking them how they were doing. To some poor-looking men and women he gave a few crowns.

At the beginning of January 1917, my name appeared in the official military gazette, the *Streffleur*, among those who were promoted to higher ranks. I had advanced to the rank of lieutenant. With it came the acquisition of new equipment, such as field glasses and a handgun, items which I had already received from the military depot at no charge some time before. Furthermore, I was to acquire a parade uniform and a sword, but who needed such things at the front? The promotion also meant that I would now receive a large salary, good rations of rum, fine cognac, and cigarettes. Also, a permanent orderly was assigned to me. Because I had everything I needed for myself, I sent all my money and cigarettes to my parents.

The Studienurlaub. At the end of 1916 I learned about a decree granting students whose studies had been interrupted by the war, and who had at least one year's service at the front, the right to a three-month furlough in order to go back to the university for a condensed course for which they would receive credits for an entire semester. I availed myself of this opportunity and applied for the furlough, which was granted, and before the end of January 1917, I left for Vienna.

I had a week's time before enrolling for the course and wanted to make as much of it as I possibly could. I made my way from the far south of Austria to her most northern part, to Oberleutensdorf, close to the Austrian-German border, where my parents lived. There I could only stay for two days. Bidding my parents farewell was heartrending. They were worried about me, and when I was leaving and already on the other side of the door, my father looked at me and said: "Who knows if I shall see him again?"

In Vienna I rented a room with a Jewish family whose son was in the army. They rented his room as they needed a few crowns. The landlords were nice people, but the bedbugs were not quite so nice to me. I had to change my lodgings a few times because of this same problem, the bedbugs. At that time Vienna was infested with bedbugs. Lights on or off didn't matter. That was my trouble with lodging, but the board which I had at the Jewish student's mess didn't give me any reason for complaints, considering the shortage of foodstuff in general.

The university was filled with students, mostly military men of all ranks from captain down. Some of the professors were ready to turn a blind eye to a not perfectly correct answer, respecting the student's uniform and medals, if he happened to have some dangling on his breast, or if he was on crutches. They were guided by a feeling of guilt for not being in the army. Older professors were of the opinion that knowledge could not be acquired in the trenches and were as demanding as usual.

Pesach happened to come up during the time of our courses. The Jewish community arranged communal Seders for the soldiers of the garrison and those in hospitals. Some Jewish families offered to entertain one or two soldiers at their family Seder. A few days before Pesach a note was placed on the bulletin board at the *mensa academica,* asking students who wanted to spend the Seder with a Jewish family to register in the office of the *mensa,* which is what I did.

The Hofrat (privy councillor, a title of honor in Austria). Distributing the addresses of the families to whom the soldiers were invited, the secretary first asked some questions. When my turn came to receive my invitation, the secretary asked me if I had attended *cheder* and if I knew the Jewish traditional rituals and prayers. When I answered in the affirmative she smiled and showed me a letter from a *Hofrat.* The letter came, she told me, from an elderly gentleman who was the owner of a steel mill in Silesia. In his letter of invitation he expressed his preference for an officer, possibly from Galicia, who would be familiar with Jewish traditions and knew the prayers.

I ordered a dozen roses at a flower shop and made sure to have them delivered to the *Frau Hofrat* on the eve of Passover. When I arrived at the *Hofrat's* residence in the evening of the eve of Passover, the butler showed me into the "salon" (the drawing room) and announced the arrival of the invited guest. I introduced myself to the *Hofrat*, and he in turn introduced me to the members of his family. Shortly after, it was announced that supper was ready and we went into the dining room.

Under the glitter of silver girandoles and candelabras a big table was laid for supper. Fine china, crystal glasses, silverware, a huge plate with matzos, separately three matzos in a silk bag with three compartments, a few bottles of wine which were marked *kosher shel Pesach*, and a plate with the symbols of Pesach: *karpas, maror, kharoses*, an egg and the shankbone. Everything was ready to start the Seder.

Before starting the Seder the *Hofrat* said that he felt obliged to explain to his family the reason why he had decided to celebrate Passover this year. He had come to Vienna with his parents from a little town in Galicia when he was still a child. His father was not a religious man and didn't observe any Jewish traditions or holidays. His father had belonged to the temple, as he too did, but he only attended services on New Year's day and Yom Kippur. He bestowed substantial donations to Jewish and non-Jewish institutions, hospitals, orphanages, and the home for the aged, but no matter how much he donated to these charities he somehow had the impression that only his money was appreciated, not his personality.

His father had told him stories of his grandfather, how pious a Jew he was, and the poverty in which the family had lived. But he didn't want to have anything in common with the *Ostjuden* (Jews from the eastern part of Austria, Galicia). But when, about a year before, he had seen the trains passing through Vienna with cars overcrowded with poor Jewish refugees from Galicia he became nostalgic and somehow had a feeling of being close to them. If his father had not left Galicia he could have been among those refugees.

A few weeks earlier he had seen his grandfather in a dream, with a long white beard, as his father had described him in his stories. The grandfather told him: "Repent my son, repent, and don't stray from thy folk. I remind you that on *shabbes chol hamoed* [the Sabbath between the first and the last two days of

Passover] is my *yahrzeit* [the anniversary of a dead person]." And this was why he had decided to have at least a symbol of Galicia, and that was the reason why he invited me for the Seder with his family.

He assured me that the food was kosher, as it had been prepared by an expert cook from the best Jewish restaurant in Vienna. He asked me to conduct the Seder as it was done in a Jewish home in Galicia. I must confess that I felt a little uneasy, being for the first time in my life in a home of such splendor.

I first explained the meaning of Passover, retelling briefly the story of *yetsias mitsrayim* (the delivery from bondage in Egypt), and of the symbols of Passover, which had been laid out correctly. There were a few Haggadahs with German translation, and when I mentioned that the man of the house was supposed to start with *kiddush* he asked me if it would be all right to read it in German from the Haggadah, to which I replied that God understood all languages. The host read the *kiddush*, and when I raised my glass and, making the blessing over wine, asked everybody to repeat the blessing and then to drink the first *kos* (cup) of the compulsory four cups (*arba kossiot*) of wine, everybody followed me. My shyness was gone.

After we read a few passages from the Haggadah, supper was served. Everything was as it was at my father's home, and I liked it very much. If the others did, I don't know, but I do know that what they liked best was the wine.

After supper the *Hofrat* took me aside for a chat and asked me how I was doing in Vienna and to tell him of the acts of bravery I had performed for which I had been decorated with medals. He said that he was proud of me because the German "patriots" who used any means to keep their sons at home and away from the front line could see how Jewish patriots were sacrificing their lives and blood for the fatherland. (His sons, too, were not in the army.)

When asked how I was doing in Vienna I, in my naivete, mentioned the bedbugs. He then promptly invited me to be his guest for the duration of my stay in Vienna, which I gratefully accepted.

He told me that on the upcoming Sabbath he planned to go to the temple and would be called up to the Torah because of the *yahrzeit* of his grandfather. He wondered if maybe I would write down the *brachot* (blessings) he was to say, in Latin spelling, so that he could learn them by heart and pronounce them clearly. The next day I moved in and the lessons started right away. On Sabbath evening he told me how his friends in the temple were amazed that he could recite the blessings over the Torah. They asked him if he had ever attended a Jewish school in his childhood and remarked on how good a memory he must have.

The *Hofrat* took a liking to me. After the war, when I finished the last year of my studies, he gave me a job in his main office, so that I could get acquainted with his business, and later, when he needed a Polish-speaking representative in Warsaw for his mill, I got the job.

I later learned that he poisoned himself when the Nazis entered Vienna, and that none of his family escaped. All, including the ones who had converted to Christianity, were exterminated by the Nazis.

Just when I returned to the front from my *Studieurlaub* the Italians tried once again to overtake our positions in the hope of opening a way to Trieste. In this offensive, the last one on the Isonzo front, the attacks lasted for a month. The losses in manpower were enormous, but as was the case in all previous offensives on the Isonzo, the gains that resulted were minimal.

The Death of My Father, alav hashalom (may he rest in peace). When these fierce battles were going on a telegram was received by the commander of the regiment with the message that my father was seriously ill and a request to allow me to come and visit him even for a day or two. Because of the ongoing battle I was refused permission to leave the front. In the little town where my parents lived as refugees there was no doctor; all the doctors were in the army. By the time a doctor was brought from a nearby city it was too late. A few days later a second telegram was received, requesting my release for the funeral, which had been delayed until my possible arrival. Again I was refused. The battle was not yet over, and, as the colonel said, since I could no longer see my father alive there was really no reason for me to leave the front at such a critical time.

We had enough Jewish officers and soldiers on different duties at the headquarters of our regiment. Putting together a *minyan* (a quorum of ten men) was no problem. After an hour of *shiva* my colleagues came to my shelter, where we prayed *mincha* and *maariv* (evening prayers) and I said *kaddish*.

Two weeks later I received a letter from my mother in which she informed me that she was going to put up a gravestone on my father's grave and that the unveiling would take place on *shloshim* (the thirtieth day after the death). The battle was already over, and when I applied for a furlough I was given a leave of seven days for religious and family considerations.

In the town where my father passed away there was no Jewish cemetery, so he was buried in Brücks, a nearby city, where we went for the unveiling of the gravestone. After the war that city belonged to Czechoslovakia, the Czechoslovakia of Masaryk and Beneš. When my wife and I came to visit my father's grave a few years later, I found the cemetery well cared for by the affluent Jewish community. However, when, after the Second World War, I came again to that city for *kever avoth* (visiting parent's graves), I found a city with no trace of Jews living there or having ever lived there. I asked a taxidriver to take me to the Jewish cemetery, but he even didn't know that anything Jewish had ever existed in the city. My inquiries at the city hall didn't solve my problem either. I asked elderly passersby on the street whether they knew if there were some Jews living in the city and was given the address of an old Jewish lady, and she explained to the driver how to find the cemetery.

When I finally arrived at the cemetery I found the place devastated by the Nazis. Most of the beautiful monuments were lying around broken. Wild shrubs had grown around everywhere. The brick fence which surrounded the cemetery was broken in many places. At the cemetery there was a wall with compartments where urns with ashes of cremated deceased people were kept locked. It looked like a wall in a post office containing post office boxes. The Nazis had broken into all the lockers, slit open the urns, and dumped out the ashes. Obviously there had once been Jews there who aped the Gentiles by wanting to be cremated. They did it long before Hitler; of course, only after a natural death. Hitler had no time to wait for the Jews to die a natural death.

I knew the place where my father was buried and found the tombstone on the ground but not broken. I found in the city a retired laborer who helped me in raising and cementing the stone in its place. My wife cleaned the place nicely. From that time on we went every year to the nearby Karlsbad spa, but the main aim of our trip was *kever avoth*.

In the past three years, due to my bad health, we have not been able to go to *kever avoth*, but the Jewish community in Prague has informed us that the Czechoslovakian government is taking good care of the cemetery and that it has rebuilt the stone fence around the cemetery at its own expense. The community also promised me that they would have somebody periodically look after the grave of my father, *alav hashalom*.

The burden of the prolonged war was too heavy to bear at home, as well as on the front, where the soldiers were war-weary. To take advantage of the war-weariness of the soldiers, a new weapon was introduced. We bombarded the Italian lines and rear with pamphlets from airplanes which encouraged the soldiers to put an end to the war which they could never win, as they could see from the results of the eleven offensives which they had initiated. They would be better off to come over to our side and make an end to the slaughter.

The Italians, on the other hand, knew how scarce our supplies were and showered our lines with pamphlets in which they invited our soldiers to go over to their side, where they would have plenty to eat. In addition to the pamphlets gift packages containing cigarettes, chocolates, and canned stew were dropped on our lines.

It was rare for Italians to desert to the Austrian side; Austria, however, had to suffer the desertion of many of her soldiers to the Italian side. Desertions of Czechs, Poles, soldiers of other Slav nationalities, and even Hungarians were taking place all the time and were on the increase during this third year of the war. Italians drafted into the Austrian army from the Trentino, Gorizia, and Trieste, who had to kill an enemy akin to their own nationality, often deserted to the Italians.

The Court-Martial. Not all the Italian gift packages landed in or just behind the Austrian lines. Some fell in the no-man's land located between the trenches and/or just in front of our barbed-wire rows. Once a few packages fell on a spot just in front of the lines which were held by a Hungarian company. The soldiers in our trenches discussed how ironic it was that when bombarding the lines the Italians most often achieved direct hits, but when it came to giving away some goodies, they just missed the target. Then they would discuss how fine it would be to get the packages.

A gypsy soldier from that company, tempted all day by the packages, decided that there was really no great risk in going out at night to bring them back. After dark, when there was no shooting, he took a wire cutter, went over the ramparts, cut an opening in the barbed wire and started to quietly crawl toward the packages. Suddenly a rocket flared up which lit up the terrain as bright as daytime. The Italians realized that somebody was crawling toward the packages and didn't open fire. Instead an officer in the adjoining entrenchment held by Tyrolers, suspecting that a soldier was deserting to the Italians, ordered his men to open fire. The man panicked and ran back into the trenches. All were happy to see him back unharmed, although they were disappointed that he hadn't been able to get the packages.

The Tyrolers reported to the command of the regiment that they had prevented the desertion of a man from the adjoining Hungarian battalion. The next morning the company to which the gypsy belonged received an order to put the deserter under arrest and send him down under guard to the command of the regiment.

There, without any delay, a court-martial was held. The soldier was charged with desertion to the enemy. Three officers, with a military judge presiding, heard the case. Another military judge functioned as defense attorney. The accused assured the court that he had never given thought to deserting his unit and that the only reason he had left the trenches was to collect the packages which were lying in front of the barbed wire. All his colleagues knew what his intentions were, and they could testify and confirm that he was telling the truth. The court didn't want to believe his story. Based on the report of the Tyrolian officer they rejected the defense attorney's request to call as witnesses the soldiers from the accused's company and sentenced him to death by a firing squad.

The defense attorney's plea for mercy, based on the fact that the accused was one of the bravest soldiers, who had voluntarily gone out with a patrol and brought back a "tongue," and who had been decorated many times for bravery, went unheeded. The evident innocence of the accused didn't matter. It was a preconceived affair to set an example. In a matter of minutes, not hours, the brigadier sanctioned the verdict.

The cruelest thing in this case was that six comrades from his platoon were ordered down from the trenchline to form the execution squad, with the commander of the platoon in charge. A regiment from the reserve was brought to the place of the execution to watch and witness the procedure. The poor gypsy was fastened to a tree, hooded, and blindfolded. He didn't utter a single word during the time the execution was being prepared. A priest approached the condemned man, but the only word he spoke to the priest was, *"Weg!"* ("Away, get lost").

True to the maxim of the army, *Maul halten und weiter dienen* ("hold your tongue and carry on"), his comrades did what they were told to do. The command "Aim and fire" was barely audible. After the shots were fired the soldier was cut loose, and laid on the ground. A doctor went over to him and, after five minutes, he pronounced the executed man dead. This show of inhumanity didn't boost the morale of the soldiers who had witnessed this cruel act of injustice. Later, whenever I saw an execution in the concentration camp, it brought back to my mind the execution of the alleged deserter.

The Austrians, desperate on the Italian front, turned to Germany with a request for help. The Germans dispatched in great secrecy an army with a huge quantity of artillery and equipment to the Austro-Italian front. The German General Staff took over the joint command of both their own and the Austrian forces.

A weak spot on the Italian front between the Isonzo plateau and the Julian Alps at Caporetto was chosen for the starting point of the attack, which began with a heavy bombardment of poison gas and explosives from the massed artillery batteries and airplanes, killing everyone in the Italian lines. Up till then the struggle was only in the mountains, but when the mountainous positions were broken through there was no longer any resistance. The combined Austrian and German forces pushed the Italians farther back, reaching the Tagliamento and then the Piave River. The entire northern part of Italy from the Trentino in the west to the mouth of the Isonzo River in the east was in Austrian hands.

After entering the captured regions the conquerors, German as well as Austrian, began to immediately plunder the military depots and the civilian population. Loading themselves with things which they would never need, they only increased the ballast they were already carrying. One could see some soldiers with a broken tube from an old phonograph under one arm and a chicken under the other.

Wherever a cow or a pig could be found it was carried away, slaughtered, and cooked in the field kitchens. To see the eyes of a helpless peasant when his last cow or pig was taken from him was extremely depressing. It reminded me of the Russian occupation of our shtetl, with only one difference. The houses were not burned down, the people were not beaten, nor were the women raped. Later, during the occupation, when the population depended on the meager rations doled out to them and was starving, no force was needed to win a girl's favor. A bread, a roll of sausage, a piece of meat, a few bars of soap, or chocolate closed the deal.

Officers could do nothing to stop pillaging. The marauders were drunk, and laughed at them, especially when the marauder was a German, and the officer, an Austrian. The Germans looked down on the Austrians and treated them as inferiors. Name calling and pushing became frequent.

Sometime after we had reached the Piave, a regrouping of our forces took place, and my regiment was moved again to the western section of the front. The aim of the Austrians was to cross the Piave, invade the valley of the Po River, and so open the way into the heart of Italy. However, after their debacle, the Italians reorganized their forces and were able to maintain strong resistance. A stalemate developed which lasted for about a year. Then in order to save the Italians from defeat, French, British, and later American troops were dispatched to join the Italians.

Again a Hero. Our line of defense ran on the south side of a hill. I had installed my communication post in a blasted-out cavern on the north side of the hill. Near the end of November 1917, our trenches came under a strong artillery bombardment which rained explosive shells and gas bombs upon us. The reports which started to come in from the front lines were very disappointing. We were attacked by units of the French army. Our losses were enormous, and our men were surrendering without any resistance. Most of the phones were silent or were answered in French.

When the connection from my cavern to the command post of our regiment ceased to function I realized that the enemy was in our trenches along nearly the whole length of the front. I knew that it would not take long before they came over to our side of the hill. I ordered that our equipment be smashed and that we should be ready for an escape.

We had only one possible escape route. A few steps from my

cavern behind a bend was a steep, snow-filled gorge running straight into a valley, on the other side of which, on the ridge of a mountain, our next line of defense was entrenched. I had with me a sergeant, two telephonists, and the orderly. In order to get out of the loop we had only to slide down the gorge as fast as possible before the French came over to our side. I got a spade on which to slide and my men were supposed to used their canvas tents.

Just as we left the cavern for the edge of the ridge, a French soldier with his rifle shouldered suddenly appeared before us from the bend on the other side of the ridge. A few more Frenchmen followed, whom we noticed only later because they were still behind the bend of the hill. The Frenchman, who found himself two steps in front of the sergeant, a giant of a man, became frightened. Without allowing the Frenchman any time to use his rifle, the sergeant, in a split-second decision threw his canvas tent, on which he was to slide down the gorge, upon the Frenchman. He sprang on him and entangled him in the tent as if in a straitjacket. Jumping into the snow he slid down on his pants, carrying behind him the Frenchman who was wrapped up in the tent. The rest of us followed at once. By the time the other Frenchmen realized what had happened, we were already out of their sight at the bottom of the valley. There, with the Frenchman unwrapped, disarmed, and frisked, we marched to the command post of the regiment. The colonel was pleased to have a prisoner taken and ordered me to write a report, describing all that had happened.

The remnants of the regiment were replenished with new arrivals, and a few weeks later, in the order of the day, all five of us who had escaped and brought with us a French prisoner were heralded as heroes. What we did was described in a story, not taken from my report, but in a version written by the propaganda officer from his own imagination. What the staff of the regiment intended to do was to cover up the shameful mass surrender at the first attack of the French by showing that in the ranks of our regiment there were heroes. The sergeant received the highest distinction which could be bestowed on a noncommissioned officer, the Golden Medal for Bravery. I was amazed that I too received the highest medal which could be bestowed on an officer for bravery in battle, the big Silver Medal with a golden *K* on it, the initial of the Emperor, Karl. The telephonists received high distinctions as well, and my orderly received the lowest one, although we all had, with the exception of the sergeant, distinguished ourselves with the same degree of passivity.

With the so-called *Karl Truppenkreuz,* a medal given to everyone who was at the front for at least a year, I had a collection of four medals. With them I was to have qualified for a lifetime monthly pension, which, of course, was never paid, since there was no longer an Austro-Hungarian monarchy after the war. I did, however, make good use of my medals; my sons used to play with them.

Colonel Kurmanowycz, a Ukrainian who came to the front from the Austrian General Staff, took over the command of my newly pieced together regiment. He never talked about his nationality and didn't care about anyone else's nationality. I later met this man under entirely different circumstances.

The colonel brought with him *Oberleutnant* Abel, an Austrian from Graz, as his first adjutant. The duties of second adjutant were given to me. The command post of the regiment was a multinational one, a mix of Germans, Jews, Poles, and Ukrainians. *Oberleutnant* Abel and I became friends. In the spring of 1918, I got a furlough for three weeks. *Oberleutnant* Abel gave me a letter to his parents, and a few Edelweiss he had plucked high up in the mountains for his fiancée. *Oberleutnant* Abel's parents were delighted to receive the personal greetings from their son. They invited me to stay with them and brought tickets for the opera for themselves, their son's fiancée, and me.

After the *Anschluss* (the annexation of Austria to the German Reich), I noticed among the names of important Nazis in the newspapers that of my former friend, *Oberleutnant* Abel.

I spent the rest of my furlough with my mother and aunt, who were still living as refugees in the Sudetenland. I also managed to spend a few days in Stryj with my uncle and my fiancée. On the way back to the Italian front, I stopped in Vienna for a day and visited with some friends.

At the Kadimah, a student society, I heard news which touched me deeply—news which hadn't filtered through to us at the front at all. I learned about the Balfour Declaration. As a result I now saw in an entirely different light the news that our allies, the Turks, had been beaten by the British and driven out of Palestine, which was now in British hands.

I also learned about, and was impressed by, President Wilson's Fourteen Points, which he proposed as a basis for a peace treaty to be imposed on the Central Powers. The main points of his proclamation included self-determination for all nations, with frontiers drawn along recognizable lines of nationality; the creation of a Polish state inhabited by Polish nationals; protection of minorities; reduction of national armaments to forces needed for domestic order; and the creation of an Association of Nations with the purpose of guaranteeing political independence to all states. For me all these news items were rays of hope that the war was not being fought in vain, and that we might look ahead to a better future, hopefully with no more wars.

When Colonel Kurmanowycz was called back to the General Staff, I regretted it very much. In his place we got a new regimental commander, a von: Colonel von der Eltz, a German from the Sudetenland. An old gentleman who had been taken out of cold storage, he was an anti-Semite, and didn't make any attempt to hide his feelings. He knew a little Yiddish, a few words which he had acquired when stationed as a young officer in Lwów. On the day of his arrival at our regiment he held an *Offiziersrapport* in order to become acquainted with his subalterns. He asked every Jewish-looking officer what his real name was. When he was told, say, Max so and so, he asked, "Are you sure it isn't, maybe, Moishe so and so?"

17

The End of World War I

THE SWALLOW WHICH ushered in the end of World War I was the Russian Revolution of 1917. There were over a million Austrian prisoners of war in Russia, most of them of Czech nationality, who formed a Czech Legion to fight against Austria. After the revolution, the prisoners, soaked in Russian revolutionary propaganda and convinced that the war was over, started to move westwards and headed back home. Since the Austrian army had suffered substantial losses in manpower, they were put through a short period of retraining and sent to various units dispersed over the entire length of the Italian front.

These reconditioned defenders of the fatherland were infected with antiwar propaganda and were carriers of a contagious virus: disobedience. Whenever they were able to gather an audience of even only one or two men, they told their listeners time and again their version of the Russian Revolution. With an ambiguous grin, they repeatedly retold the story of how the Russian soldiers had come to understand that the war was being fought not in the interest of the people but solely in the interest of the nobility, represented by the officers. The soldiers used their own brains, said "enough is enough," and refused to obey orders. They took revenge on their officers, killing many of them, and simply left the front and headed home.

As prisoners of war, the returnees said, they had it good in Russia and there was no reason to think that they wouldn't be even better off as prisoners of war in Italy. Thus the returnees didn't stay long at the front, especially those of Czech nationality.

At the first opportunity they surrendered and went over to the Italian side, where they could join the Czech Legion fighting in French uniforms in the ranks of the Allied forces. With the Czechs went also Poles, Slovaks, Ruthenians, and members of other Slav nationalities, and even Hungarians.

The soldiers at the front shivered in their uniforms made of textiles with a mixture of nettles, which seldom got dry in the prevailing rainy days. The daily ration of an Austrian soldier was 150 grams of bread baked from a mixture of flour, cornmeal, and ground dried beans, a soup made from dried vegetables, and 70 grams of meat. If meat was not supplied, which was often the case, a double portion of bread was given instead.

The Austrian High Command, therefore, decided that the only solution to the calamity would be a decisive attack over the Piave River which would open the way deep into Italy to the American provisions stocked there. In June 1918 the Austrians began the attack and crossed the Piave River, but they were beaten back. Nonetheless the provisions behind the Italian lines lured like a fata morgana, and in October 1918, the Austrians tried once again. They crossed the river at many points, built pontoon bridges, and brought over equipment and supplies. However, the water in the river rose and swept away the bridges.

Also, Italy got help from her allies. British, American, and French forces joined the Italians and launched an attack on the whole length of the front, crossing the Piave to the island of Popadopoli and advancing to the Tagliamento River.

The British army brought a new weapon to this front which they had previously used against the Germans on the western front—the tanks. Invulnerable to machine guns and capable of crossing trenches, they couldn't have been used on the Italian front as long as the fighting was in the mountains. Now that the front had been brought down onto a flat region, they were put into action. The Austrians, seeing these monsters, panicked and started to run, soon to be captured and taken prisoner by the attacking forces.

On October 28, Austria asked the Italians for an armistice, the acceptance of which the Italians delayed, wanting to gain back more territory before the armistice lines would be drawn.

My regiment was once again on the western sector of the front at Trento, where I had first been introduced to the Italian front in

1916. We managed to keep the Italians at arm's length as we fell back and withdrew to positions in the Tyrolian Alps. There, on November 2, we started to build new positions near Meran.

However, the first order we received the next day from the brigade was to inform all the units that an armistice agreement with the Italians had been concluded. The next day the commandant of our regiment, Colonel von der Eltz, ordered the officers to a meeting at which he declared that the war had not yet ended. What was taking place was only a temporary cease-fire, he said, and we could be called at any time to take up our arms once again. Although we had lost the battle, we would fight and win the war.

A captain of German nationality from Tyrol, and not one of the minorities, asked the colonel how it would be possible to win the war if we were not able to feed our troops. If our mess still functioned, it was only by what we obtained from our own people, who were starving. There was no longer an army with which to start any further activities. Discipline was nonexistent, soldiers were tearing off the rosettes from the officers' caps and the stars from their collars. Resisting officers were being beaten and disarmed. The troops were in disarray and the men were leaving for home. The colonel then said that insubordination bordered on treason and whoever committed such an act would be courtmartialed. He reminded us also that we had not yet been released from our oath of allegiance to the Kaiser.

The captain then said: "I, for one, am not prepared to wait for miracles. I am leaving for home, which is not far away from Meran; for me the war is over." He saluted and left. "For us, too!" said all the others in a chorus, and proceeded to leave, without saluting.

It was one thing for a Tyroler to leave for his home, since it was not far away, but it was something else for the majority of our regiment, Ukrainians, Poles, and Jews originating from Galicia. We were in a foreign country over 2,000 kilometers away from home. Everything was in decay. The army disbanded and became a mob of irregulars. Everyone looked for his own conveyance. With the lack of food, the ex-soldiers started plundering and robbing the civilians, and not only civilians, but other soldiers as well. Our only problem was how to get home and out of the mess with the men with whom we shared the misery of the war years.

Force of arms was used to climb onto already overcrowded

trains. Soldiers rode on buffers and on the steps, while holding convulsively onto the rails at the doors. Soldiers settled on the roofs of the railway cars and many were killed when the train unexpectedly entered a tunnel. Railway stations were seized by marauders who robbed the passing trains.

The situation of our men was desperate and hopeless. There were some 300 men, including many noncommissioned officers and sergeants, and six officers; one Pole, three Ukrainians, and two Jews, mostly if not all from eastern Galicia. Unlike units of other nationalities, our men were not rebellious and looked to the sergeants of their own nationality for help, realizing that they would undoubtedly get lost if they acted on their own.

The next day the wagoneers, who were Ukrainians, told the sergeants that they had been ordered by a group of German officers to get the train with all the supplies loaded and to await further orders to move. They were given one more day to look after the horses, feed them well, and replace the shoes where needed. Also to check the wagons for necessary repairs. The sergeants became alarmed, and told the officers what was happening.

The highest in rank among us, the Pole who was a captain, immediately called a meeting of the officers and sergeants in order to decide what should be done. The meeting concluded that the wagons and the horses might be useful for short distances, but that we would have to rely on railway transportation. But under no circumstances should we allow the provisions to be taken from us right under our noses. We decided to outsmart the Germans. If they wanted the train, let them have the wagons and horses. We, however, should secure for ourselves all the supplies which were still on the wagons. We would do to them what they had intended to do to us.

Everything should be done in secret, but in case they found out about our intentions and tried to use force against us, they would be no match for us. They were only a group of officers, whereas we had all our men behind us. The wagoneers were called in and told to go ahead with the preparing of the train for the trip as ordered by the German officers, and to have the wagons loaded and ready to leave that evening, not the next day as requested by the Germans. They were to keep quiet about any of the actions planned by us.

The captain located a big warehouse behind the railway station, and all our men were brought there in small groups. In the evening, as soon as it became dark, the wagoneers rolled up to the warehouse with the loaded wagons. In no time everything that was considered necessary for our trip was unloaded into the warehouse. Two field kitchens were also brought from the train into the warehouse. We were interested in the large quantities of food, as well as tobacco, and some liquor which was still on the train. We knew that we would be passing through some hostile places on our way home and decided to hold on to our rifles, and also to take a couple of machine guns and a quantity of hand grenades with us.

Armed sentries were posted around the warehouse. The empty wagons were driven back to where they had been taken from and the wagoneers returned on foot to the warehouse. Everything was done quietly and secretly at a time when the German officers were dancing and drinking at a farewell feast to celebrate the end of the war. For us, however, the question was how to get out of Meran as soon as possible, and to avoid an encounter with the Germans.

The captain, who was sitting at a table beside the machine guns in the warehouse, called in the stationmaster and asked him to assemble a train consisting of two flat cars and ten cars of whatever type was available, freight or passenger cars, plus a locomotive with plenty of coal, an engineer, and brakemen. At first the stationmaster tried to wriggle out of the task, saying that there were no cars at the station. The captain used the carrot and stick method, offering him the alternative of cooperation "or else," but not spelling out what the "or else" meant. A bargain was struck. He was promised two sacks of potatoes, a case of sugar, and some cigarettes under the condition that everything would be ready before midnight. It took him nearly two hours to assemble the train as ordered, but he had no men who were qualified to run a train for a long distance. After he received his bribe, he told us that in about an hour a goods train was supposed to arrive at the station from Innsbruck. The crew would leave the train in Meran, take on water and coal, and return the locomotive to Innsbruck. We decided to load and board our train right away so as to be ready when the expected train arrived.

The two flatcars were put at both ends of the train. On each of them a field kitchen was loaded and secured against moving; five men with a machine gun and ammunition were stationed on these cars for security.

The men boarded the freight cars, and we waited for the arrival of the expected train and its crew. The stationmaster, wanting to get rid of us, undertook to mediate and to help us strike a deal with the engineer. When the train arrived it didn't take very long to come to an agreement with the engineer to carry our train to Innsbruck. After he received a thousand cigarettes, he told us that he should have been the one to bribe us because he was scared that he might be attacked by marauders on his way back, who would force him at some station to assemble a train and carry them to Innsbruck, maybe even farther. But now he felt safe with our guards.

We left Meran just before daybreak and were in Innsbruck in the evening. We asked the stationmaster there to secure a locomotive and a crew for us. He phoned the new city council, asking them for advice as to what he should do. The mayor soon arrived at the station and, after a brief discussion, was persuaded that it was in his own interest to let our train move. The next day we were on our way via Linz to Vienna. At some smaller stations we encountered problems. Only after we threatened to use our machine guns were we able to continue our journey. At the larger stations we had to deal with citizens' committees. There we met no resistance but only cooperation and goodwill; the locomotive was changed and a new crew of railwaymen was assigned to haul our train a stretch farther.

It took us six days to reach Vienna, where our train was put on a side track at the marshaling yard. We were only halfway on our journey home. Here again we were met by a friendly committee whose only worry was that they were not able to supply us with any kind of provisions. When they were told that our kitchens were working and we only needed to move a step farther on our way home, they promised us help but told us that under the circumstances that was not a simple thing, because in eastern Galicia a war was going on between the Ukrainians and the Poles. The railway went past Cracow only till Przemyśl. Whoever wanted to go farther east or to districts south of Lwów had to take the route via Budapest and Slovakia.

The Poles from our train disembarked in Vienna and looked for a train heading in the direction of Cracow. For the rest of us who wanted to proceed to eastern Galicia there was a big problem which the citizens' committee at the railway station in Vienna tried to solve as best they could.

An agreement had to be reached between the railroad authorities in Vienna and Budapest to allow the passage of the train through Hungary. It took many days to complete the transactions with the Hungarians, mainly with regard to the question of the ownership of the cars of our train. In order to avoid complications a train of Austrian cars was assembled similar to the one on which we had arrived in Vienna. We transferred onto the newly supplied train and after a week's stay in Vienna left for Budapest. In Budapest we didn't encounter any trouble. The locomotive was sent back to Vienna, and we received a new one with a crew.

The next day we were on our way to Miškolc, but there we ran into real trouble. A representative of the local national committee came to our train with an ultimatum: We had to hand over the rifles, the machine guns, and every piece of ammunition to the committee. We were given three hours to have all the weapons brought into the warehouse at the railway station. The Ukrainians refused. They wanted all the weapons which we had brought with us from the Italian front for their compatriots who were fighting the Poles. They declared that they would fight for the right of free passage home. However, when shown that on a hill behind the station there were three cannons aimed at us, to which our machine guns were no match, they agreed to surrender the weapons.

We were brought under escort to the border station of Lawoczne. After we were stranded at the Lawoczne station for another two days, a locomotive was called in and our train was carried to Stryj. As soon as the train halted at the railway station, a Ukrainian officer ordered us to march to a nearby school, where we would be housed for a few days, and then join the Ukrainian army.

I, for one, didn't ask any questions. I walked away, aiming for my uncle's home, which was only a few blocks from the railway station. But on the way I was stopped by a military patrol. They asked me if I knew there was a curfew, and where I was going.

After deciding that I was a Polish spy, they took me to the military police station, where they locked me up in a solitary cell. I overheard someone in the corridor behind the door to my cell mentioning the name of a General Kurmanowycz. It dawned on me that it could well be the former commander of my regiment, Colonel Kurmanowycz, the Ukrainian. I knocked at the door and told the guard that I wanted to see General Kurmanowycz, whose adjutant I had been on the Italian front. Soon an officer arrived and asked me why I wanted to see the general. I told him that I intended to complain about being unlawfully arrested. The general would vouch that I was not a Polish spy, and I requested to be connected with the general by phone. The officer told me that the general was in Stanislawów and would not be returning to Stryj. He refused to let me phone but promised that he would call the general first thing in the morning. He didn't wait until the morning, however. In about an hour he returned and told me that the general would be away from Stanislawów for three days and that he wanted to see me a day or two after his return. I was set free and received marching documents to Stanislawów which were valid for five days.

At my uncle's home they were surprised but glad to see me. They told me that it would have been better to remain in Vienna and not to enter voluntarily into the lion's den. Didn't I know that a war was going on between the Ukrainians and the Poles? Each side was accusing the Jews of helping the other, and Jews were being beaten, robbed, and even killed by both the Ukrainians and the Poles.

The Ukrainian newspaper had just published a report from Lwów that the Poles had perpetrated a pogrom in that city and that 100 Jews had been killed, and many hundreds more had been wounded. At first we didn't believe it, considering it to be another Ukrainian propaganda trick because they wanted to induct Jews into their army. But to our sorrow a Jew who had fled Lwów and arrived in Stryj confirmed that the tragedy had really happened. Jews were leaving our city, trying to evade a draft into the Ukrainian army, which, according to rumors, would be decreed in a day or two. It didn't matter whether or not General Kurmanowycz was Colonel Kurmanowycz, the former commander of my regiment; if I were to go to see him in Stanislawów, I would become an officer of the Ukrainian army which was killing Jews.

The next morning I contacted some people who had connections with smugglers and were in the business of facilitating the passage out of Galicia through the Carpathian Mountains to Carpatho-Russ, which was previously Hungary. After having paid a substantial amount of money in the old currency (people didn't want to accept the new Ukrainian currency, the *griwny*), I said goodby to my relatives and left with a guide, who brought me via a rarely used foot path in the mountains to the first railway station on the other side of the border of Galicia. I boarded a train which was filled with home-going soldiers and arrived via Budapest in Vienna, in time to register for the second semester of the school year 1918/1919. The university was bursting at the seams with demobilized soldiers. Everyone was in a hurry to finish his education, get a job, marry, and forget the events of the war. And, so was I.

The crucial factor in the outcome of the war was the entry of the might of the United States of America. In the autumn of 1918 the Allies were able to strike blow after blow at the weakened and war-weary Central Powers on all battlefields.

Based on President Wilson's fourteen points, the Austro-Hungarian and the German Empires asked the Allies, in October 1918, for an armistice. In response to this request the Allies asked for unconditional surrender of the Central Powers, to which the latter agreed. Armistice agreements with the Austro-Hungarian monarchy and Germany were signed, with the former November 3, 1918, and with the latter November 11, 1918.

The eleventh of November, the day of the signing of the armistice agreement by Germany, was supposed to mark the end, not only of the First World War, but of all war. This "war to end wars," however, was only a prelude to a more terrible and devastating war which took place only twenty years later. The eleventh of November was proclaimed "Remembrance Day."

The war ended with a military victory for the Allies. As a result the map of Europe changed completely, and thrones and empires collapsed. Emperors, Tsars, and Sultans had reigned over their subjects "by the grace of God." At least, that was their conviction and what they asked their subjects to believe.

In the name of "God and the Monarch" people had been sacrificed and forced to give their lives to the insatiable demon, the Moloch of war. However, when the burnt offerings on the battlefields, during the four years of World War I, amounted to millions, God withdrew His grace from the Kaisers, the Tsar, and the Sultan, and let their thrones collapse. The God of the Russian Orthodox Church began the process. He was soon followed by the God of the Austrian Catholics and that of the Prussian Lutherans. Mohammed, however, showed more compassion with the Moslems of Turkey.

The first of the monarchies to fall was that of Russia. It was replaced by the Communist regime headed by Lenin. Next to topple was the Habsburg dynasty.

The Habsburg Empire was destroyed by war-weariness, shortages, hunger at the front, and centrifugal actions by the many nationalities of the monarchy whose representatives openly declared in the Parliament in Vienna that their aim was to smash and destroy Austria.

Around the middle of October 1918, Kaiser Karl issued a manifesto granting the nationalities of the Austrian part of the monarchy the right of self-determination in a common monarchy under the umbrella of the Habsburgs. It was too late, however, and too small an offer to induce the antagonistic nationalities to hold on together. All of them aimed for total independence. The Austro-Hungarian monarchy was falling apart. Different republics were formed and carved out of the monarchy in which they had been united.

In Prague, on October 28, 1918, Professor Masaryk, proclaimed the Czechoslovak Republic, consisting of the provinces of Bohemia, Moravia, Silesia, Slovakia, and Carpatho-Russ, the latter two still under Hungarian rule. He was appointed President, and Beneš, Foreign Minister.

The Poles in Cracow issued a declaration proclaiming that Galicia was separating from Austria to join the new sovereign Polish state proclaimed in Warsaw.

The Slav nations of Serbia, Croatia, Slovenia, and Bosnia proclaimed a sovereign state, the Kingdom of Yugoslavia, with Belgrad the capital of the kingdom. The Italian-populated parts of Austria joined Italy, Transylvania joined Rumania. The Ukrainians in eastern Galicia proclaimed an independent and sovereign Ukrainian Republic to be united with the Russian part of the Ukraine. Hungary proclaimed its separation from Austria but declared that it would remain a kingdom.

On November 11, 1918, Kaiser Karl abdicated.

What was left of the monarchy was her German provinces, and they too proclaimed an independent republic known as *Deutschoesterreich* (German Austria).

On the same day, November 11, 1918, that Emperor Karl of the

Austro-Hungarian Monarchy signed his resignation papers. Wilhelm II, the German Kaiser, fled into exile in Holland. Thus the dynasty of the Hohenzollerns came to an end and the wings of the arrogant German Empire were clipped.

It was, in fact, the end of the Hohenzollern Dynasty and at the same time the end of the reign of the heads of the different German states. Vienna, the once bustling joyous and proud capital of a great country now became the capital of a minuscule country. It was like a huge head sitting on the remnants of a body whose limbs had been amputated, or had fallen off when the body was rotting.

Thousands of army officers of all ranks, and tens of thousands of functionaries of the monstrous Austrian bureaucratic apparatus, whose services had suddenly become superfluous in the little new Austria, flocked to Vienna, claiming pensions and seeking help from the once rich, but now empty, treasury. Austria, by provoking the war, had gambled away the monarchy and had to give up her luxurious style of life.

The Austro-Hungarian monarchy had been a market for about 50 million people, but after her collapse the successor states put up trade barriers between one another. Import and export restrictions of many goods were introduced. Custom duties were clamped on merchandise which had previously moved freely, not hampered by borders.

Means of communication were crippled and in some places nonexistent. Before the war there had been freedom of movement, not only inside the monarchy, but across all of Europe. Passports were not required when crossing most of the borders of the European countries. On a trip one could use any of the main currencies everywhere in Europe. To cross the border from one country into another, with the exception of the Russian borders, was no problem.

Now each newly born state issued its own passports and its own currency, which underwent rapid devaluation. The borders were only 200 or 300 kilometers apart, and in many cases even less, and a collection of visas for exit, transit, and entry in any state was required. Moreover, miniwars now began to break out between many of the breakaway states from the Austro-Hungarian monarchy. On top of the many millions of lives lost during the war, there were new battles claiming new losses of life and material. A few months later the Austrian government confiscated all the properties which had belonged to the Habsburgs and expelled the ex-Kaiser and his family from Austria. They found asylum in Switzerland. Karl, however, slipped twice into Hungary in an attempt to regain the crown of Hungary, but failed. Consequently he was exiled with his family to the island of Madeira, where he died in 1922. This was the end of the reign of the dynasty of the Habsburgs.

The Ottoman Empire was sliced into pieces and all non-European parts of it were cut off. The French got the mandate over Syria and Lebanon. Many Arab states were created, and Britain got the mandate over Palestine, where they were supposed to build a Jewish homeland. Unfortunately the British didn't build the Jewish homeland. A Jewish state had to be won by the Jews on their own at a high price, paid in blood and Jewish lives.

The Armenian Holocaust: The Turks, aiming to eliminate the Armenians through pillage, robbery, and simply by mass murder, annihilated, in 1915 alone, one and a half million Armenians with no regard as to age or sex. After the war the Turks, wanting to get rid of the Armenians once and for all in a "Final Solution," encouraged their beaten army to manifest their heroism by perpetrating cruel atrocities behind the lines. In cases where the Turkish heroes were not sure whether a man whom they had just captured was a Turk or an Armenian, they used the same method of identification later used by the Germans in the Second World War. The man was ordered to pull down his pants. The foreskin of his penis or the lack of it was the identification mark and, at the same time, the death sentence of the individual being questioned. The Turks were circumcised, the Armenians were not.

I shall never forget the sadness and emotion I felt for months after I read a book written by Franz Werfel entitled *Muza Dagh* in which the author laid bare the cruelties perpetrated by the Turks on the Armenian people. Nearly two million Armenians were mercilessly and cruelly killed. It seems to me that only Jews, who have experienced Hitler, are able to really understand the Holocaust brought on the Armenians by the Turks.

After the disintegration of the Austro-Hungarian Monarchy, the law of the jungle prevailed in her previous territories. Each of the newly born successor states wanted to grab for itself the biggest possible slice of the inheritance pie. Quarrels over disputed territory took place: Hungary wrangled with Rumania, Serbia, and Slovakia; Czechs with Poles, Yugoslavs with Italians, and Poles fought Ukrainians.

In Hungary the Reds, under Bela Kun, took over the regime after the liberal government of Count Karolyi resigned when the Allies asked him to evacuate territories inhabited by minorities. Fighting between the big powers had ended, but for the Jews of Middle, and especially Eastern, Europe, dark clouds were forming. Anti-Semitism raised its head in many countries of Europe, especially Germany.

Paris was filled with White Russian reactionary immigrants who, holding jobs as taxi drivers, dishwashers or waiters, denounced the Bolsheviks. Guzzling vodka, they busied themselves with the dissemination of anti-Semitism in Europe. Any lie was good enough to be used in the anti-Jewish campaign. They brought with them the so-called "Protocols of the Elders of Zion," a proven falsification and an accumulation of lies. They translated them into German and many other languages, and fueled the fire of anti-Semitism. The Protocols contained a story of an alleged secret gathering of Jewish leaders who conspired to organize a Jewish world empire by exploiting the Jewish monopoly of the world's finances, by their control of the press, by using terrorist tactics, by creating wars and revolutions, by overthrowing governments, and by seizing power during the resulting chaos. They were published in Russia at the time of the terrible pogrom in Kishiniev, by the notorious "Chornayay Sotnya" (the Black Hundred). The Protocols found a ready market in postwar Germany and were used as a tool in anti-Jewish propaganda. They were praised by Hitler, who referred to them in his *Mein Kampf*. Translated into Polish in Poznań, they were widely used by the anti-Semitic *Endecja* (the National Democrats).

The Protocols found their way to America and fed anti-Semitism there. The Ku-Klux Klan, and many others, found inspiration in the Protocols. They also prompted Henry Ford to publish a series of articles about the International Jewish Conspiracy which, though later retracted, did a lot of harm to Jews. By coincidence, or not, immigration to the United States was restricted in the early years of the 1920's. Immigration quotas dealt a harsh blow to the Jews. It happened just at a time when homeless masses were fleeing and needed refuge. Their lives were endangered and their future uncertain. Also, another place of refuge, Palestine, became subject to restricted immigration.

Europe was sick; sick in the real meaning of the word. In 1918/1919 grippe, or the Spanish flu, as it was called, hit Europe, along with the worst of the epidemics, such as typhus and cholera. They spread to the overseas countries as well, killing, in addition to millions of casualties fallen on the battlefields, another ten million people.

Epidemics, lack of food, hunger bordering on starvation, industries destroyed, unemployment rising, currencies devaluated, and prices rocketing sky-high made the situation hard to bear. Somebody had to be responsible for the prevailing misery. Who else but the Jew could be the scapegoat? Jews were blamed for causing the war, for the collapse of the front, for the epidemics, for the lack of food, and for any other misery which happened. Jews were called shirkers and traitors, Bolsheviks, and capitalists. This was the case throughout Central and Eastern Europe in the immediate aftermath of the war, particularly in the Ukraine and the new Polish republic. Prior to the portrayal of Jewish life in interwar Poland as witnessed and remembered by me it is also worthwhile for a better understanding of the situation of the Jews during these turbulent years after the war to consider some other countries where anti-Semitism had been rooted for centuries.

I had the sad opportunity to refresh my memory about these painful events from clippings from the presitigious Viennese *Neue Freie Presse* and the *Wiener Morgenzeitung* when I was recently in Vienna on a stopover during a return trip to Canada from Israel. First a look at Germany and Russia, and a short recollection of the pogroms in Hungary, Slovakia, Rumania, and even in the Czech provinces. This will be followed by a narration of the terrible slaughter in the Ukraine by the hordes of Petlura and, of course, of the pogroms and oppressions Jews have been subjected to in Poland.

In Germany the communists tried in nearly all the provinces to create revolutions. Reactionary and anti-Semitic forces, in collaboration with the white emigres from Russia, raised their heads. Everywhere throughout the length and breadth of Germany massacres were commonplace. Communists murdered the Freikorps and they, in turn, massacred the communists. But all the organized gangs from the left, as well as from the right, were jointly engaged in brutal and ruthless killings of Jews.

In Russia, after the Bolshevik Revolution White generals, all fervent anti-Semites, organized counterrevolutionary armies and fought the Reds on different fronts. Wherever they set their foot, their main task was killing Jews. During the fighting, places changed hands from the Reds to the Whites, and vice versa. The Whites killed Jews, treating them as Bolsheviks. The Bolsheviks did likewise to Jews, capitalists, speculators, exploiters, and counterrevolutionaries. It didn't matter how poor a Jew might be. If he was a merchant he had to be rehabilitated and reeducated, which meant that he was sent to a labor camp.

Rumania was known for centuries as an anti-Semitic country in which equal rights were denied to Jews, where pogroms often occurred, and the governments were bent on forcing the Jews to emigrate. The worst riots against Jews were perpetrated by the Iron Guard organization, which was subsidized by the government. Jews were murdered and synagogues burned in Czernowitz and Orade Mare. The Rumanians were specialists in robbing, beating, and killing Jews and burning and demolishing synagogues. The government did nothing to quell anti-Jewish riots, and anti-Semitism became a part of the Rumanian official policy.

A terrible pogrom was perpetrated in Budapest by the Rumanians, when they were asked by the Great Powers in July 1919 to march into Hungary against the Bolshevik regime of Bela Kun. Upon entering the city the soldiers began robbing and plundering stores, offices, and apartments. The Rumanians incited the Hungarian mob, who fell upon Jews and delivered them into the hands of the Rumanian soldiers. Arrested Jews, without exception, were tortured, and many were beaten to death. Jewish property worth millions of crowns was loaded on military trucks and carried away to Rumania. Gangs of plunderers, under the leadership of Hungarian students and protected by Rumanian soldiers, stormed the Technical University, beating Jewish students, wounding fifteen, and leaving four of them past the hope of recovery.

Hungary itself was not standing idly by; the apostles of anti-Semitism in Austria were Dr. Lueger and Dr. Schoenerer. Hungary had her Istoczi and the Catholic clergy who fanned the fires of anti-Semitism. In the 1920s the white terror spread over the entire country, resulting in more than three hundred dead and thousands wounded.

Officers of the White Guard pulled Jews from the trains and beat them severely. In Kleinzell, 250 soldiers under the command of their officers scoured the streets with the cry, "We want to see Jewish blood running." They broke into Jewish houses, robbing and destroying them. Many Jews were wounded. Two brothers were badly beaten, and their eyes gouged out with bayonets. A lieutenant with five medals for bravery in defense of the Magyar fatherland was murdered on the street, as was a Jewish captain of the Hungarian army who had eight medals. Until then he was the pride of the city, which had bestowed on him the title of an Honorary Citizen. The police did not intervene and looked on with passivity. In various cities throughout the country Jews were robbed, mercilessly beaten, many killed, and a large number wounded. In Janosaga four Jews were killed and six were badly wounded. In Sarval a Jewish teacher was stabbed to death.

Slovakia: The Hungarian-brewed strain of anti-Semitism was very active in Slovakia. Riots occurred frequently through the centuries, with the exception of the time that the country was under the sovereignty of the Habsburgs. At the end of the First World War, pogroms took place in nearly all the cities and villages of Slovakia. The mobs robbed, plundered, and killed Jews. What couldn't be carried away was burned. Anti-Semitism was simmering all over Moravia and Bohemia. Even in this part of Czechoslovakia a major pogrom was carried out in the city of Holleschau in December 1918. It was a well-organized action carried out with military precision under the command of officers for the benefit of the city mob and the peasants from surrounding villages, who came to the city for the market day. They were invited by the ringleaders to do what they wished with the Jews. The telegraph and telephone lines were cut, and the police and gendarmes were disarmed and locked up in the city hall building. At the railway station a command post manned by an officer was set up; weapons and ammunition were taken from the depot and given to the civilians. Roadblocks were established and manned by soldiers at all exits leading from the city in order to prevent any Jews from escaping the city. Two Jews were killed, many others were wounded, and multi-millions in property damage was suffered.

A few months later the participants were brought before the court, the soldiers appearing before a military court and the civilians before a civil one. Sentences from one-and-a-half to fifteen years imprisonment at hard labor were meted out.

The government of Czechoslovakia was in the hands of such true liberals and democrats as Thomas Masaryk and Beneš. The trial of the hooligans was not a mockery, as was the custom in some of the other countries where pogromczyks were seldom brought before a court. And, if they were, they were either freed or given nothing more than a token punishment. When Beneš was asked about pogroms occurring in many places in Europe, he said that the treatment of its Jews in any given country showed the measure of the culture of that country. Masaryk, when offered the honorary citizenship bestowed on him by Holleschau, refused to accept it.

The Ukraine: The soil of the Ukraine has been soaked with Jewish blood throughout history. The Ukraine was the home of the Zaporozhian Cossacks, who in 1648, under Chmielnicki, massacred hundreds of thousands of Ukrainian and Polish Jews. It was the home of the Haidamaks, who a hundred years after Chmielnicki, tortured and beheaded 75,000 Ukrainian Jews. The Ukraine was the place where the Russian tsars established, toward the end of the eighteenth century, a huge ghetto, the Pale of Settlement. The Jews were barred from residing in other parts of the Russian Empire and were squeezed together in a limited area, thus becoming easy prey during the frequent pogroms. There, at the beginning of the current century, the terrible pogroms in Kishinev occurred in 1903, and the ritual-murder accusation of Beilis in the capital city of the Ukraine, Kiev, took place in 1912.

Petlura. After the German Empire collapsed in 1918 and the German forces withdrew from the Ukraine, a new government was formed, the East Ukraine Republic, ruled by a Directorate, the Rada.

Petlura became the Chief Commander of the Army, the *Holovni Ataman* and "little batko" (father), as his men lovingly and obediently used to call him.

As soon as the German forces withdrew, the Red Army marched

on the Ukraine. Petlura ordered a mobilization and built up an army of over 100,000 well-trained Cossacks, gangs of cutthroats, bandits, and murderers, under the command of atamans. A large Galician detachment was formed from prisoners of war taken by the Russians from the Austrian armies.

The Ukraine became the battlefield for various armies. The Reds fought the Ukrainians, and the White generals fought the Ukrainians and the Reds. Cities, towns, and villages changed hands constantly. This region in the former Pale of Settlement was densely populated by masses of impoverished Jews, and each change of the occupying forces resulted in terrible pogroms. The soldiers of the warring forces, the Whites, the Reds, and the *Petlurovtsi* (Petlura's forces), all of them, regardless of the color of their flag, were adherents of the prerevolutionary *Chornaya Sotnya* (Black Hundreds). The bacillus of anti-Semitism, suckled with their mother's milk, still circulated in their veins. For the chiefs of the different gangs and of their elite, the *Kurenyi Smerti* (the Corps of Death), under the direct command of the *Holovni Ataman*, Petlura, the annihilation of the Jews became the axiom.

It is impossible to describe the horrors of the pogroms perpetrated by the *Petlurovtsi*, which began in 1918 and intensified in 1919 and 1920. These were the most severe pogroms Jews anywhere had ever endured. Their cruelties were worse than those perpetrated by the hordes of Chmielnicki and the Haidamaks. They were surpassed only by the Nazis twenty years later. Jews were slaughtered in the multiples of thousands. Before being allowed to die they were tortured in a refined manner of inflicting pain and with cruelty which had never been known before. To remove rings, fingers were cut off; lobes of ears were ripped off for the removal of earrings; women of all ages, including those under the age of ten, were raped; eyes were put out, bellies cut open, people hacked into pieces, tongues cut out, old and young were drowned in rivers. Still others were beaten to death and their corpses fed to the pigs. Jews were herded into locked synagogues and burned alive. Petlura, the *Holovni Ataman*, didn't restrain his gangs of murderers from their devilish deeds, though he knew very well what was going on. He took no measures to quell these crimes. It was impossible in those chaotic days to compile exact statistics of the Jewish deaths. It was estimated by some to be 300,000. The number of crippled victims was twice as large. But does it matter how many thousands were butchered? Would Petlura's responsibility have been less if there had been fewer victims?

Petlura's heroes were not as successful on the battlefield as they were in slaughtering Jews. Beaten by the Reds, Petlura withdrew as far as he could into Galicia. There, however, he met the resistance of the Polish forces and, not being able to withstand their attacks, he decided to follow the maxim: if you can't beat them, join them! For the price of renouncing the claim of the Ukrainians to sovereignty over Galicia, he concluded an alliance with Pilsudski. Kiev, which should have been the reciprocal price the Poles promised Petlura, was captured.

The expedition, however, ended in failure when the Bolsheviks recaptured Kiev and, in a counteroffensive, succeeded in driving the attacking forces as far back as Warsaw. The defeat was the death knell to Petlura's forces and Petlura himself. He took refuge first in Warsaw and later in Paris, the dumping ground and watering point of all strains of anti-Semites whose hands were stained with Jewish blood. These included Russian princes, dukes, archdukes, survivors and relatives of the Romanovs, and generals of the different White armies. They felt themselves safe and secure under the rights of asylum France had granted them, regardless of what crimes they might have committed.

There were, however, also living in Paris, some survivors of the pogroms, close relatives of the victims, and other witnesses of the horrors inflicted on Jews by the *Petlurovtsi*. One of them was a watchmaker named Sholom Schwarzbard, a French-naturalized Russian Jew, decorated with the Croix de Guerre, France's highest decoration for bravery, which he had obtained while serving in the French Foreign Legion during the war. After the Russian Revolution of 1917, Schwarzbard went back to Russia to be with his family, but there he found no peace of mind when he learned that his family had been murdered by the *Petlurovtsi*. He left the Ukraine for France, where he opened a shop in Paris. During sleepless nights the atrocities of the *Petlurovtsi* came back to him in nightmares, and he dreamed of taking revenge for what had been done to his family and his people.

When Schwarzbard learned that Petlura was living in Paris, he decided that the best way of taking revenge was to kill Petlura himself. He bought a revolver, and one day in May 1926 he tracked down Petlura and shot him to death. Schwarzbard was arrested, and after a year he was brought to trial before a judge and jury of twelve Frenchmen. He was charged with premeditated murder, a crime for which the punishment was the death sentence. The prosecution tried to persuade the jury that Schwarzbard was a criminal who had killed an innocent man who had tried unsuccessfully to control an undisciplined army which had to live on the land and wouldn't obey his orders. In no way was Petlura responsible for the bad treatment Jews had been subjected to in those turbulent days. Most of the atrocities had been carried out by Denikin's army and the Bolsheviks. Schwarzbard was no avenger of his people but an agent of the Bolsheviks and had killed an innocent man.

Having characterized Schwarzbard as a simple murderer, the prosecution called a number of character witnesses who, while not denying the terrible pogroms, testified that Petlura was favorable to Jews. He had even condemned pogroms, which were the result of anarchy in the Ukraine. Petlura should be absolved of any guilt for what had happened to the Jews.

In his own defense Schwarzbard described the horrors of the pogroms he had witnessed and to which he had also been subjected. Petlura was the chief of the Haidamaks, and they had acted under his direction. As the Chief Commander, he was responsible for the murders committed by his soldiers. He, Schwarzbard, had personally lost more than twenty relatives in the pogroms of 1919; yes, he had, with premeditation, killed a murderer, but this was because the murderer had to atone for the crimes perpetrated on his people.

The team of defense lawyers was headed by Henri Torrés, a grandson of the founder of the League for the Defense of Dreyfus. The defense called only a few witnesses. Among them were victims of the pogroms who described in detail the horrors committed by the *Petlurovtsi*. Jews had been killed indiscriminately under the battlecry: *"Khaai zhive batko Petlura!"* ("Long live our Father, Petlura!")

Torrés pointed out a few places, such as Proskurow, where, during three days of rampaging 4,000 Jews had been murdered while Petlura was in the city; or Fastow, where 2,000 Jews had been hacked to death; or Zhitomir, with 1,500 victims. And there had been many other places. Had Petlura wanted to put an end to the mass killings of the Jews, he could have easily done so. Instead he allowed the pogroms to be committed as an incentive for his gangs, who were able to bathe freely in Jewish blood. As Commander-in-Chief, he was answerable for his soldiers and their deeds.

The trial ended with a verdict of "Not Guilty!"

The West Ukraine (Galicia). In October 1918, when the Austro-Hungarian monarchy was on its deathbed but clinically still alive, the Ukrainians in Galicia were swift to proclaim eastern Galicia as the National West Ukrainian Republic, to be united with the eastern Ukraine in an independent Ukrainian State, *Samostiyna Ukraina.*

Military detachments from the *Sichovy Streltsi* (riflemen), trained and armed with weapons taken over from the departing Austrian armies, established their regime in Galicia and occupied Lwów, its capital city. Fierce fighting between the Ukrainians and the Poles developed, and the Poles succeeded in capturing the city. But the Ukrainians were able to hold on to the rest of Galicia for seven more months.

During the fighting between the Poles and the Ukrainians, the Jewish National Council in eastern Galicia declared complete neutrality of the Jews in the war between these two Slav nations. This, however, gave both sides an excuse to declare Jews as their enemies, each side accusing them of spying for and giving help to their opponents. On both sides of the front severe oppression of the Jewish population began.

The Ukrainian press, with the priests chiming in, incited the townspeople and the peasants with inflammatory anti-Jewish propaganda. Ten commandments binding on the Ukrainians were published from the pulpits in the churches. The Jews were enemies of the Ukrainians and should be expelled. The money, gold and jewelry they possessed belonged to the Ukrainians and should be confiscated. Jews were spies and should be imprisoned. Nothing should be bought from or sold to Jews, and so on. It was no wonder that Jews were beaten, robbed, and killed. Their cattle and horses were taken, and then they were driven from the villages. A boycott of Jewish stores was declared. On market days roadblocks were set up on the streets which led to the marketplaces and to the streets where Jewish stores were located. The peasants were directed to those parts of the cities where Ukrainians had opened stores.

When the Ukrainians were unable to withstand the pressure of the advancing Poles, they withdrew to the east and joined Petlura's forces, abandoning their territory but not the pogroms.

18

Jews in the Reborn Poland

HAVING GIVEN A brief account of the history of the Jews in Galicia and their status under the Austro-Hungarian government, I shall now undertake a description of Jewish life in Poland, and particularly in Galicia. This description, based on my own memories and experiences, is a *yizkor* in memory of the millions who perished in the Holocaust.

After the signing of the armistice agreements between the Allies and the Central Powers, a Peace Conference was convened in Paris. It was supposed to work out an enduring peace based on President Wilson's Fourteen Points but failed to achieve its aim. Obviously the time of Isaiah's "when swords are turned into plowshares and spears into pruning hooks" had not arrived yet.

Over thirty states, including representatives from the breakaway states of the defunct Austro-Hungarian monarchy, sent delegates to the Conference. The delegation of the United States of America was led by President Wilson. The French Prime Minister, Clemenceau, the founder of the League of Defense of Human Rights, who had published, in his paper *l'Aurore*, Zola's "J'accuse" in defense of Dreyfus, headed the French delegation. The British delegation was headed by the British Prime Minister, Lloyd George; the Italian delegation, by Italy's Prime Minister; and the Prime Minister of Japan headed the delegation of his country. The Polish delegation was headed by the well-known pianist Ignacy Paderewski and by Roman Dmowski, a friend of the former Russian Tsar, Nicholas II. Both the Tsar and Dmowski were arch anti-Semites.

Jewish interests were represented by delegations from the United States and from many European countries, all under the chairmanship of the President of the Zionist Organizations of America Judge Mack. Professor Chaim Weizmann, a member of the Jewish delegation from England, came to plead for the speeding up of the creation of the Jewish homeland in Palestine. Dr. Ozjasz Thon of Cracow headed the Jewish delegation from Poland.

The Paris Peace Conference was the midwife, and three Wise Men from the East (i.e., the east of Poland) stood godfather to the reborn Poland. They were Roman Dmowski, Ignacy Paderewski, and Józef Pilsudski. Each of these men brought gifts for the infant; namely, well-trained army forces.

All three were born shortly after the Polish uprising in 1863 against Russia. They had all been raised in an atmosphere of patriotism and hoped, sooner or later, to regain their fatherland. But each of them had different ideas on how to reach that goal.

Dmowski had been a member of the Russian Duma (parliament) and a friend of the tsar, with whom he shared a common hatred of Jews, the God-killers. Before the war of 1914 Dmowski founded the National Democratic Party of Poland, the *Endecja*, which had already at that time initiated a boycott of Jews, under the slogan *"Swój do swego po swoje"* ("Go to your kin. One's own is always best"). In 1915 he went to France and organized there a Polish military force from prisoners of war of Polish nationality taken by the Allies on the western front from the Germans and on the Italian front from the Austrians. Dmowski's nationalistic doctrine was *"Ruat Caellum Fiat Endecja."*

Paderewski, the world-renowned pianist, was living in Switzerland when the First World War broke out. He formed a Relief Committee, with the aim of sending food and clothing to his countrymen in Poland through the International Red Cross.

In order to gain funds for his relief activities, Paderewski went to London and Paris, gave concerts, and pleaded with statesmen in both countries for help to the Polish cause. From Paris, he sailed to the United States. His concerts and his oratory made dollars flow into the chest of the Relief Committee. When he played before President Wilson in the White House he spoke to the President after the concert, pleading for the cause of Poland. His eloquence won the President over.

After the United States declared war on Germany, Paderewski received permission to form a Polish expeditionary army from Polish American recruits. Over 30,000 American and Canadian volunteers, trained in military camps, were transported to France and joined there the Polish forces which had been organized earlier by Dmowski. Together they formed a Polish army of over 100,000 men.

Pilsudski was a left-wing socialist and a Polish nationalist devoted to the restoration of Poland's independence. He formed an underground organization, the Polish Socialist Party. Hunted by the Russian police, Pilsudski managed to escape and fled over the border to Galicia. He settled in Cracow and started to organize the nucleus of a Polish army.

When the war broke out in 1914, Pilsudski, as the Commander-in Chief of a secretly organized Polish army brigade, marched out of Cracow on the first day of the war, leading a detachment of his army, the *Bojówka* (the storming squad), against Russia. He crossed the border, drove the Russians back, and captured the city of Kielce.

The Poles in Austria approached the Austrian government with an offer to form a Polish Legion which would fight on the side of Austria against the mutual enemy, Russia. Austria accepted the offer and agreed to arm the Legion under the command of Pilsudski. Many Poles, instead of being drafted into the Austrian army, joined the Legion voluntarily. So did many Jews, who fought in the Legion side by side with their Polish comrades. Many of them became high-ranking officers in the Legion. The Legion fought gallantly, gained more and more volunteers, and soon reached the strength of three brigades under Pilsudski's command.

In the middle of 1915 the Central Powers successfully expelled the Russians from Poland, occupied Warsaw, and a few months later divided Congress Poland between themselves. The Germans were in dire need of fresh cannon fodder, and in the hope of replenishing the losses they had suffered in the West with hundreds of thousands of Poles, the Central Powers proclaimed the creation of an Independent Kingdom of Poland with a Polish Council of State in Warsaw, in which Pilsudski was named Minister of War. The Germans insisted on a condition—that the Polish army to be formed must take the oath of allegiance to the German

The Big Three in Paris, 1919: Clemenceau, Woodrow Wilson, and Lloyd George

Judge Julian Mack

The synagogue on Zolkiewska Street, Lwów

Marshal Pilsudski

and Austrian Empires. But Pilsudski demanded a Polish army loyal to the Polish state only. When the Germans refused, he resigned from the Council, and his adherents followed suit. The Germans then arrested Pilsudski and his staff, imprisoning them in the fortress of Magdeburg.

In November 1918, Austria was the first to collapse, and a Polish Liquidation Commission, the Provisional Government of West Galicia, was set up in Cracow. In Lublin a Provisional Government of the Polish Republic, headed by a Socialist, Ignacy Daszyński, was proclaimed. A week later the German Empire collapsed; the Poles in Warsaw disarmed the German occupation forces and declared that the existing Polish Council of State, a German creation, would now function as the Provisional Government of the independent Poland.

Pilsudski, freed from his imprisonment in Magdeburg, returned to Warsaw on November 11, 1918, to a hero's welcome. The reactionary Council of State in Warsaw, the Socialist Provisional Government in Lublin, and the Liquidation Commission in Cracow united under Pilsudski. They appointed him Head of State in a Provisional Government of the Independent Poland, and the Socialist, Daszyński, as Prime Minister, until a legislative *Sejm* (Parliament) could be constituted.

The country was devastated by war. Men were drafted into one army or the other and were not available to work the fields, which lay uncultivated. Hunger, bordering on starvation, plagued the country.

A great effort was needed to build from the fragments of three empires, with different grades of culture, a united country. Rivalries and quarrels split the population into many political parties.

The *Endecja* (National Democrats), led by Dmowski, aimed at building a Poland of one nation, a Poland for Poles only. The country should be polonized by any means possible. Jews who could not be polonized were to be eliminated from every sphere of activity. Poland had to get rid of the Jews.

The Left, represented by the Polish Socialist Party, was under the influence of Pilsudski, who dominated the Polish scene until his death in 1935. He was convinced that *l'État c'est Pilsudski*.

Pilsudski spared no efforts in organizing a functioning administration and building a democratic government. As a starter he introduced the so-called Little Constitution in 1919. His difficult task was compounded by the meddlings of Dmowski who, although in Paris, was able to hinder his program.

The question of defining Poland's western borders was the responsibility of Paderewski and Dmowski through diplomatic channels at the Peace Conference in Paris. Pilsudski understood that Poland might expect some resolutions favorable to her with regard to her western borders with Germany. But he didn't believe that Poland could rely on the goodwill of the great powers in connection with the demarcation of her eastern borders. Here not only the interests of Soviet Russia but also those of the Belorussians, the Lithuanians, and the Ukrainians had to be reckoned with.

Recognition of Poland and her boundaries had to be decided by the Peace Conference, and a form of understanding between Pilsudski and Dmowski had to be worked out. Paderewski, therefore, went to Warsaw, and after prolonged haggling a compromise was reached between him and Pilsudski. A government of National Unity was formed, with Pilsudski as Head of State and Paderewski as Prime Minister and Minister of External Affairs.

Pilsudski had no alternative but to come to terms with Paderewski. The treasury was empty, not enough food was available in the country, and a war had started with the Ukrainians. The arms and ammunition available to the army were insufficient (although enough was available to shoot Jews during the pogroms).

Back in Paris, Prime Minister Paderewski became a member of the Conference Council. Soon monetary and material help were granted. Food and armaments began to roll into Poland in considerable quantities.

Dmowski presented the Peace Conference with the demand that it restore Poland to the borders which had existed prior to her partition in the eighteenth century. Since the Allies were eager to present Germany with a peace treaty as soon as possible, the Conference decided only on Poland's borders with Germany. The question of Poland's eastern borders was left unresolved.

Gdańsk, which once had belonged to Poland and then had been under German rule, became a free city under the protection of the League of Nations, with a corridor for free access to the sea allotted to Poland.

The duchy of Cieszyn was divided between Czechoslovakia and

Poland, and the city of Cieszyn was divided between these two countries.

Poland was reborn and now became an independent country with a variety of ethnic groups—Ukrainians, Belorussians, Germans, Jews, Czechs, Lithuanians, Tartars, Karaits—under her sovereignty. Taken together these minorities made up more than 30 percent of the total Polish population.

The birth of the new Poland was accompanied by rivers of Jewish blood. Polish independence was celebrated with pogroms in more than 150 places. Hundreds of Jews were killed and thousands were maimed, not to mention the material damage of multi-millions of crowns. Encouraged by articles in the anti-Semitic press charging Jews with communism, soldiers instigated mobs and led them in the killing and robbery of Jews. Jews had lived in Poland for over a thousand years and contributed to the development of her trade and commerce, to the banking system, to industry, the arts and the sciences, in numbers far out of proportion with their numbers. They had fought side by side with the Poles for the freedom of their mutual country. Nevertheless, they were looked upon by the anti-Semitic majority as foreigners, tolerated only on a temporary basis. As soon as the Germans were chased out of Warsaw in November 1918, anti-Jewish disturbances occurred in that city and in many other places of Central Poland.

The Jews in Galicia, who under the Austrian regime had enjoyed full rights at least formally, couldn't believe that their Ukrainian or Polish neighbors, with whom they had lived in relative harmony, could become murderers overnight. Such things had happened in other parts of Poland and in the Ukraine under the Tsar's regime, but law and order had usually prevailed in Galicia. Though disturbances caused by drunk peasants occasionally took place, these were never very serious, and the gendarmes were on hand to restore order.

The Poles, who had been the actual rulers in Galicia under the Austrian monarchy, were no less anti-Semitic than the Ukrainians, but they were kept in line by the Austrians. Besides, a large number of Jewish volunteers had fought side by side with their Polish comrades in Pilsudski's legions under the motto, *"Za naszą i waszą wolność"* ("For our and your freedom"), and Pilsudski was now the Head of State in a free Poland. And yet, the

Jews didn't have to wait too long to be taught a lesson, proving how mistaken they were and how venomous a Polish bite can be when the muzzle is removed.

As already related, a week before Austria surrendered to the Allies by signing the armistice agreement on November 3, 1918, the Austrian forces turned Lwów, the capital city of Galicia, over to the Ukrainians, who then took over eastern Galicia and proclaimed it a Ukrainian National Republic. The Poles claimed Galicia for Poland, and fighting broke out between the Ukrainian and the Polish population, especially in Lwów, where the Poles were in the majority. The fighting in Lwów lasted for about three weeks. The Jews, not wanting to be caught between the hammer and the anvil, declared their neutrality.

After three weeks a Polish military column advanced from Przemyśl, captured Lwów, and forced the Ukrainians to retreat. Immediately after taking over the city the Poles faulted the Jews for their declared neutrality, accused them of espionage in favor of the Ukrainian enemy, of having shot at the Polish defenders of the city (they called the defenders *Orlęta*, "Young Eagles"), and of having poured boiling water from windows of upper floors onto the heads of Polish soldiers marching on the streets below. The soldiers were given three full days for robbery, plunder, arson, and taking revenge on the Jews.

A pogrom lasting for three days began in Lwów on November 21, 1918. Its ferocity surpassed even the terrible pogroms of 1903-1905 in Kishinev, Odessa, and other places in tsarist Russia. Soldiers and civilians—the women among them were even more cruel than the men—marching to the ringing sound of the Polish National Anthem, *"Jeszcze Polska nie zginęla póki my żyjemy"* ("Poland is not lost yet as long as we are alive"), entered the Jewish district of the city. Stores were broken into and looted, everything which could be moved was taken, houses were plundered, and Jews were beaten, hacked down, and many were shot to death. The Jewish district was put to the torch. The temple, from which the Torah scrolls had been thrown into the street and trampled upon, was set ablaze. The water supply was deliberately cut off, and Jews were not permitted to leave their homes. Those who dared to do so were shot at. The blood of hundreds of men, women, and children, old and young alike, terribly maimed, wounded and killed, colored the cobblestones of the streets of the

Jewish district of Lwów. During these gruesome "free-for-all" three days the authorities didn't interfere with the *pogromczyks*. Only after protests from all over the world was martial law proclaimed. These unforgettable three days left 400 Jews maimed and crippled, and 80 killed. The material damage from looting, robbery, and fire amounted to millions of crowns. Strange as it may seem, only Jewish businesses were looted. Spared from any harm were not only the Poles but also their enemies the Ukrainians, and their businesses and homes.

In a special plot at the Jewish cemetery in Lwów, the murdered

Photographer Bojm. Nasz Przegląd June 15, 1930

A Jew whose beard was cut off by Polish soldiers, Lodz, 1923
Reprinted by permission of Schocken Books, Inc., from Image before my eyes by Lucjan Dobroszycki and Barbara Kirschenblatt-Gimblett. Copyright © 1977 by Schocken Books, Inc.

Jews were laid to eternal rest. The author of this book saw the many rows of tombstones marking the burial places of the martyrs of the pogrom in Lwów while he was working at the removing of tombstones as a prisoner of the Janowski concentration camp during World War II. They still stood untouched, after twenty-five years. Who knows whether the resting place of these martyrs has not been plowed under by now, during the last forty years of Soviet rule?

After the pogrom the Polish press wrote that the Polish soldiers in Lwów had never perpetrated a pogrom. Before retreating from Lwów, it was claimed, the Ukrainians had opened the prisons and set more than a hundred criminals free. Once free, these felons changed clothes, donning Polish military uniforms, and started looting and burning. (The newspapers didn't explain where the criminals had obtained Polish military uniforms.) Fighting had ensued, during which a few dozen people on both sides were killed, but the Polish military command had declared a state of emergency. Fifty looters were shot and the disturbances were brought to an end. Many bandits were arrested—Ukrainians, Poles and Jews. The majority of them were Ukrainians.

The Ukrainians told an entirely different story. The Ukrainian National Council proclaimed the West Ukrainian National Republic, encompassing the territories of eastern Galicia and the Bukovina. Under the pressure of superior Polish forces the Provisional Government had been forced to evacuate Lwów. As long as Lwów was in Ukrainian hands, they said, all was calm and order had prevailed in the city. After Lwów was evacuated, the Poles provided the riff-raff and criminals with arms and ammunition and instigated a pogrom.

These were the Polish and Ukrainian versions of the pogrom. However, anybody who knows the truth about what actually happened in Lwów on the days of November 21-23, 1918, will reject both versions with contempt.

In May 1919, the Ukrainians regrouped their forces and attempted to recapture Lwów from the Poles. The *Poznańczyki*, Polish troops from Poznań, were dispatched to beat off the attackers. During this period Jews were attacked on the streets and mercilessly beaten, houses and stores were broken into and plundered. Again the authorities declared that the disturbances had been committed by hooligans but were brought to an end by the energetic intervention of the heroic soldiers who represented the best guarantee for peace and order in the city.

The pogroms in Galicia were not restricted to her eastern part only. Neither middle nor western Galicia was immune to pogroms, which spread like a brush fire and engulfed the whole country.

During a pogrom in Brzesko, the commander of the troops called in from Bochnia and Tarnów to quell the riots instructed his men on how they should act: "Killing is not allowed, looting may be tolerated, but under no circumstances should you fire on your brethren." Under such protection the riots went on undisturbed, and many Jews were wounded, eight of them seriously. Five were murdered.

In Strzyżów, rumors were spread at the end of April 1919 that Jews had killed a Christian for ritual purposes. Four Jews were killed, and a large number wounded, fifteen of them seriously. In the neighboring towns six Jews were killed. In Kolbuszowa, peasants from the surrounding villages looted stores and houses, and barbarously killed Jews.

At the beginning of May 1919, a huge crowd gathered around the police station in Rzeszów and demanded the American food supplies which had arrived the day before. The commandant of the police station pleaded with the angry mob to leave him alone. He told them to go to the Jews, who had plenty of food, as well as many other good things. The rabble went immediately to the Jewish district and ran amuck when, in addition, rumors were spread that the Jews had lured a Christian girl into the synagogue to use her blood for ritual purposes. The same officer who had previously encouraged the mob to go and rob the Jews investigated and found that the girl involved had spent the night with an officer. Being afraid of her mother she had dreamed up the story of the blood libel as an excuse. But there was no stopping the maddened mob. The hooligans broke into the synagogue, demolished everything inside, and tore the Torah scrolls into pieces. Then they went on a rampage through the city, beating and robbing Jews, leaving four killed and 400 wounded.

A Jewish delegation went to the district authority asking for protection. The answer was, "Until now you were neutral," an allusion to the Jewish declaration of neutrality with respect to the war between the Ukrainians and Poles, "from now on, we will be the neutrals." And really, the local authorities remained neutral and did nothing to stop the riots. Finally, a military detachment was called in from Tarnów to quell the riots, but the soldiers encouraged the mob to go ahead with the beating and molesting of the Jews. An officer offered the storeowners protection if he would be paid. He got what he asked for but was unable to prevent his soldiers from joining the looters.

At the end of May 1919, a committee of delegates from the cities in western Galicia, under the chairmanship of Dr. Rafael Landau, president of the Jewish congregation in Cracow, heard testimony about pogroms in every town of western Galicia. From many places loss of life was reported. Robberies had taken place everywhere.

A boycott of Jewish stores and a prohibition on selling food to Jews had been ordered. Many Jews who had worked for years with the military command in Cracow had been fired, and a mass expulsion of Jews from the villages began. The committee decided to intervene with the central government in Warsaw, asking for protection of Jewish life and property.

Under pressure from some socialist deputies in the *Sejm* (parliament), Prime Minister Paderewski decided to send his own commission to Galicia in order to discover the cause of the tragic riots in Rzeszów and the other cities in Galicia. The commission came to the conclusion that false rumors of Jews using the blood of a Christian girl for ritual purposes had caused riots in which not only Jews, but Christians, were wounded or killed. It reported that thanks to the intervention of the military forces the riots had been brought to an end.

A month after the pogrom in Rzeszów, a terrible pogrom took place in the ancient capital of Poland, Cracow, the site of one of the oldest universities in Europe. Anti-Jewish riots in Cracow were not new. They had occurred as early as the fifteenth century. The Jews of Cracow lived mainly in a suburb of the city called Kazimierz. The pogrom in Cracow was committed by the *Hallerczyki*, as the soldiers from General Haller's army were called.

During the war the Poles had formed Polish Army units in Austria, Russia, and France. In Austria Pilsudski's Legions fought on the side of the Central Powers. In Russia a military force formed mainly from Polish prisoners of war taken by Russia from the Austrian armies who fought under General Dowbór

Muśnicki on the side of Russia. In France the Polish corps sponsored by Roman Dmowski was formed from Polish prisoners of war taken by the Allies from the German army. Dmowski's corps was later joined by the expeditionary army brought over from America, formed by the endeavors of Paderewski from American and Canadian volunteers of Polish origin.

As already related, when Pilsudski refused to take the oath of allegiance to the Central Powers, he was arrested. General Haller, formerly an Austrian officer, also refused to take the oath of allegiance to the Central Powers. He managed to break through the Russian front, which at that time was already in disarray, and via Murmansk reached France.

In Paris, Dmowski's National Committee entrusted Haller with the command of the Polish forces in France, already over 100,000 strong. In Paris, Paderewski frightened the Allies with the threat of Bolshevism, which, if not halted, would soon submerge the whole of Europe. He argued that such a disaster could be averted only by making Poland a bulwark against Russian communism, and that this could be done by transferring the Polish forces from France to Poland. The Allies readily agreed, and the Polish army was equipped and armed as best as possible, and under the command of General Haller was shipped via Gdańsk to Poland.

Once in Poland, General Haller's soldiers, soaked in anti-Semitic propaganda, fought against the Ukrainians and Bolsheviks, and with even more vigor attacked, robbed and killed Jews. They were not far behind the *Petlurovtsi*.

The *Hallerczyki* developed a special system of their own for the molesting of Jews. Arriving at a railway station they would encircle its compound so that nobody could leave. Passengers at the station were herded together in the station hall. Jews were picked out and beaten. The Christians were asked to go through the cars and pull out any Jew who might be hiding. One of their many sources of fun was cutting off the beards of pious Jews, sometimes together with a piece of skin. Then they would ask the victims to pay ten crowns for the barber service. Bearded Poles had a difficult time proving that they were not Jews, and many shaved off their beards. When Jewish deputies brought up the matter in the *Sejm*, they were accused of deliberately lying for the sake of defaming the Polish nation in the eyes of the world.

After the arrival of General Haller's army in Poland from France, a part of it was dispatched as reinforcement in the war against the Ukrainians in Galicia. On May 20, 1919, the victorious *Hallerczyki* occupied Stryj. That evening riots began. Stores and houses were plundered, and Jews were brutally beaten. On the following day soldiers, going from house to house, pulled out Jews, young and old alike, and led them away to dig trenches at the outskirts of the city. On Saturday the soldiers invaded the synagogue and dragged away the men; also the women, to do some cleaning. All were beaten. They began to play their wild tricks with the beard-cutting. They did it, among others, to a well-known sixty-year-old jeweler, Sobel. The beard-cutting job administered to him was fatal. The beard was cut off together with a piece of skin; the wound became infected and then gangrenous.

On vacation in Stryj, a friend of mine and I, in the company of our fiancées, were on our way to the railway station to find out whether there would be a train for Budapest. We were met by a military patrol. The soldiers asked us what our nationalities were. When the answer was Jewish, the girls were ordered to leave immediately and we were led away to the goods station. My friend asked the soldiers to let him go because he had to prepare for his exams. The soldiers then asked him what he was studying because they too were students. Hearing that he was studying medicine, the soldiers said, "Who the hell needs Jewish doctors! Anyway, you shall have work right now which is just in the line of your chosen profession."

He was led away to a latrine, given a bucket with a piece of rope on it, and ordered to ladle out the contents of the pit, as another Jew was already doing, into a barrel. A third Jew had to cart away the barrel when it was filled and empty it in a nearby field. These trips had to be repeated until the pit was empty.

When the pit was nearly empty, the soldiers pushed my friend into the pit and, laughing, yelled at him, "Get out and run you stinking Jew doctor." And he did so, running through the field.

I was taken to the warehouse, where another Jew was already unloading heavy sacks of flour from a railway car, carrying them on his back into the warehouse, and I was told to do the same. After the flour was unloaded from the car, we were released and allowed to go home. To leave the station we had to go via the passenger platform. As luck would have it, the moment we stepped onto the platform, a train with *Hallerczyki* pulled in and halted alongside the platform.

The soldiers jumped out and encircled us. Covered with flour, we looked the very picture of misery. They began to beat us. We were knocked down, kicked with boots, and given blows with rifle butts on the head, the back, and the groin. An officer encouraged them with the words, "All right, boys. Go ahead. These Jews sure deserve it." The sound of the whistle announcing the departure of the train was probably responsible for saving our lives. The *Hallerczyki* hurriedly boarded the train, leaving us in a pool of blood on the concrete floor.

After a while we were helped by some civilians to leave the station. My fiancée, who was waiting for me outside the station, took me in a *fiaker* to the hospital, where I was refused emergency treatment because the hospital had been taken over by the military. I had to be taken home, where the wounds were washed. Due to the curfew which was in force, I was unable to get any further help. The next morning many stitches were needed by a doctor to close the cuts on my head. The black eyes and the swelling of the face lasted for weeks.

In June 1919, General Haller arrived in Cracow with a large detachment of his army. On Friday, the day after their arrival, a pogrom began in the afternoon. It started in the *Sukiennice* (the Cloth Hall) in the center of the city. There was an argument between a peasant woman and a Jewish woman stall-holder. Two *Hallerczyki*, who had just entered the hall, not knowing what the reasons for the argument were, attacked the Jewess. The mob in the hall began looting the stores. Soon a large crowd of riff-raff filled the hall and joined the looters. In no time a throng of nearly a thousand had gathered around the *Sukiennice* and, directed by the *Hallerczyki* and their officers, spread all over the city, robbing, looting, and beating Jews.

The *Hallerczyki*, under the command of their officers and joined by soldiers from other units and by civilians, marched on the Jewish quarter, Kazimierz. Some soldiers started shooting, and many Jews lay wounded on the pavement of Grodzka Street, the one leading to the Jewish district. The *Hallerczyki* brought tools with which they were easily able to break into the stores. The mob, with cries of hurrah, flooded the premises thus opened and helped themselves to everything they could find inside. On the next day, Saturday, it became clear what had happened in the Jewish district of Cracow. Over 200 wounded, thirty of them seriously, needed medical attention. The stores had been cleaned out of everything removable, and their doors were wide open. But the synagogue remained closed on that Sabbath day because no Jew dared to leave his house.

The speaker for the General Staff of General Haller's army, Colonel Modelski, described what had happened the previous day and night in Cracow. He said that behind this whole affair lay German propaganda and Jewish provocation to stir up trouble in order to smear the good name of Poland abroad. (It would follow that the Jewish tailor found among the wounded with cuts on his belly had committed harakiri only to smear the honor of the *Hallerczyki*.) He went on to say that actually the police were to blame for not acting promptly to prevent Jews from provoking his brave soldiers who were out sightseeing in the city. As soon as the soldiers appeared on the streets, he said, Jews yelled, "Watch out, here come the bandits, the *Hallerczyki!*" Undoubtedly, a German-Bolshevik-Jewish provocation had caused the whole affair.

The contents of a communiqué published by the press department of the Haller army repeated Colonel Modelski's version, adding that the brave units of the army restored order and that, on searching Jewish houses from which shots had been fired, weapons and ammunition had been confiscated. As a matter of fact, no weapons had been found and therefore none could be confiscated. What had actually been confiscated was jewelry, money, and valuables which had been found in Jewish homes.

Dr. Thon was received by General Haller and described what actually happened. The general issued an order that all soldiers and officers who had participated in the riots were to be court-martialed. Since none of the *Hallerczyki* had left their visiting cards at the places of their crimes, the order was meaningless.

The socialist deputies proposed in the *Sejm* (parliament) the withdrawal of the Haller units from Cracow. When the headquarters of the Haller army was moved to Lublin, Prylucki, a Jewish deputy, went to Lublin to see the general. He complained about the pogrom which had taken place in Lublin and told the general that on the way to Lublin, he himself had witnessed mistreatment of Jews by the general's soldiers. Jews were pulled out of trains, beaten, kicked, and had their beards and earlocks cut off. Again the general promised to restore peace and order.

The Poles fought the Ukrainians with success on the northern front in Galicia. In order to gain a fast victory and drive the

Photographer Roman Vishniac

**Entrance to the Jewish quarter in Cracow,
1938**

*Reprinted by permission of Schocken Books, Inc., from Image
before my eyes by Lucjan Dobroszycki and Barbara Kirschenblatt-Gimblett. Copyright © 1977 by Schocken Books, Inc.*

Ukrainians out of Galicia entirely, it was decided to attack them at the same time from the south.

The Polish military force formed previously in Russia was engaged in fighting the Bolsheviks in the eastern Ukraine and had recently withdrawn via Bessarabia into Rumania, which occupied Pokucie the southern districts of Galicia.

The Rumanians allowed the Polish forces to move to Galicia by rail transport, except for the cavalry, which had to use the highway. On their way from the border station in Nepolokoutz, through Śniatyń, Zablotów, and Kolomyja, the Polish cavalrymen molested and mistreated Jews. Upon their arrival in Kolomyja, the uhlans dispatched a unit of horsemen under the command of an officer to nearby Slobódka Leśna. There, on an estate owned by the Jewish Colonization Association, an agricultural school which prepared Jewish boys and girls for emigration to Palestine had been established many years before the war and was still functioning.

At the estate the soldiers told the girls to leave, and then herded the boys into a barn and discharged a volley at them. Two boys were killed and many wounded. The uhlans left after they had plundered and totally ravaged the estate. A seriously wounded student lying on the floor begged the departing Poles to help him. His request was answered with a shot, which ended his sufferings.

On their way back to Kolomyja six more Jews were killed in Turka and in Rakowice a Jewish girl was raped. On the day following the murders in Slobódka and Turka the corpses were taken to Kolomyja. At the autopsy the Polish physician implied that death had occurred many days earlier. This meant that the murders must have been committed by the retreating Ukrainians. However, the Rumanian military doctor who was present at the autopsy proved, and the Pole had to agree, that death had occurred less than twenty-four hours before. Therefore, the victims had been killed by the Poles.

In those days pogroms were committed everywhere in Poland. They were not restricted to eastern and western Galicia, but also occurred in the center, the west, and the east of Poland. The pogroms had a common pattern: breaking into Jewish houses and stores, looting, molesting, beating, wounding, and, in many cases, killing Jews. The police did not lift a finger to protect the

Jews. In most cases soldiers of the Polish armies instigated the pogroms and participated in them. To give a detailed account of all the pogroms which took place in Poland, especially during the first three years of her existence, would be an enormous task. But some of them need to be told about.

In Częstochowa seven Jews were brutally murdered. Among them was a doctor who was dressing the wounds of a wounded Jew. Twenty were wounded, nine seriously. An official Polish communiqué gave Jewish provocation as the cause of the riots.

On the Shavuot holiday in 1919 a pogrom in Chelm left many Jews dead and a large number wounded.

In Piotrków, a Polish doctor was not allowed to render any help to the victims of a pogrom there on the same Shavuot day.

At the beginning of June 1919, the *Hallerczyki* encouraged a mob to join them in robberies in Warsaw. Two Jews were killed and eighteen seriously wounded. Carrying on with the pogrom the next day in Praga (a suburb of Warsaw), thirty Jews were seriously wounded. A pogrom in Zawiercie left two Jews killed and twenty-one wounded.

Asserting that Jews in conspiracy with the Germans were plotting a surprise attack, the Polish authorities in Poznań arrested all Jewish lawyers as hostages. In the city of Poznań 300 prominent and respected Jewish citizens were arrested and interned in a camp together with Germans.

It would be a serious omission not to mention the terrible pogroms which occurred around the end of April 1919 in Wilno, Lida, Wlodzimierz, Wolyński, and Pińsk: On the day when the Polish Legionaires entered Wilno, the soldiers distributed arms to a mob of civilians and instigated a massacre of Jews in the city.

Terror against the Jews included a constant barrage of rioting in which 2,000 Jews were killed and many more were wounded. As usual, the Polish authorities asserted that the riots were due to Jewish provocation and arrested 3,000 Jews who were driven to Lida. Among those murdered was the well-known writer, Weiter. Another writer, Niger, was among the arrested.

The daily *Nowy Dziennik* in Cracow, which published an account of the pogroms in Lida during which thirty-five Jews had been murdered, and five times as many wounded, was suspended. The *wojewoda* (head of the provincial administration) denied that there had been a pogrom in Lida and asserted that only a few Jews had been killed because they had cooperated with the Bolsheviks.

Immediately after the Polish forces entered Wlodzimierz Wolyński, Jewish houses were searched and robbed. Jews who couldn't find a hiding place were taken to a mill at the outskirts of the town. Sixteen were shot dead and many seriously wounded. There would have been more victims if it hadn't been for the intervention of a Polish priest who put a stop to the riots.

On the day when the Polish army entered Pińsk, the commandant declared that all Jews were Bolsheviks, enemies of Poland, and that each Jewish house sheltered a spy. Jewish houses were searched and plundered, and every store was looted. Jews were beaten and taken away, allegedly for the purpose of performing some sort of labor. Eighty to ninety of them never returned home. They simply vanished, and no one was able to find out what had happened to them.

On April 5, 1919, in the same city, the Zionist organization held a meeting at the Bet-Am for which it had previously received permission from the military commander of the city. Just as the gathering was breaking up, soldiers broke into the Bet-Am and arrested everybody who was in the building. All were terribly beaten and tortured, and thirty-four were shot. Most of the others who were released were wounded or crippled. Six went mad. Order in the city was not restored and atrocities against the Jews did not stop. The synagogues were ordered closed, and Jews had to pay a huge amount of money as a contribution.

The Polish *Sejm*, acting under pressure from world opinion, decided to send a parliamentary committee to Pińsk to investigate the massacre. It included the Jewish deputies Grynbaum and Prylucki.

Correspondents of Polish and foreign papers who at first were allowed to go along with the commission were halted in Brześć by the commandant, General Listowski. They were not allowed to proceed to Pińsk. He arranged a press conference and declared that Pińsk was a war zone and that there was no need to go there.

He then gave the correspondents his version of what had happened in Pińsk. The Jews shot in Pińsk, Listowski said, had been sentenced to death by a court set up by martial law. (As a matter of fact, there was no such court.) What the major who executed the order did, he, Listowski, would have done himself.

Jews were usurers and blackmarketeers, and it was tactless for the correspondents to talk so much about these events or the alleged injustice done to the Jews. One cannot make an omelette without breaking eggs. If the killed hadn't been Jews, nobody would have talked about it. It was also in the interest of the Jews not to cry wolf. No questions were allowed to be asked, and the correspondents were ordered to return to Warsaw.

Before the parliamentary committee arrived in Pińsk, the general asked the rabbi to sign a document that the meeting at the Bet-Am was a Communist meeting, but the rabbi refused. He also refused to agree to the general's condition for allowing two synagogues to open for the holidays, namely, that the events of the murder would not be discussed or even mentioned. The synagogues remained closed.

The committee examined witnesses, widows and orphans of the murdered Jews, and listened to their heartrending description of the pogrom. The military persons responsible were not available and couldn't be heard. They simply left the city, and the general refused to bring them back. The committee opened the common grave where the victims had been buried. Most of the dead were maimed, and one had his belly slit open. The victims were identified; thirty-two belonged to the Zionist party, two to the *Bund*, but none of them had anything whatsoever to do with communism.

Back in Warsaw, Deputy Prylucki was received by Pilsudski, reported to him the findings of the commission, and asked him to cancel the contribution order. Pilsudski promised to look into the matter, and that was all.

In Plock, in 1920, when the old Orthodox rabbi, Shapiro, was praying in *talles* and *tfillin* on his balcony, raising his hands in ecstasy to the Almighty in heaven, he was arrested and accused of signaling military secrets to the Bolsheviks. He was immediately brought before a military court, which found him guilty of espionage and sentenced him to death. He was executed without delay.

Paderewski, with the self-assurance of righteousness, asked President Wilson to dispatch an impartial commission to investigate the alleged pogroms. President Wilson appointed as head of the commission the well-known anti-Zionist, Ambassador Henry Morgenthau. Paderewski's government received Mr. Morgenthau and the commission with honors and the utmost courtesy and hospitality. Among the Jews, the arrival of the Morgenthau Commission awoke a ray of hope that something would finally be done to alleviate their situation.

The commission decided that it should visit some of the places where pogroms had occurred. After visiting a few towns where pogroms had taken place, it arrived in Wilno. The Jewish community in Wilno had well prepared its case and by bringing before the commission all the available witnesses enabled it to get a true picture of what had occurred.

The commission learned from eyewitnesses how the wife of a murdered Jew had been shot dead at her husband's open grave during his funeral and how his seventeen-year-old niece had been pushed into the same grave while still alive after being wounded by a gunshot. A fifty-eight-year-old man taken for forced labor and severely beaten on the way had been left in terrible pain to die on the ground. A butcher was tied by his hands with a rope to a horse and then dragged through the streets by a soldier, and so on and on, all stories of the horror which was the lot of the Jews in Wilno.

The Poles suggested that for Morgenthau to go to Pińsk would be an undertaking in futility, since there were no witnesses to the events there. Ambassador Morgenthau heeded their advice. But back in Warsaw he couldn't avoid hearing about the pogrom in Pińsk. Therefore, contrary to his previous plan, he decided to visit the city, together with two members of his commission.

In Pińsk the three gentlemen went to the old Jewish cemetery where the thirty-four victims of the massacre had been interred. The entire Jewish community went along with them. It is impossible to describe the heartrending scene at the martyrs' grave and later at the bloodstained wall in the city where the victims had been tortured and murdered. Until then the Jews had not been allowed to visit either of these places.

In the evening a memorial service was held at the synagogue, which had been opened for the first time since the day of the pogrom. The synagogue was filled to capacity, with more people crowded outside the building. After the *El molay rakhamim* (the prayer for the dead), Professor Johnson, a member of the commission, said in his speech that the commission had come to Pińsk to tell the Jews on behalf of President Wilson that the Americans understood their sufferings and would help.

Ambassador Morgenthau spoke about the economic situation of the Jews. He too promised help. The next day the commission left for Lida, Grodno, and Galicia. Wherever they went they heard complaints of pogroms and persecution. Nevertheless, Mr. Morgenthau, in his desire to whitewash the Poles—although acknowledging that vicious pogroms had taken place in all parts of Poland—concluded his report with the remark that it was as wrong to condemn the whole Jewish population of Poland for a certain number of undesirables among them as to hold the whole Polish nation responsible for the regrettable acts of violence committed here and there by a wild mob and some undisciplined units of the army.

Mr. Morgenthau thus implied that the pogroms were the result of wrongdoing by some undesirable Jews and that the Polish authorities were not in a position to handle the undisciplined mobs or army units. But the pogroms were not committed as a reaction to wrongdoing by any group of Jews; they were caused solely by ingrained anti-Semitism. He neglected to mention that the entire Polish army was well-disciplined and that it was not unusual for local authorities to encourage the *pogromczyk*s to get even with the Jews, and that help from the police was never, or seldom, forthcoming.

Another commission in Poland which tried to assess the situation of the Jews was sent by the British government. This commission, headed by Sir Montagu, came to the conclusion that Poland's treatment of her Jews was to be condemned. Pogroms had to be stopped, boycotts should not be allowed, and restrictions on admissions to the universities and violations of minority rights should not be tolerated.

In Paris the Jewish delegation urged the Peace Conference to introduce a binding clause into the peace treaty with Poland providing safeguards on the rights of the national minorities, especially the Jews. However, Paderewski and Dmowski, who regarded Poland as a country of Poles only, and who aimed at the polonization of the minorities, were strongly opposed to being bound by any obligations to minority rights. They tried to dissuade the conference from including the proposed clause concerning the minorities in the treaty with Poland. Poland was a democracy, they said, and there was no need for introducing such a humiliating clause into the treaty. Lloyd George, however, insisted on having written into the peace treaty with Poland a specially binding clause covering the rights of the minorities.

To strengthen their opposition to the signing of the Minority Rights Treaty, the Poles dispatched to Paris a delegation composed of three Jewish assimilators, Dr. Sehleicher from Lwów, Stanislaw Natanson from Warsaw, and a third one from Cracow. These three musketeers went to Paris and asserted that in spite of the pogroms there was no need for special safeguards for the minorities. However, nobody wanted to listen to them, knowing fully well what was going on in Poland.

Dmowski and Paderewski had the temerity to state that there had been no pogroms in Poland. All was exaggeration and unfounded rumors. The conference, they said, should realize that the country was in bad economic shape and if there had been any disturbances, not only Jews, but Poles too had suffered. The Jewish delegation to the Peace Conference, influenced by the Polish delegation headed by Dr. Ozjasz Thon of Cracow, insisted on iron-clad guarantees for the minorities in general and for the Jews in particular.

In view of the pogroms and massacres of Jews in Poland, the guarantee of rights to the minorities in Poland was made a condition of the recognition of Poland's independence. Forced to take it or leave it, the Polish delegation signed the Minority Rights Treaty. The treaty stipulated that the law of the country should apply equally to all Polish citizens, without prejudice as to religion or creed. There should be no curtailment of the use of languages other than Polish in the courts and in all other institutions. Minorities were also entitled to establish schools at their own expense, and to use their own language in them. Jews were not expected to perform any acts which violated the Sabbath except for those when in the military service in connection with national defense. The Minority Rights Treaty must be made an integral part of the Polish constitution.

The anti-Semitic press protested the acceptance of the treaty, claiming it would turn Poland into a Judeo-Polonia. The Poles were not ready to allow the *parszywi Żydzi* (scabby Jews) equal rights. They accused the Jews of trying to form a *państwo w państwie* (state within a state).

The *Sejm* nevertheless ratified the treaty, and it was made a part of the Polish constitution of 1921. But why abide by a democratic constitution if it is theory only? The treaty was violated before the ink of the signatures on the document had a chance to dry. It was regarded as a mere piece of paper which Poland had signed under duress.

While the ratification of the treaty was being debated in the *Sejm*, minority schools were replaced with schools of a bilingual (Polish) character, and Polish was imposed as the language of instruction. The universities introduced restrictions on the admission of Jews, though an official law to apply a *numerus clausus* was rejected.

When I came back from Vienna to Poland I was obliged, as a demobilized officer from the Austrian army to register with the Polish military command. A war was going on and there was a shortage in officers, but because I entered into the questionnaire Jewish as my nationality I was told that for the time being they had no assignment for me and that I would be notified later to which unit I would be assigned. I never was.

Moreover, the Poles may claim to have been first to intern Jews in special camps. In 1920 tens of thousands of Jews, men and women who had served in regular military units on the front lines fighting for an independent Poland, were segregated and interned in a detention camp in Jablonna under the pretext that they were Communists and might support the enemy. Many were sent to disciplinary labor battalions. Three years ago I met a Jew in Miami who was incarcerated in Jablonna, and he told me about the annoyances and vexations he was subjected to there. The military was never concerned with having an official order with regard to the discrimination of Jews. They made up their own rules in a policy of brutality against, and humiliation of, the Jewish soldiers who served in the army.

In 1920, in violation of the Minority Rights Treaty, a bill was passed denying citizenship to Jews who at the end of the nineteenth century fled the pogroms in the Ukraine, in Lithuania and Belorussia, into the Polish portion of Russia, now a part of Poland. The pretext was that they were not listed on the permanent population register. It was the so-called "*Litvak* Question."

Crowning the resolutions arrived by the Peace Conference in Paris was the creation of the League of Nations along the lines proposed by President Wilson. President Wilson's idealistic dream of eternal peace never came true. The Senate of the United States of America refused to ratify the Peace Treaty, and thus the United States did not become a member of the League of Nations. The treaty with Germany was signed in Versailles on June 28, 1919, exactly five years after the murder in Sarajevo of the Austro-Hungarian Crown Prince, Franz Ferdinand.

Danzig (Gdańsk) was made a free city under the League of Nations and Poland received a part of Pomerania as a corridor to the sea. The district of Poznań was assigned to Poland. Upper Silesia was later, after three uprisings, led by the known anti-Semite, Korfanty, divided between Germany and Poland. The Duchy of Cieszyn was divided between Czechoslovakia and Poland, as was the city of Cieszyn divided between these two countries.

Paderewski, supported by his American friends, and Dmowski by the French delegation, gained many important concessions favorable to Poland. A variety of ethnic groups, such as Ukrainians, Belorussians, Germans, Jews, Czechs, Lithuanians, Tartars, Karaits and splinters of other nationalities were placed under Polish sovereignty. Taken together they made up more than 30 percent of the total Polish population.

Meanwhile, although Pilsudski had originally advocated a *modus vivendi* with the ethnic groups, a kind of federalism with the Ukrainian, White Russian, and Lithuanian minorities, he abandoned his tolerance vis-à-vis the minorities after his successful war with the Bolsheviks. True to the spirit of the Polish anthem, *"Jeszcze Polska nie zginęla . . ."* ("Poland is not lost yet, as long as we are alive; what foreign force has taken from us, with force we shall regain"), he decided that Poland's eastern borders should be carved out by force of arms. As Commander-in-Chief of the armed forces he built up a strong and disciplined army. In Galicia the Poles had recaptured Lwów in November 1918. But as of May 1919, the Ukrainians were still in possession of the part of Galicia south of Lwów.

As soon as General Haller's army arrived from France, Pilsudski launched an offensive against the Ukrainians, and in July 1919 the whole of Galicia was conquered. Having annihilated the West Ukrainian army, Pilsudski turned against Petlura's East Ukrainian army. Petlura, being hard-pressed by Denikin and the Bolsheviks, asked the Poles for an armistice. This was accepted and led to an alliance between the *pogromczyk* Petlura and Pilsudski. As a result, the Polish army, accompanied by Petlura's *haidamaks*, marched on Kiev, the capital city of the Ukraine, which they captured in May 1920. However, a month later the Reds launched a counterattack and recaptured Kiev. The badly beaten allied forces of Pilsudski and Petlura retreated hurriedly, with the Bolsheviks in pursuit.

One attacking Russian army reached the outskirts of Lwów, and in July 1920 the Bolsheviks reached the banks of the Vistula River on the outskirts of Warsaw. The Allies were in no hurry to extend any help to Poland, and the situation became critical and threatening. No material help could reach Poland in any case, since the dockers in Gdańsk refused to unload any shipments destined for Poland, nor would Germany or Czechoslovakia allow any transport of war materials through their territories.

A government of National Defense under the premiership of Wincenty Witos, the leader of the peasant party, *Piast*, was formed. He declared that the reason for the defeat of the offensive against the Bolsheviks was treason and espionage by Jews. Pilsudski, who was named Marshal, worked out a plan which he felt would get him out of the snare. He then launched a counterattack and in August 1920 succeeded in defeating the Russian invaders in the battle known as the *Cud nad Wisłą*, (the "Miracle on the Vistula").

The Russians asked for, and the Poles agreed to, an armistice. A peace treaty between Poland and Russia was signed in March 1921 in Riga. It established very favorable eastern borders for Poland.

Now, Pilsudski ordered one of his trusted generals, Lucjan Żeligowski, to occupy the central part of Lithuania, including Wilno. This city, a center of Jewish learning and the seat of *gaonim* (great Jewish scholars), was proudly called *Yerushalaim de Litha* (Jerusalem of Lithuania). The coup d'état was allegedly carried out by Żeligowski against the will of Pilsudski. Later this part of Lithuania was annexed by Poland.

One might assume that with the wars successfully ended, the time had arrived to unite all Polish citizens in healing the wounds inflicted on the country during the six years of war (1914–1920), and all efforts would be directed to the building of a democratic and prosperous country. Unfortunately, this was not the case.

An anti-Semitic campaign in violation of the Minority Rights

Treaty was carried out, though without the vicious pogroms of the preceding three years. In 1921 a new constitution was legislated. It gave equal rights to all citizens and incorporated also the terms of the Minority Rights Treaty. Of course, it was an excellent constitution but only on paper.

After the elections to the first *Sejm*, held on the basis of the so-called Little Constitution of 1919, Jews were represented by only a few deputies. The new constitution of 1921 provided universal suffrage with equal, secret, and direct elections. Yitzchak Grynbaum organized and cemented a bloc of all minorities—Lithuanians, Czechs, Ukrainians, Germans, White Russians, and Jews—which in the elections in 1922 succeeded in winning eighty seats in the *Sejm* and Senate.

The *Endecja* came out with a substantial number of deputies, but with no absolute majority. The balance of voting power fell, therefore, into the hands of the minority bloc. When the National Assembly had to choose a President, a friend of Pilsudski's, Professor Gabriel Narutowicz, was elected, with the votes of the minority bloc tipping the scale.

The Poles couldn't agree to the fact that Jews had their own representatives in the parliament, who had the right to take part in the debates and could vote and decide in matters of concern to the Polish state. The election of Professor Narutowicz was said to be the best proof that Jews were already ruling Poland.

Two days after his election, President Narutowicz, who was dubbed "The Jewish President" by the anti-Semitic press, was assassinated by Eligiusz Niewiadomski, who was hailed by the *Endecja* as a national hero. At the next election of a President, Stanislaw Wojciechowski, also a friend of Pilsudski, was elected. Again, the minority bloc cast the decisive votes.

After the victorious war over Russia, Pilsudski was heralded as the Saviour of the Fatherland. But the *Endecja* was always a dominant power, and it continued its efforts to tarnish his reputation. The *Sejm* was split into too many parties. Pilsudski, not seeing any possibility of playing the decisive role in the government, resigned in 1922 and withdrew to his estate in Sulejówek.

The economic situation of the country, which had been bad when the Republic was born, worsened because of the wars with the Ukrainians and the Bolsheviks. The rural portion of the country was overpopulated, and there was no industry to absorb

Henry Morgenthau, flanked by American officers, Poland, 1919. Morganthau headed a commission sent by President Wilson to investigate anti-Semitic pogroms.

Studio Broudner, Vilna. Gustav Eisner Collection

Yitzchak Grynbaum (front row, third from right) with other members of the Jewish Agency
Executive

Jewish soldiers and officers in the Polish army who had fought for Polish independence and were
later interned because it was feared that they might support the enemy. This incident aroused
heated protest in the Polish Parliament and the men were released.

*Reprinted by permission of Schocken Books,
Inc., from Image before my eyes by Lucjan
Dobroszycki and Barbara Kirschenblatt-
Gimblett. Copyright © 1977 by Schocken
Books, Inc.*

the unemployed peasants. The revenue from taxes was low, because there was no real basis for taxing the impoverished population. The only remedy the government could apply was the printing, at high gear, of banknotes, which led to a constantly rising inflation.

Although the inflation in Poland didn't reach the heights of the runaway German inflation, it was bad enough, reaching its peak in 1923. Prices rose, and all over the country strikes broke out.

The Finance Minister, Grabski, introduced a currency reform, replacing the Polish mark with the zloty. In the beginning of 1924 he was able to balance the books. It worked, however, for only a short time, and the printing presses were set in motion again. The zloty dropped by 50 percent and unemployment rose. There was almost no base for revenue except levying high taxes, and this meant taxing Jews. As a result of this tax burden, and the economic boycott, Jewish businesses were ruined. Jews lost their livelihood, and many emigrated to Palestine. This wave of emigration was called the *Grabski Aliyah*.

The government, under the influence of the *Endecja*'s mania for Polish superiority, introduced a strong oppressive policy against all minorities. As a result an anti-Polish movement developed, especially among the Ukrainians in Galicia, who responded with acts of terror.

One of their terrorist acts was the bomb thrown at President Wojciechowski when he came to Lwów for the ceremony of the opening of the *Targi Wschodnie* (the Eastern Fairs) held in the city every year.

To greet the President the population filled the streets of the city along the route by which he was to drive to the fair grounds. At one point a bomb was thrown at the President but missed him, and the perpetrator escaped. Suddenly a Polish woman pointed at a Jewish student as the one responsible. The mob then started to yell, "It's the Jews who want to kill our President!" As at the blood-libel trial in Kiev, when a bigoted woman, Czeberiak, a thief, testified falsely against Beilis, now in Lwów a woman of ill reputation, Pasternak, falsely accused a Jewish student, Stanislaw Steiger, as the bomb thrower.

Soon, other bigots and fanatical anti-Semites joined Pasternak in asserting that the would-be killers were Jews. Steiger and many other Jews who came to greet, not to assassinate, the

President, were arrested. The mob, as usual, started to attack and molest Jews all over the city, and in all corners of the country a violent anti-Semitic campaign with a wave of wild harassment swept over the Jews.

Despite the fact that a Ukrainian organization claimed responsibility for the bomb-throwing, and that no evidence other than the deposition given by the hysterical woman, Pasternak, could be brought up, Steiger, as well as the other Jews who had been arrested at the scene of the bomb-throwing, was prosecuted and brought to trial.

At the trial, the defense lawyers, Dr. Woźniakowski from Cracow, a Pole, and two Jewish lawyers, Dr. Landau from Lwów and Dr. Axer from Przemyśl, easily proved Steiger's innocence. He, as well as the other Jews, was acquitted, to the disappointment of the anti-Semites, who were prepared for pogroms not only in Lwów but in the whole country. Polish Jews remember the trial as "The Steiger Affair."

The economic situation was steadily worsening, and the government was in dire need of international loans. Aware that Poland's reputation abroad was tarnished by the bad treatment of her minorities, and especially that of the Jews, Prime Minister Grabski declared his intention to come to an understanding with the Jews.

In 1925, the government signed an agreement with the Jewish parliamentary club, known as the *Ugoda*. The government promised the granting of credit to Jewish merchants on equal terms with non-Jewish merchants; the reinstatement of Jewish officials who had been fired when Poland took over Galicia; the abolition of discriminatory laws against the Jews from the time of the tsars which were still on the books; and taxation of Jews on an equal basis with non-Jews.

None of these promises were special privileges for Jews but merely rights which they were entitled to according to the constitution. Nevertheless, even for these promises the Jewish parliamentary club had to support the budgetary laws and to abolish any independent policy in general matters of state.

However, the *Ugoda* couldn't be put into effect due to the events which took place shortly afterwards.

While in Sulejówek, Pilsudski secured the support of some army regiments, and in May 1926, in a coup d'état against the government, led a large rebel force on Warsaw. The Jews and the entire Left supported him in his endeavor. When troop reinforcements ordered by the government from Poznań couldn't arrive because the railway workers went on strike, the government succumbed. President Wojciechowski resigned, and Professor Ignacy Mościcki, who held this post until the end of the Polish Republic, was elected President, again with the help of the Jewish parliamentary club.

Professor Kazimierz Bartel, known for his favorable position in the question of granting equal rights to the minorities, formed a new government in which Pilsudski took over the portfolio of the Ministry of Defense, which post he held until his death in 1935. From then on no decision was made without Pilsudski's advice. The hopes of the Jews were riding high, expecting that his followers, known as *Sanacja* (Moral Sanity), would introduce political and economic stability.

Premier Minister Bartel condemned all forms of anti-Semitism, and proclaimed a radical change in policy concerning the national minorities. He declared that the government would strictly abide by the provisions of the constitution. Jews, like all other citizens, would enjoy equal political, social, educational, and economic rights. Thus secret *Ugodas* were not needed. The situation of the Jews greatly improved, but the calm was not to last for very long.

Pilsudski, the revolutionary socialist, made a turn to the right and started his new regime with an alliance with the aristocrats, who possessed enormous wealth and influence. The agreement with the landowners killed any hope for introducing land reform, which was the only possible way by which the problems of the landless peasants could be solved. Instead, the expropriation of Jewish businesses and shops was heralded as the panacea for all of the country's economic ills.

A new political party, the *Bezpartyjny Blok Wspólpracy z Rządem* (Nonparty Block of Cooperation with the Government), was formed. In the elections of 1928, it emerged as the strongest party in the parliament, but did not obtain a majority.

The opposition parties formed a united opposition bloc, stiffened their stand against the government, and in 1929 succeeded in toppling the government.

To counteract them, Pilsudski decided to abandon democracy

and introduced authoritarian rule. When the leaders of all the opposition parties convened in the Slowacki Theater in Cracow, Pilsudski ordered the arrest of those who were present at the convention. The arrested leaders of the opposition were transferred to the fortress of Brest-Litovsk, where they were mistreated by the commandant of the fortress, Kostek-Biernacki. New elections, held in 1930, gave the government an absolute majority. It was formed from colonels, hence the nickname, "The Colonels' Regime." In 1933 Professor Mościcki was reelected President for another term of seven years.

On the advice of Goebbels, who visited Poland in 1934, a concentration camp was installed in Bereza Kartuska, where the same methods of torture used in the German concentration camps were put into practice. The treatment of non-Jews in Bereza Kartuska was harsh and unbearable. No one can imagine how bad were the tortures the Jews were subjected to. Upon their release, many came out crippled for life. In justifying the existence of Bereza Kartuska, the government declared that only hooligans, Jewish anarchists, Communists, and Ukrainians who disturbed the public order were imprisoned, but insisted that they were treated humanely.

The Ukrainians in Galicia resisted the policy of polonization. To combat their resistance, punitive expeditions of cavalry detachments were sent to Ukrainian villages. In retaliation the Ukrainians launched a guerrilla war. Many young Ukrainians escaped to Germany, where they received military training under the command of General Kurmanowycz, a former member of the Austrian General Staff, and later a high-ranking commander in the West Ukrainian army after the First World War. The ranks of the Ukrainian emigrés in Germany steadily grew. Under the command of Stefan Bandera they marched side by side with the Germans into Lwów when the latter occupied Galicia in 1941.

When Hitler came to power in 1933, Pilsudski thought that relations with Germany would improve because Hitler was an Austrian. Dr. Thon wrote in an article in the *Cracow Jewish Daily*—in Polish, the *Nowy Dziennik*—that the Nazi hooligans would stop their harassment of the Jews because Hitler, elevated to such a prestigious post, would find it unfit for the Chancellor of Germany to tolerate hooliganism. It didn't take too long, however, to learn how mistaken both of them had been. Instead of becoming a democracy, Germany became an autocracy. Hitler didn't change his behavior, but Pilsudski changed his and, following the Nazi pattern, introduced a dictatorship in Poland.

The treatment of Jews by the government took a turn for the worse, as did the relationship between the Jews and the other minorities. There was no longer any cooperation between the minorities in the *Sejm* as there had been when the minority bloc initiated by Yitzchak Grynbaum was functioning.

The Ukrainians revived their anti-Jewish activities, and the Germans, influenced by Nazi propaganda, joined the Polish anti-Semitic line.

In Galicia and Belorussia the Jews were not only victims of Polish persecution, but were subjected to Belorussian and/or Ukrainian boycotts as well. A Ukrainian brand of Hitlerism was introduced in Galicia. Slogans and propaganda imported from Germany were used, and swastikas decorated many Ukrainian institutions and businesses.

In 1934 the "Government of the Colonels" hosted Goebbels, and a year later Göring was invited and received with great pomp. He was wined and dined, and a special hunting party was arranged for him in the Puszcza Bialowieska. Ribbentrop was also one of the Nazi VIPs who was hosted by the Polish government.

National Socialist doctrines influenced some leaders of Polish political circles. Like their German counterparts, they proclaimed that the rights of Jews must be drastically restricted. Jews had to get out of Poland.

Anti-Semitism was steadily increasing. Spreading Nazi propaganda was not restricted, but taking part in the anti-Nazi boycott of trade with Germany was liable to punishment with a long jail sentence.

In 1935 a new constitution gave the President unrestricted right to govern by decree.

In May 1935, Marshal Józef Pilsudski died. He was not an outspoken anti-Semite, but neither was he a philo-Semite. He disliked anti-Jewish demagoguery and was generally regarded by Jews as being favorably disposed toward them. On the other hand, he didn't view the Jews as a nationality, never openly condemned the discriminatory treatment of Jews, and did not commit himself to their defense, because he was not prepared to antagonize the anti-Semites.

During the first three years after the First World War, when Poland was engaged in wars, Pilsudski's soldiers went on a rampage, robbing Jews, murdering hundreds of them and wounding thousands. The Commander-in-Chief, Pilsudski, didn't react. He didn't want to displease the army and risk his political popularity. Had he introduced legislation against the mistreatment of Jews, he would have been regarded as a defender of Jews.

In connection with Pilsudski's failure to stop the pogroms, it should be remembered that during the trial of Schwarzbard, the assassin of Petlura, Pilsudski's ally, the question of Petlura's responsibility for the pogroms was put before the jury in Paris. The prosecution insisted that Petlura had been against pogroms but was unable to restrain his army, which was composed of wild, cutthroat Cossacks. The defense, however, argued that no matter how wild and undisciplined the soldiers may have been, Petlura, by not taking drastic measures and by not court-martialing and punishing his *pogromczyks*, bore the responsibility for their acts. Schwarzbard was found not guilty by the French jury.

Now, what about Pilsudski? His armies were well disciplined, and it may be assumed that there was no need for any exemplary court-martials for perpetrators of pogroms. A strongly worded order with a decisive warning issued by Pilsudski would have been enough to prevent pogroms from being committed and/or instigated by the Polish armies in the years of 1918 to 1921.

Because of the ills the Jews had been subjected to by the governments which were under the influence of the rightist parties, they backed Pilsudski after his coup d'état in 1926. They expected from him more justice, fairness, and humanity. Unfortunately, he later changed colors.

Before and during the First World War, Pilsudski had friendly relations with Jews. Many Jews had fought as gallantly as their Polish comrades for the independence of Poland. But this was forgotten. In a few years, Pilsudski destroyed the parliamentary system and didn't hesitate to introduce a dictatorship. He also did nothing to prevent the evil and harmful treatment of Jews.

Exceptions prove the rule, and one Jew was elevated to the rank of general. General Mond, the only Jewish general in the Polish army, enjoyed friendly relations with Pilsudski until the latter's death, and was responsible for arranging Pilsudski's impressive funeral.

Pilsudski believed in democracy only so far as it served the interests of the Polish nation. He gave in to the demands of the anti-Semites, anxious not to antagonize them, and to win their support. Nevertheless, numerous Jewish delegations from all over the country and many rabbis came to the funeral. The Jews reasoned that Pilsudski had kept the *Endecja* in check and that without him it could have been much worse.

Pilsudski was a man of contrasts, idolized by some and damned by others. A revolutionary socialist, a champion of the autonomy rights of minorities, he became later a champion of the polonization of the minorities. An opponent of violence, he turned a blind eye to the pogroms and did not lift a finger to stop them. It was, therefore, interesting to examine and conduct a study of his brain. A Jewish doctor from Cracow, the world-renowned Dr. Rose, later professor at the University of Wilno, was given this job.

After Pilsudski's death, Ignacy Mościcki remained President; Edward Rydz-Śmigly, named Marshal, became Commander-in-Chief of the army; Felicjan Slawoj-Skladkowski became Prime Minister; and Colonel Józef Beck the Minister of External Affairs. (By the way, Skladkowski lived in Tel Aviv during World War II and was even a member of the civil defense.)

The government, seeing the popularity gained by the *Endecja*, jumped on the anti-Semitic bandwagon. The relationship between Poland and Germany was formally a friendly one, and Minister Beck visited Germany and brought back new ideas about the treatment of Jews. Racial principles in the Nazi manner were introduced. Jews, it was said, had too strong an influence in the economy, and therefore had to leave the country. In the meantime, however, their political rights must be curtailed. The Jews, however, refused to bend their backs before the *pooritz* (squire) any longer and rejected the maxim of the older generations, *"Mir zehnen dokh in goolis, m'miss shwahgen"* ("We are in dispersion, and better keep quiet"). Since they fulfilled all their duties as loyal citizens, the Jews insisted on having equal rights with all other citizens.

There was, however, a small minority among the Jewish population who called themselves "Poles of the Mosaic Faith" and disassociated themselves from the Jewish nationality. But these assimilators found themselves in a vacuum: not part of the Jewish nation and not accepted into the Polish one. The mere declaration of being Polish was not enough. Conversion to Christianity was the price a Jew had to pay for being recognized as a Pole. Conversions on purely religious grounds were nearly nonexistent. Apostatizing was always the only way in which a Jew could reach a high position in the civil service, a professorship at a university, a high rank in the army, and so on.

A *mekhes* (slang for "convert") could rarely wash off his or her Jewishness. Even gossiping friends would never fail to remark that Mr. so-and-so was of Jewish descent. Their personal relations were usually limited to their own circle of *meshumadim* (converts). Converts and their descendants, however, were abundantly represented among the renowned and most prominent intellectuals, artists, poets, writers, university professors, industrialists, and bankers. The well-known Jewish daily *Nasz Przegląd*, published in Warsaw in the Polish language, printed a series of columns in 1936 under the heading, *"Galeria Przechrztów"* ("A Gallery of Converts"). Hundreds of Jewish apostates were listed, the majority of whom had long forgotten their roots. It was astonishing to learn how many prominent personalities among the higher echelons in all walks of life in Polish society, hitherto considered to be of pure Polish origin, had Jewish blood in their veins and Jewish brains by inheritance.

In the 1930s, conversion alone was no longer enough to be considered Polish. One had to have baptised ancestors for two generations back, as set out in the Nüremberg laws.

Because it brought a Trojan horse into the Polish nation, assimilation of Jews was rejected. A Jew always remained a Jew. After World War I anti-Semitism was used as a tool to avert the attention of the impoverished masses from the real cause of their misery.

The Church could have terminated anti-Semitism, but would do so only if Jews would first accept Jesus as their Messiah. The constantly burning pilot of anti-Semitism burst into flames from time to time, turned on by sermons and appeals by the priests, even by the princes of the Church, such as Cardinal Kakowski, Cardinal Hlond, and Archbishop Sapieha, who declared that rioting was not Christian conduct, but that the economic boycott of Jews, who were swindlers and usurers and were spreading immorality, was all right. One did well, they said, to adhere to the principle, *Swój do swego po swoje* ("preferring his own kin") in commercial dealings.

Premier Slawoj-Skladkowski followed suit and, in a speech in the *Sejm*, defined the government's attitude toward the Jewish problem as being in principle against violence, but when it came to the use of other means against the Jews, such as economic boycott, *Owszem!* ("Yes, why not!") With *owszem* pronounced from the rostrum of the *Sejm*, a new slogan in the anti-Semitic vocabulary was coined.

Another minister, when asked by a Jewish delegation to take measures in order to prevent a pogrom which, as they knew, was being prepared in their city, answered that first of all, it was the fault of the Jews themselves if some disturbances did occur because by their behavior they were provoking the people's anger. Secondly, nothing had yet happened and blood was not running. Finally, did the Jews think that he should post a policeman behind every single Jew as a bodyguard? Moreover, he could not hang people for being anti-Semites.

Nevertheless, it would be incorrect to assume that all Poles supported rabid anti-Semitism. There were political parties, such as the PPS, and also the trade union, that opposed anti-Semitism. There was no lack of decent men who spoke up in protest and condemnation of anti-Jewish riots and anti-Semitism. Dr. Bilinski, former Finance Minister in the Austro-Hungarian monarchy, Professor Bartel, many times Polish Prime Minister, Professors Kotarbinski, Rudnicki, Zaderecki, and many others, as well as a host of enlightened personalities, were not unfavorable to Jews.

The memory of the widow of Count Krasiński should be honored. At the time of the worst pogroms in Poland in 1919, she called the president of the Jewish community and told him that in protest she had decided to donate her palace in Warsaw to the Jewish community. That action made her a white crow, since up until then no Pole had ever made a donation to specific Jewish institutions, in contrast to Jewish philanthropists, who very often had donated substantial sums to Polish establishments. Some even participated in funding the building of churches.

Poland entered the path of *Gleichschaltung*, i.e., political coordination, with respect to the treatment of her Jews, and in the League of Nations renounced the Minority Rights Treaty. In 1936, Mrs. Prystorowa, the wife of a former Prime Minister, herself a deputy to the *Sejm*, introduced a bill by which the Kosher slaughter of animals, allegedly inhumane, would be prohibited. Under strong pressure and protests from abroad, the government slightly modified the bill.

In connection with the *Shechita* Bill a priest, Trzeciak by name, issued a pamphlet full of invectives against the Jewish religion and the Talmud. Jews sued Trzeciak for libel and asked for the prohibition of the pamphlet as based on falsehoods. Together with Jewish experts, Professor Zaderecki of the Catholic University in Lódź appeared before the court and proved that Trzeciak was ignorant about the Jewish religion.

After the *Anschluss*, the union of Austria and Germany, the Polish government was afraid that Jews of Polish citizenship fleeing those countries would return to Poland. It also feared that the Nazis would expel Jews who were Polish citizens living in Austria and Germany. Therefore, wanting to outmaneuver the Germans, Poland issued a decree stripping all Polish nationals who had lived out of Poland for more than five years of their Polish citizenship.

The Germans, on the other hand, were not concerned with such niceties as valid or revoked citizenship. At the end of October 1938, they picked out 20,000 Polish Jews living in Germany for expulsion to Poland. With no warning, and given only minutes to grab some personal belongings, these Jews were loaded onto trains and brought close to Poland, where they were ordered to run toward the border. They found themselves in a no-man's land, facing machine guns from the Polish border guards who wouldn't allow them to reenter the country, their country; from behind they were threatened by the Nazi machine guns if they attempted to turn back. Finally the Poles allowed the Jews to cross the border, but put them into a camp in the border town of Zbąszyń.

It took months until the Polish government, under pressure from public opinion abroad and protests by Polish liberal circles and Jewish mass demonstrations across the country, allowed the internees from Zbąszyń to reenter the country. A student in Paris, Hershel Grynszpan, whose parents had been expelled from Germany, entered the German embassy in Paris and shot vom Rath, a Nazi official of the embassy. The Nazis ordered anti-Jewish riots in Germany.

On the evening of November 8th, 1938, nearly one hundred Jews were murdered and many hundreds wounded, two hundred

Jewish refugees from Germany in Zbaszyń on the German-Polish border

Policemen arresting a 70-year-old Jew who had fought with the rioters during the pogrom in Przytyk

Forward Collection upper as well as lower pictures

synagogues were set on fire, thousands of Jewish businesses were destroyed, and thousands of Jews were sent to concentration camps. Sacred scrolls, and religious as well as secular books were burned. On that night the streets of the German cities were strewn with shattered glass. It is remembered as the *Kristallnacht* (the Night of Glass).

Aping the Nazis, there were already, in 1938, some coffee houses in Warsaw with signs reading, JEWS NOT ALLOWED. In the city of Żywiec, not far from Cracow, the law of *de non tolerandes judaeis* was in force long before Hitler. No Jew was permitted to reside in that city. A Jew who came to the city for business purposes—for instance, a lawyer to appear before the court—was not allowed to stay overnight; no hotel would accommodate him. Though not recommending violence, the government did nothing to prevent it, and Jews were not safe on the streets of the cities.

In April 1936, the author of this book, who at that time was living in Warsaw, on Niecala Street, noticed from the balcony of his apartment, from where he had a clear view down to the *Ogród Saski*, the Saxonian Garden, that a gang of a few boys, probably high school students, was molesting Jews in the park. He saw them attack a Jewish lady who was pushing a pram with her baby. The boys chased her from the park, and when she resisted, they overturned the perambulator with the baby. They began to beat the mother, knocked her down, and kicked her aimlessly. My older son, who had also witnessed the incident, grabbed a cane and ran down into the park to rescue the lady. Soon a group of Polish strollers, young and old, came to the defense of the attackers and befell my son, kicking him and knocking him to the ground. The police took their time in responding to my telephone call and arrived at the scene an hour later. The ambulance responded quickly, but the medics were jeered, abused as Jew servants, and called names. Upon leaving for the hospital, the ambulance was pelted with stones by the mob.

To create a *Judenrein* (free of Jews) Poland, the anti-Semites put into practice a manifold arsenal of measures against Jews: vicious pogroms, economic boycotts, cultural discrimination and forced emigration.

Violent pogroms and ruthless anti-Jewish riots, which began on the very first day of the rebirth of the independent Polish Republic resulted in many thousands of murdered and wounded

Jews. It quieted down temporarily only after three bloody years, after which the situation appeared to have improved. But in 1921 pogroms were committed in Mińsk Mazowiecki, and in Katowice and Siedlce in 1922.

In 1932 anti-Jewish excesses broke out in Warsaw, Wilno, Częstochowa, and in other places. The year 1935 saw pogroms in Grodno, Lwów, Poznań, and Łódź. There was never a complete respite from pogroms during the entire twenty years of Poland's independence.

A pogrom of a special type took place in Myślenice, near Cracow. There, a landowner, Doboszyński, from a nearby village, not satisfied with the government's "mild" anti-Semitism, decided to teach the government how to deal with the Jews. In bygone days, when a *szlachcic* (nobleman) had grievances against his neighbor, he merely armed his servants and organized a *najazd* (foray) against him. He put his enemy's estate to the torch, followed by murder and pillage. Doboszyński did the same thing. He armed his peasants and farmhands and led them in a raid on the city of Myślenice. He occupied the government buildings, dismissed the civil servants, disarmed the police, and proclaimed himself the governor of the district.

He allowed his gangs to do with the Jews whatever they pleased. Immediately the crowd befell the Jews, beating them terribly, and under the slogan, "Long live Poland without Jews," all Jewish stores and houses were looted. Those Jews who couldn't find a hiding place in time were wounded, some seriously, and material damages amounted to hundreds of thousands of zlotys. Doboszyński was not in a hurry to relinquish his authority, and when he finally did, after three days, his *Endek* protectors saved this three-day king of Myślenice from even being charged for his "bravery."

During the 1930s there were hundreds of anti-Jewish riots in Poland. The worst took place in March 1936 in the little town of Przytyk, near Radom. Peasants from many surrounding villages were met by agitators on their way to the market. The agitators incited them against the Jews and gave some of them firearms. The enraged mob of peasants went into the town to put an end to the Jewish presence in Przytyk and to show the whole country how to treat Jews. When the peasants, led by the agitators, reached the center of the town and began to harass Jews, they were met with strong Jewish resistance. Shots were fired from both sides, and one peasant and three Jews were killed and ten badly wounded.

The district governor reported that Jewish Communists had provoked the peasants, who fought back and, in revenge, demolished a few Jewish stalls at the marketplace, but that the police had brought the disturbances to an end and arrested ten Communists, who were sent to Bereza-Kartuska. As a matter of fact, however, not only stalls had been demolished, but all the stores had been looted and emptied to the bare walls. There was no police intervention, except for arresting Jews.

At the trial, which was held shortly after the pogrom, nine Jews were sentenced to periods from six months to eight years imprisonment. Twenty-five peasants were sentenced to six months to one year imprisonment and the sentences were suspended.

The year 1937, however, surpassed the previous years as far as pogroms were concerned. In Częstochowa, during three days of rioting, seventy-five Jews were wounded, most of them seriously. After a pogrom in Brest-Litovsk, the Polish press heralded that the majority of Jewish businesses would never be able to come to life again. In Lwów, pogroms erupted also. Slogans such as "*Żydzi do Palestyny*" ("Jews, go to Palestine"), and "*Bij Żyda*" ("Beat up a Jew") were pasted on the walls in cities across the country.

The countryside was overpopulated with hungry and unemployed peasants living in great misery. The Jewish population lived in the towns and cities and were occupied in industry, trade, crafts, and the professions. The economic situation in the cities was not much better than in the rural areas.

A radical solution to the country's economic problems was urgently needed—a redistribution of the land. Also, it was necessary to utilize the invaluable know-how of the Jewish population, which was willing and ready to participate in the reconstruction and restoration of the country and able to do so through experience in trade and business. However, the *Endecja* saw the complete elimination of the Jews from the economy as the only cure for the nation's ills. The government agreed. Thus, when a token agrarian reform was implemented, the Jewish estates were parceled out first, but poor Jewish peasants were excluded from the distribution of the land.

Similarly, any Pole who opened a new business could count on a generous loan from the state banks. Being Polish was collateral enough for these freshly baked merchants. But Jews with the best tangible collateral were refused loans. The new businessmen, riding high on the wave of patriotism, expected through dejudaizing the Polish economy to become rich overnight. They charged unreasonably high prices, counting on the Christians to pay whatever they were asking. They met with sharp competition from the Jewish merchants, whose principles were, *"duzy obrót, maly zysk"* ("Small profit, quick turnover"). Superior quality was also the weapon used by the Jews against their new competitors, who were riding high on patriotism. The credits which they had received were, in most cases, quickly used up. What was left of the merchandise was sold at less than cost and the businesses were closed.

In order to help the Polish *owszem* merchants, the government, applying Skladkowski's *owszem* formula, brought into the field a large arsenal of heavy weapons. Some priests preached that buying from and selling to a Jew was a sin, and asked their parishioners to stay away from Jewish stores and abstain from using the services of Jewish craftsmen. The word *Żyd* (Jew) was painted on showcases of Jewish shops and stores with paint that was hard to wash off. Jewish stores were picketed. Those who insisted on entering the store were pushed back brutally and had small placards, stating I SUPPORT JEWISH BUSINESSES glued onto their backs.

Another method of marking Jewish businesses without the need of painting *Żyd* was made possible by a special law. All businesses and enterprises were forced to have a sign on the outside of their buildings which indicated not only the family name of the owner, and/or all partners, but also their first names as registered on their birth certificates. The same applied to letterheads and other forms used by the firms.

The government stopped doing business with Jewish businessmen. In order to circumvent this measure, Jews took in Poles as partners and registered their firms, using the Pole's name first, for example, "Wladyslaw Kozlowski and Company," or registered the firm under a trademark, such as "Import-Export." But this loophole was quickly plugged by ordering that the first and family names of all the partners were to be published along with the trademark. The anti-Semites boasted that there would be no more shelter for the Jews under fictitious firm names. It must be known whether the name "Import-Export" was hiding a Rappaport.

The introduction of monopolies restricted commerce in staples of various kinds, formerly in the hands of Jews, to those who held government concessions. By law concessions were to be given to only war invalids. However, when Jewish war invalids applied for concessions they usually were refused. The new Polish concessionaires rented their concessions to the previous Jewish owners of the business. Because the stores had to be open on Saturdays, Jewish owners were forced to hire non-Jews to replace them on Saturdays. What was left over for the Jew was too little to live on, but still too much to die.

Heavy, unjust taxation of Jews—in contrast to non-Jews, who were granted various exemptions—was a bitter pill for the Jews to swallow. Taxes were levied by way of assessments or in accordance with bookkeeping records kept by the taxpayer. The tax inspectors, however, used tricks in order to disqualify the books. After this happened (and it happened in ninety-nine cases out of a hundred to Jewish businesses), business taxes were levied through assessments. A Tax Assessment Commission was composed of functionaries of the taxation department and members of the Polish Merchants' Association, usually competitors of the taxpayer involved. Needless to say, the sky was the limit for the taxation of Jews. Often the amount to be paid exceeded the substance of the whole business.

One was entitled to appeal the unjust assessment, but appeal or no appeal, the payment of the taxes was due within thirty days from the date of delivery of the notice of assessment. Missing this deadline resulted in the visit of a sequestrator to the business and the home. The entire stock of merchandise which was found in the business, as well as furniture and even objects of a personal nature, found in their homes, were seized, and the debtor and members of his family were searched for hidden money. Sewing machines were taken from tailors, horses and wagons from coachmen, and tools from shoemakers, carpenters, and other craftsmen. Everything that was seized was sold at auctions to gangs whose attendance at these auctions became their profession. Everything was sold for close to nothing, and the amount gained from the sale was never enough to cover the amount owed.

Polish cooperatives, such as *Spóldzielnia Mleczarska, Spolem,* and others, were organized. These cooperatives enjoyed unlimited credit at the state banks, were free from taxes, benefited from special railway tariffs, and had many other privileges. They refused to have any dealings with Jewish wholesalers and pushed the small storekeeper out of business.

The Ukrainians followed suit and built up a chain of cooperatives of their own, the largest one called *Maslosoyouz,* which took business from Jews by using the same propaganda slogans as the Poles.

To carry on a craft independently, one had to have a "master's diploma." If not, one had to pass an exam given by the appropriate guild. The problem was that the examiners nominated by the guild, craftsmen themselves, didn't like to have Jewish competitors. Besides, the examinations were conducted exclusively in Polish, which the Jewish applicants, especially the older ones, didn't understand well. The result was that a Jewish craftsman was seldom able to pass the exam and therefore lost the right to work in his trade. Those who carried on behind closed doors and curtained windows were fined heavily if caught. If they were unable to pay the fine, jail was the alternative.

"Markets without Jews" was the battlecry of the anti-Semitic hooligans. Jews from other places were prevented by force from entering the city. Jews in their own cities were not allowed to display their merchandise at marketplaces. When some did, the stalls were overturned and the merchandise destroyed. The marketplaces were relocated to new sites where no space was rented to Jews.

Similar acts of oppression were also carried out against workers and employees. When Poland became independent, a new administration had to be built up. There had been no civil servants of Polish nationality in the German sector of the partitioned Poland, and very few in the Russian one. Galicia, however, under the tolerant Austrian occupation, had been ruled by a Polish administration, and thus was the only source of experienced and well-trained civil servants. It provided all ranks of civil servants for the restored Poland, though not enough to fill the shortage. Jews were represented among teachers, railway employees, and civil servants in Galicia. They responded with enthusiasm to the newborn Poland and offered their services to the authorities. However, for them there were no openings. A few thousand Jews, who had been employed in the civil service in the part of Galicia occupied by the Ukrainians, were released from their positions, but employees of Polish nationality and even Ukrainians who had also worked during the Ukrainian occupation, were not fired from their jobs. There were no more, or very few, Jews employed by the government, the courts, the post, telegraph, telephone, railway, urban transportation system, utility works, state-owned banks, or the postal savings bank, where Jewish deposits amounted to more than 60 percent of all the deposits.

Contractors who worked for any level of government could not employ Jews. Jewish lawyers, doctors, architects, engineers, sworn-in accountants (the equivalent of chartered accountants), and so on, were also subject to discrimination.

Tricks similar to those used against other Jewish occupations were used, such as entering on signs and letterheads the first names as spelled out on the birth certificate, disproportionate taxation, and so on. Even the Aryan paragraph brought over from Germany was used by many branches of the Medical Association to deprive doctors from practicing. Lawyers' associations followed suit. They also introduced the Aryan paragraph and got a helping hand from the government. The list of candidates for lawyers was closed, and any new lawyer had to be approved by the Minister of Justice. It goes without saying that no Jewish applicant was accepted.

In 1919, after the Poles took over eastern Galicia from the Ukrainians, Jewish schools were ordered closed, in spite of the Minority Rights Treaty. At the University of Lwów, all Jewish students were excluded under the pretext that only students who had served in the Polish army could be admitted. The catch was that Jews, under the pretext that they didn't belong to the Polish nationality, were not accepted into the army.

Anti-Semitism existed and blossomed in all Polish universities throughout the country. In 1921, the *Endeks* introduced in the *Sejm* (parliament) a bill providing a *numerus clausus* for Jews at the university, but the government revoked the bill. Nevertheless, the rectors of many universities introduced their own regulations and continued to apply Jewish quotas.

In the 1930s the *Endecja* reintroduced a bill in the *Sejm* asking for the implementation of a *numerus clausus* at the universities. During the debate on the bill, tempers became red-hot. Dr. Ozjasz Thon brought up the subject of the riots at the University of Lwów, the seat of the terrible pogrom of 1918 in that city, and pointed out that no measures had been taken by either the university authorities or the police to quell the riots. Concluding his speech, he contested the right of the *Endeks* to close the doors to higher learning to Jews whose forefathers possessed a high grade of civilization at a time when there was no Polish nation in existence, only single tribes hunting in the deep forests, armed with clubs. A tumult broke out in the *Sejm* upon hearing such truth, and Dr. Thon was censured. In fear of adverse world reaction, the bill was rejected.

Incited by *Endek* propaganda, Polish students, armed with sticks, mailed fists, knives, razor blades mounted on long canes, and revolvers, attacked fellow Jewish students, male and female alike. In Lwów three Jewish students were killed and many were wounded, at the Polytechnical Institute. At the Wilno University, when a Christian student was killed, terror spread from the university into the streets of the city. The student hooligans threw bombs into Jewish stores and apartments, and beat, wounded, injured, and crippled any Jew who got in their way.

Anti-Semitic riots at the universities intensified. *Endek* students began to oust Jewish students from the classrooms, declaring that they would, under no circumstances, tolerate Jews occupying seats on the same benches with Polish students. At the Polytechnical school in Lwów, the administration ordered Jewish students to sit on especially assigned benches. The Jewish students refused to accept the "bench ghetto," and in fights with the *Endeks* over one hundred Jewish students were wounded. Soon all universities introduced bench ghettos. In protest, Jewish students listened to lectures standing for hours, behind the benches or along the walls.

It may be hard to believe, but the Jewish students were tried and disciplined by the universities' academic disciplinary courts for the offense of not obeying the rector's orders, i.e., for standing and not sitting on the benches. Even the Wawelberg Technical School, founded by Jewish philanthropists, Wawelberg and Rotwand, and later donated by them to the Polish state with the condition that there be no discrimination against Jews, expelled students for refusing to occupy the ghetto benches. It was only after strong protests by the descendants of the founding families that the administration allowed Jewish students to stand behind the benches while attending classes.

In the laboratories at the universities, Jewish medical students were permitted to work only with Jewish corpses. "Jew Free" days and weeks were proclaimed from time to time at universities, and at these times Jewish students were forcibly barred from entering the classrooms.

In the year before World War II, anti-Jewish riots in all the Polish universities led to the complete elimination of Jews from the universities. Some professors excluded Jewish students from their classes for refusing to sit on the ghetto benches. On the other hand, there were also non-Jewish students and non-Jewish professors who defended Jewish students, but they were assaulted the same as Jews were.

The Polish Socialist Party, intellectuals, and many university professors, protested the persecution of Jews at the universities. Hundreds of French, British, and American professors joined in the protest, but the American professors of Polish descent opposed the protest against the ghetto benches. In any event, regardless of where the protests came from, they were ignored in Poland.

The corporants (students belonging to fraternities), adorned with green ribbons and with their caps tilted to one side at an angle, didn't limit their terrorist activities to the campuses, but went out hunting for Jews on the streets of the cities. Again, Lwów scored a record. Turning to the streets, the corporants attacked and beat up every Jew they could find. Especially dangerous were the streets in the vicinity of the Polish students' dormitory, which was located on Loziński Street.

Hunting for Jews, the corporants operated in the vicinity of the railway station and the intercity bus terminal. There, in company with the riff-raff, these educated gangsters found plenty of Jews arriving and leaving the city. Jews were pulled out of cabs and, after receiving a terrible beating, were warned not to dare show up in the city again.

The main task of the corporants was not studying but beating Jews. Studying or not, they could rest assured that as defenders of Polish honor they would pass the exams in any case. But Jewish students were subjected to stiff exams, first at the *matura* (graduation) exams at the high school, and then at the university. By determination and very hard work Jews were able, in spite of the ghetto benches, the beatings, and the fighting, to overcome all the barriers and to achieve a higher education.

Jewish students who were not accepted at the Polish universities left Poland for foreign countries. They entered universities in places such as Italy, France, Belgium, and largely in Czechoslovakia. Before the end of the 1930s, there were over 10,000 Jewish students from Poland studying outside their own country. Jewish organizations took care of them and extended all possible help. These students were admitted to the foreign universities with the condition that their diplomas would not entitle them to reside in that given country and practice their profession, so the freshly baked engineers, accountants, economists, pharmacists, and doctors had to return to their Polish homeland. However, when these young men and women returned home they found that their diplomas were not recognized in Poland.

In 1920, 25 percent of the university students were Jews, but due to the constantly applied curtailment of the admission of new students, the attendance of Jews at the universities was constantly dropping, and the *numerus clausus* from the previous years became, by 1939, a *numerus nullus.*

The goal of the Polish government—the destruction of the Jewish population by the means described above—was achieved, in that the economic well-being of a great part of the Jewish population was undercut. Poverty was widespread and desperation prevailed. Jews were driven out of industry, commerce, trade, and the professions. Shops and stores closed down, and thousands of businesses went bankrupt. The number of unemployed workers and intelligentsia was constantly rising. However, in spite of all the difficulties, and perhaps even because of them, Jews were able to persist. Help from their brethren abroad and well-organized self-help were of great value.

Kitchens where free meals were dispensed to the hungry were established. *Gmilas-chasudim* banks, distributing interest-free loans, were organized.

Cultural life thrived. Scientific institutes, libraries, yeshivas, secondary, elementary and trade schools, such as ORT, were functioning well.

At the Hebrew *Gymnasium* (high school) in Cracow, for example, where Hebrew was the language of instruction, mathematics and natural sciences were taught in Polish. Its *matura* (certificate of graduation) was recognized as equivalent to the *matura* from state schools and accepted at any university abroad. Magazines, newspapers in Yiddish, Hebrew, and Polish, and books from Jewish publishing houses, had a large readership. Concerts, courses, and lectures on many subjects were given, and the Yiddish theater was widely patronized. Many political parties were active. Well-functioning medical and social institutions, such as Jewish hospitals, *Toz-Towarzystwo Ochrony Zdrowia* (Society for Health Care), and orphanages were maintained. Artists, musicians, painters, doctors, and professors of international renown in many fields of science continued working.

Commercial agencies with firm connections abroad and financially sound Jewish banks, some still patronized by some Polish clients, also functioned. For example, the *Szereszewski Bank* in Warsaw and the *Holzer Bank* in Cracow. Many important branches of industry were still in Jewish hands, and a residue of craftsmen and merchants were still holding out against the government-subsidized *owszem* competitors.

Although on their knees, the Jews were not yet beaten. The backbone of the Jews remained unbroken. As a result, the fascist government of Skladkowski-Slawoj and Company decided to find a more effective and final solution to the Jewish question. Polish citizens were to be divided into three categories: those of true Polish nationality for at least three generations would enjoy full rights; the national minorities, with the exception of the Jews, would have limited rights; and the Jews would be deprived of any rights. This matched the Nazi scheme of *Deutsche, Arier, und Juden.*

Poland was fascinated with the German solution to the Jewish problem through emigration. (Gas ovens had not been brought into the picture yet.) In the *Sejm*, forced emigration of Jews was debated, and the Prime Minister, Slawoj-Skladkowski, declared that the government had resolved that the final stage of getting rid of the Jews would be by forced expulsion.

First the Jews would be deprived of all their political rights and would be excluded from economic activities. After which a mass emigration of Jews would follow. However to organize a mass exodus of 3.5 million Jews was not a matter which could be quickly accomplished.

Jews emigrated from Poland in 1920-1921, 75,000 to the United States before the doors to that country were closed. But now, in their hour of distress, Jews had nowhere to go. In the country in which they, and their ancestors, had been born and had lived, even before the Poles had a government of their own, the right to live and work as any other group was denied to them.

A conference was convened on the initiative of President Roosevelt in Evian, France, to deal with the brewing refugee problem. A considerable number of countries sent delegates to take part in the discussions. Poland sent a team of observers who asked that the conference include in its deliberations the question of the emigration of Jews from Poland and not be confined to the question of refugees from Germany.

Minister Beck of Poland threatened that otherwise, a wave of anti-Semitism in Poland would be provoked, resulting in more refugees from Poland than from Germany. Anyway, the participants, including the sponsor of the conference, America, did not act wholeheartedly, and it ended in a fiasco. The participating countries expressed their deep sympathy with the plight of the refugees and, burying their heads in the sand, did not commit themselves to any solution.

And so the doors remained closed to Jews everywhere. Even the British, who had been entrusted with the mandate to restore to the Jews their homeland in Palestine, had the doors to it double-locked. The United States, which previously had so magnanimously admitted millions of Jews fleeing the tsarist pogroms, remained imperturbable to the plight of the European Jews facing destruction. The Statue of Liberty, proclaiming an invitation to the poor and tired people to come and find freedom in America, obviously got an invisible rider: *Kromyeh Yewrayew*—"except Jews." Thousands of Jews on board the S.S. *St. Louis*, with entry visas to Cuba for which they had paid substantial amounts of money, were refused entry to that country. Only relatives of Cuban citizens could embark, but at an additional price. They had to show up before the immigration officer with a cross hanging from their neck. Canada's policy toward accepting Jewish refugees was: "None is too many."

And so, with nowhere to go, only the way leading to Nazi gas ovens in Poland was open for the Jews.

The Polish anti-Semites were impatient, and cries of "*Żydzi do*

Palestyny" ("Jews, get out. Go to Palestine") reverberated through the streets of the cities in Poland. The government tried everything it could think of to get Jews out of Poland. The Minister of Foreign Affairs, Colonel Beck, urged the British to lift the restrictions on Jewish immigration to Palestine and urged the League of Nations in Geneva to create, as soon as possible, a Jewish State there.

At the League of Nations, Poland also asked for colonies in which her Jews could be resettled. The Polish government approached France with a proposal to assign Madagascar for the settlement of Jews, and with the agreement of the French government, a committee of Polish experts went to Madagascar to explore its suitability for the settlement of Jews.

The Polish government supported a Committee for the Emigration of Jews, the *Żydowskie Towarzystwo Emigracyjne*, and negotiated with the leader of the Zionist Revisionist Organization, Zev Jabotinsky, to find a way of organizing the emigration of Jews from Poland. The question, however, was not how to organize the exodus, but where the expelled could be sent. Jews, "either you liquidate the diaspora or the diaspora will liquidate you," was Jabotinsky's prophetic warning.

Jabotinsky appealed to the Jews to leave Poland, describing it as a volcano about to erupt. But there was no place for them to go. Opening the doors to Palestine was not within his or Poland's power, and the doors to all other countries were closed too.

There is no question that if efforts for emigration had succeeded, hundreds of thousands of Jews, if not millions, would have been saved from the *gehenna* of the Holocaust.

Postcard Yehudia Verlag Warsaw

Vladimir (Zev) Jabotinsky (1880–1940), world leader of the Zionist Revisionist movement and founder of the Jewish Legion in Palestine during World War I

Reprinted by permission of Schocken Books, Inc., from Image before my eyes by Lucjan Dobroszycki and Barbara Kirschenblatt-Gimblett. Copyright © 1977 by Schocken Books, Inc.

Epilogue

When the Second World War began,
in no time the Germans Poland overran.
To avoid the Teutonic deluge,
Jews had no place to refuge.
Escaping from the Nazi beast
we ran to the east.
Alas, on our long, seemingly endless way,
German Messerschmitts bombarded us everyday.

On September 17th, fleeing over the Rumanian border,
Polish ministers and generals
left Poland in terrible disorder.

With the Polish government gone into exile,
The Russians didn't lose a while.
On the 18th of September,
as I do remember,
in the early morning, to be precise,
they took East Galicia as their Polish slice.

From west the Nazis, from east the Russian Bear,
the poor refugees could go nowhere.
Out of the frying pan into the fire we fell,
from the Nazi inferno into the Russian hell.

Tired, desperate, and of everything deprived
about a hundred thousand refugees in Lwów arrived.
"Capitalist spies you are," said the NKVD,
"to Siberia with all of you, that's our decree."

Knocking at night at every door,
refugees were grabbed more and more.
Reeling with fatigue, in cars overcrowded,

on trains into Siberia they were loaded.
My family and I, born in the district of Lwów,
were saved from the Siberian move.

What seemed to be luck when being left behind,
ended tragically under the Nazi scum of mankind.
The 1939 Ribbentrop-Molotov pact
was still intact,
but before two years of it ran to an end,
Nazi Germany fell upon Russia her friend.

From Lwów the Russians hastily retreated,
and the Germans entered,
by the Ukrainians joyfully greeted.
At once Jews were laid under heavy contributions,
followed up by different kinds of persecutions.
The German *Herrenvolk* started
looting, and killing,
and their Ukrainian friends,
helping them readily and willing.

While in ghettos squeezed and
in concentration camps to death tormented,
the world with closed eyes kept quiet as Jews lamented.

160,000 Jews lived in Lwów
at the beginning of the Nazi invasion;
only 800 of them could be
counted for, at our liberation's occasion.

When liberation from the Nazis arrived
we were only six close relative who the Holocaust survived,
not counting one in Rehovot, a niece of mine
who before the war went up to Palestine.

When searching after the war everywhere around
only six relatives of mine could be found.

Niece Anita, the little, then a child,
by honest people sheltered,
was saved from the Nazi beast the wild.
From the Nazi horrors she escaped,
and a new life in Toronto had shaped.

A family of her own she had founded,
by husband and three fine children
with love surrounded.

Cousin Joachim was in Hitler's hell
and under Stalin's regime as well.
For the loss of his wife and son he paid a terrible cost
he himself was lost.

In 1942 cousin Norbert, escaping
from the burning ghetto in Warsaw,
although chased by the cruel Nazi law,
joined the Slovak partisans in the fall,
finally found asylum in Montreal.

Cousin, sister-in-law Chana and
daughters Szanka and Jetusia,
having been hidden underground,
a new life in Australia have found.
For the life which was cruel and hard,
the children's and grandchildren's love is their reward.

Among the six million Jews murdered in the Holocaust,
my wife and two sons I lost.

Now, what am I doing here,
when gone are all to me so dear?
Why exempted was I,
when all others had to die?
Why spared was my life, When dead are my sons and wife?

The first impulsive thought of suicide
was, however cowardly, put aside.
Life became a must,
to which time forced to adjust.

The burial places of my dears I do not know;
and to lay a flower on their graves where should I go?

Your birthdays, our wedding anniversaries
just today the sixtieth,
forever I cherish precise;
alas, unknown to me remain
the exact day of your demise.

I hallow your memory with *Yisgadol w'yiskadosh Shmay Rabba*,
when remembering the *yarzayt* of my Grand Abba,
from whose roots in Lenczyce we are today
over 150 years away.

Out of the camps the survivors again had nowhere to go,
sorry said every country, refugees, absolutely no!
Wherever the Jewish remnants tried,
entry and refuge to them was denied.
To their homes in Poland some survivors returned,
but there the flames of anti-Semitism still burned.

There, right from the outset,
scorn, pogroms, and killings they met.
"Hitler didn't kill you all, he did a lousy job,
we will do it better," cried the mob.

"We shall finally make Poland *Judenrein*,
Zydzi do Palestyny—Jews get out, to Palestine!"
Even England, trusted with the Palestine Mandate,
closed before the survivors their old homeland's gate.

The Thousand Year Reich came to an end
divided and in pieces torn,
but out of the ashes our Nation
in our old Fatherland was reborn.

Our own land we regained anew,
into it to return is the right of every Jew.

What's left for me to remember
all of you among the *k'doyshim*
six million in number.
Among their names are yours in Jerusalem,
engraved in the Holocaust Memorial at yad Vashem.

Jerusalem, the eternal capital of Israel
the reborn Homeland of our nation,
Thee I salute, exclaiming with admiration:

Am Yisroel Chai!
Israel never shall die!

Toronto, 1980